Swinburne, Hardy, Lawrence
and the Burden of Belief

Ross C Murfin

Swinburne, Hardy, Lawrence and the Burden of Belief

The University of Chicago Press

Chicago and London

Ross C MURFIN is assistant professor of English at
Yale University.

The University of Chicago Press, Chicago 60637
The University of Chicago Press, Ltd., London

© 1978 by The University of Chicago
All rights reserved. Published 1978

Printed in the United States of America
82 81 80 79 78   5 4 3 2 1

Library of Congress Cataloging in Publication Data

Murfin, Ross C
    Swinburne, Hardy, Lawrence, and the burden of
belief.

    Includes bibliographical references and index.
    1. English literature—History and criticism.
2. Romanticism—England.   3. Swinburne, Algernon
Charles, 1837–1909—Influence.   4. Hardy, Thomas,
1840–1928—Criticism and interpretation.   5. Lawrence,
David Herbert, 1885–1930—Criticism and interpretation.
I. Title.
PR146.M87 1978   820'.9'008   78–3564
ISBN 0–226–55150–4

For Pam

In the seventies I was bearing in my breast,
          Penned tight,
Certain starry thoughts that threw a magic light
On the worktimes and the soundless hours of rest
In the seventies; aye, I bore them in my breast
          Penned tight.

In the seventies when my neighbors—even my friend—
          Saw me pass,
Heads were shaken, and I heard the words, "Alas,
For his onward years and name unless he mend!"
In the seventies, when my neighbors and my friend
          Saw me pass.

In the seventies those who met me did not know
          Of the vision
That immuned me from the chillings of misprision
And the damps that choked my goings to and fro
In the seventies; yea, those nodders did not know
          Of the vision.

In the seventies nought could darken or destroy it,
          Locked in me,
Though as delicate as lamp-worm's lucency;
Neither mist nor murk could weaken or alloy it
In the seventies!—could not darken or destroy it,
          Locked in me.

Thomas Hardy

Contents

Preface

There is a temptation, in prefaces, to go to great length explaining what the book to follow is all about. I will both succumb to and resist the temptation by saying a few words of explanation about my ambiguous title. *Swinburne, Hardy, Lawrence* may suggest, to some, an interrelationship, to others, merely the fact that all three writers share, independently, that *Burden of Belief* which could, in turn, be the burden of belief in Christianity or in that other "faith" which sometimes uplifted and at other times tortured all three poets, romanticism.

Both ambiguities are intended. That Swinburne influenced Hardy and that Swinburne and Hardy influenced Lawrence are central tenets of this book; that each of the three writers, independently, reacted against and revised an inherited set of metaphysical and aesthetic laws is equally its thesis. The *Belief* that the three poets alternately seek and dismiss is equally in Wordsworth's "life of things," Shelley's "white radiance of eternity," and Christianity.

For this latter idea I am, of course, in debt to J. Hillis Miller's important discussion of Victorian malaise, spiritual and aesthetic, in *The Disappearance of God*. While I am on the subject of debts, I should add that Miller's book on Thomas Hardy (*Distance and Desire*), together with Jerome McGann's recent reappraisal of Swinburne (*Swinburne: An Experiment in Criticism*) and two discussions of artistic influence by Harold Bloom (*A Map of Misreading*) and Richard Ellmann (*Eminent Domain*), are all studies to which, for the sake of avoiding an interminable stutter of *ibid*s later, I hereby acknowledge my profound debts.

My happiest liabilities, however, are to Cecil Y. Lang—without whose challenging thoughts, written and spoken, this study would never have been conceived—and to my family. My parents' encouragement has been, to me, a constant source of energy. And my wife, to whom this work is dedicated, has shared in the frustrations, joys—and labor—of putting this book together.

The Sins of the Fathers

1

In a tale entitled "Funes, the Memorius," Jorge Luis Borges describes a man who could remember everything. The mind of Ireneo Funes contained "more memories . . . than all men have had since the world was a world." But it is only in the haunting realms of Borges's *ficciones* that human beings can come so close to retracing, in Gerontion's terms, the "many cunning passages, contrived corridors," of history. The scholar learns quickly that no human being can determine or even guess the nature of the experiences which have combined to shape the consciousness of any artist, let alone one who has become lost to us in the labyrinths of the historical past. After such knowledge, what forgiveness?

Only the faith that analysis which *does* presume to pin down and describe even a few of these literary or cultural or personal influences—as they occur and recur as observable, consistent patterns within the artist's works—begins at the point where all humanist scholarship must begin. For whether history is, as Carlyle asserted, "the essence of innumerable biographies"[1] or, as H. G. Wells countermanded, "in essence a history of ideas,"[2] it is clear that our description of those recurring patterns or textures which bear witness to the uniqueness of their author is a potentially endless regression into the actions and thoughts of all who, directly or indirectly, left their mark. Pater implies that "nothing which ha[s] interested the human mind could" ever "lose its vitality" for the scholar. It is an idea older than Pater, older than the Renaissance.

"Homo sum," Terence's Chremes cries out in *Heauton Tim-orumenos*, "humani nihil a me alienum puto."[3]

These observations are offered partly as justification for a book which believes that only after describing the romantic sensibility as it was conceived by Victorian writers can we profitably deal with the poems of Swinburne. For Swinburne's poems offer specific, subtle, and complex examples of a more general revolt against the basic tenets of romanticism (as they were popularly conceived) and against specific romantic poems (which, because of the popular conception, often seem to have been misunderstood). These are lyrics which cry out for a fresh critical approach not only because they helped shape the critical temper of the age, but also because they were those new objects of devotion to which Thomas Hardy was drawn, with which he was enthralled, and against which he sometimes turned, schismatically, in his attempts to fulfill his own revisionary, if not quite heretical, identity. The art of D. H. Lawrence, in turn, is directly informed by Hardy's literary works and, more indirectly but only slightly less profoundly, by Swinburne's post-romantic art.

Writers of the Victorian age, presumably like all men of all ages, longed for an era in which man could believe in redemptive cosmic harmonies, but for mid-nineteenth-century sages, romantic prophecies like *Prometheus Unbound* had begun to look like the facile, fantastical daydreams of an age of innocence. Growling as usual, Carlyle referred to one of the supposedly priestly Private Prometheans of his own early period, Coleridge, as "deficient in sympathy for concrete human things either on the sunny or stormy side. One right peal of concrete laughter at some convicted flesh-and-blood absurdity, one burst of noble indignation at some injustice or depravity, rubbing elbows with us on this solid earth, how strange would it have been in that Kantean haze-world, and how infinitely cheering amid its vacant air-castles and dim-melting ghosts and shadows!"[4] De Quincey, a great admirer of Coleridge, nevertheless had wryly suggested that the poet of "Kubla Khan" "wanted better bread than can be made with wheat,"[5] and Pater wittily registers his agreement by quoting Lamb's old assertion that Coleridge "hungered for eternity."

"Coleridge," Pater goes on to say, "represents that inexhaustible discontent, languor, and homesickness, that endless regret, the chords of which ring all through our modern literature. It is to the romantic element in literature that these qualities belong. One day, perhaps, we may come to forget the distant horizon, with full knowledge of the situation, to be content with 'what is here and now.' "⁶ Pater must have imagined that Coleridge's compatriot, Wordsworth, that chronicler of cottagers, of "rocks, and stones, and trees," shared this inability "to be content with what is here and now," for he echoes in his own prose Lord Macaulay's dismissal of Wordsworth's "old crazy, mystical metaphysics."⁷ "As he dwelt upon those moments of profound imaginative power," Pater writes, "the actual world would ... dissolve and detach itself, flake by flake," until Wordsworth believed "himself ... to be the creator," thus entertaining "that old isolating thought of many a brain-sick ... mystic."⁸

Whereas Wordsworth, for Pater, showed symptoms both of brain sickness and of consequent, godly aspirations, Shelley, in Arnold's book, seemed nearly as mad and only slightly less presumptuous. We need not linger over the famous sneering caricature of Shelley as an "ineffectual angel" who vainly beats his "luminous wings" in a "void" to realize that Arnold conceives of his precursor, publicly at least, as a somewhat infirm quester after a non-existent heaven, as the poet who suffers from "the incurable want ... of a sound subject-matter."⁹ As early as 1831 Carlyle had been amused by a cherubic "Shelley filling the earth with inarticulate wail; like the infinite, inarticulate grief and weeping of forsaken infants,"¹⁰ and Ruskin, who called Shelley's lyrics "false, forced, foul," combined a horticultural analysis of "The Sensitive Plant" ("Sensitive plants can't grow in gardens! ... Dew with a breeze is impossible") with a more general (and more lively) assessment: "The blockhead—and he thinks himself wiser than God though he doesn't know the commonest law of evaporation!"¹¹ Ruskin would thus characterize his influential predecessor as a pretentious, cerebrally distressed overreacher who so wished he was in Oz that he never even looked at Kansas. Swinburne, even while seeming contrary in his praise of Shelley's ability to capture "some elusive spirit of Nature," stays within the terms of the party line by merely adding, without deriding, the "fact" that Shelley's poetry is "a rhapsody of thought and feeling coloured by contact with Nature, but not born *of* the contact."¹²

To be sure, Robert Browning says, in his scandalously ignored "Essay on Shelley," "The influence of [Shelley's] achievement will not soon die out." But while he seems to bestow glory, laud, and honor, Browning remarks that Shelley is a poet of the "spirit" after declaring, in the very same paragraph, that "it is with this world ... that we shall always have to concern ourselves." He refers to Shelley's poetry as established "doctrine," "convention," "tradition" even as he makes the claim that, once spiritual matters have become traditionalized, the world finds itself "subsisting" on "the straw of last year's harvest." What once was living bread is now over-ruminated cud, and so, finally, Browning calls out for "another sort of poet," a poet who will provide us with "fresh and living swathe," who will see that comprehension of the "objective" realm must "retain its original value.... The spiritual comprehension may be infinitely subtilized, but the raw material it operates on ... will be as desireable to know as ever."[13]

Even as Browning closes his Shelley, so Carlyle closes his Byron when he opens his Goethe. Browning had used his eulogy of Shelley to declare that it is now "with this world" that we must "concern ourselves"; Carlyle takes similar advantage of Byron, who becomes the occasion for a question in an essay on Goethe ("Why should we quarrel with our existence as it lies before us?") and the catalyst of an observation in another piece written the same year (a "poet ... striv[ing] towards the Infinite and Eternal is but mounting to the housetop to reach the stars"). Byron was—in Carlyle's terms, only one of a multitude of "Sentimentalists"—"sick children" who have finally "cried themselves to rest." He "was ... the wildest, the gloomiest, and it may be hoped the last."[14] Arnold similarly interred this infinity-prone Byron, whom Swinburne characterized as having "fancy, wit, fire ... but ... neither a note of real music nor a gleam of real imagination,"[15] when he wrote, in language vaguely responsive to Christ's Gethsemane prayer, "the hour ... has passed away for him; even for Bryon it could not but pass away." "The time has come for him," Arnold continues, even "as it comes for all poets. . . . Whatever we may think of him, we shall not be subjugated by him.... His faults ... we shall abundantly feel and unsparingly criticise; the mere interval of time between us and him makes disillusion of this kind inevitable."[16]

It would seem so. How else can we explain Arnold's flailing out at a poet apparently "wanting" in "character and self control," a "sensuous man" writing letters out of "the abandonment of all ... dignity" and poems in "relaxed self-abandonment,"[17] a Keats described by Carlyle as a "weak-eyed, maudlin sensibility"?[18] "Time," as Arnold realizes, engenders a debate with the past and "makes disillusion of this kind inevitable." And disillusion is inevitable because, in order to "abundantly feel and unsparingly criticise" the past, we seize upon its peculiar set of beliefs (all ages have them) and then, carefully misconstruing contexts, create or contribute to a popular misreading, a *post hoc* reduction, an agnostic's agonized claim that the "crazy old" faiths are, after all, mere "illusions." Carlyle, in his fascinating letters to an American romantic and Brahmin, Ralph Waldo Emerson, chastizes his transatlantic correspondent, saying,

> the roaring flood of life pours on;—over which Philosophy and theory are but a poor shriek.... I grow daily to honor Facts more and more.... Pantheism, Mydoxy, Thydoxy, are nothing at all to me; a weariness ... which I avoid speaking of, decline listening to: *Live,* for God's sake ... leave off *speaking* about Faith.... You seem to me in danger of dividing yourself off from the Fact of this present Universe in which alone, ugly as it is, can I find any anchorage, and soaring away after Ideas, Beliefs, Revelations.... Surely I could wish you *returned* into your own poor nineteenth century, its ... gigantic toilings, its laughter and its tears, and trying to evolve in some measure the hidden Godlike that lies in *it*; that seems to me the kind of feat for literary men.[19]

And Swinburne speaks to Ruskin in the same tone of voice, on the same subject, agnostically addressing himself to the very same articles of faith:

> You speak of not being able to hope enough for me. Don't you think we have better leave hope or faith to infants, adult or ungrown? You and I and all men will probably do and endure what we are destined for, as well as we can. I for one am quite content to know this, without any ulterior belief or conjecture. I don't want more praise and success than I deserve, more suffering and failure than I can avoid; but I take what comes as well and as quietly as I can; and this seems to me a man's real business and only duty. You compare my work to a temple where the lizards have supplanted the gods; I prefer an indubitable and living lizard to a dead and doubtful god.[20]

For the mid-nineteenth-century poets and men of letters, indeed for all writers of all epochs, to raze the temple erected by a bygone sect or, at least, to "supplant" those "dead and doubtful" gods who continue to haunt its recesses, is a high, perhaps even an heroic, calling. Arnold celebrates the work of Heinrich Heine for one very important reason—he carried on Goethe's supposedly iconoclastic efforts to "destroy" the "romantic school."[21] Carlyle sings praises to Friedrich Ludwig Werner, his "fundamental principle of morals . . . being little more than that high tenet of entire Self-forgetfulness," whereas romantics such as Burns, he says elsewhere, were little more than "self-seekers and self-worshippers."[22] Swinburne, a few years later, lauds Arnold for preaching the quiet "creed of self-sufficience," not "revelation."[23]

To destroy the romantic school—to eschew the role of self-seeker and self-worshipper—these two imperatives seem inseparable obligations to the Victorian agnostic. Swinburne had been incredulous at Blake's "passionate singleness of aim, the heat, and flame of faith in himself, the violence of mere words, the lust of paradox, the loud and angry habits" of "seeing everywhere the image of his own mood, the presence of foes and friends."[24] And Arnold's primary objection to Byron had been directed, after all, at what Edmond Scherer had called Byron's "inability" to be "impersonal and disinterested," at the fact that the romantic predecessor "treat[s] hardly any subject but . . . himself." It was a habit which led to a particularly egotistical sort of poetry, Arnold goes on to say, to "the promiscuous adoption of all the matter offered to the poet by life."[25]

To be sure, Arnold was fascinated with Etienne de Senancour, that Swiss romantic unique for his "profound inwardness, his austere and sad sincerity, and his delicate feeling for nature." But it was a fascination Arnold made a career of resisting, as in the first *Obermann* poem ("Away the dreams that but deceive / . . . I in the world must live"), as in his essay on *Obermann*, where he refers to this same "profound inwardness," this "delicate feeling for nature," as an "enervation" symptomatic of a time and a literature which leave the soul "maimed, incomplete, unsuccessful."[26] He admires George Sand, on the other hand, because "She regarded nature and beauty, not with the selfish and solitary joy of the artist who but seeks to appropriate them for his own purposes."[27]

To "appropriate" nature "for his own purposes," to "promis-

cuously adopt" nature for icons of "self-worship," to "see everywhere the image of his own mood," these, for later nineteenth-
century thinkers, are all tendencies of the romantic self which,
according to those same Victorian heretics, lead to that pathetic
romantic faith in metaphysical, or divine, correspondences between self and natural world. In an essay entitled "The Diamond
Necklace: Rumination on the Age of Romance," Carlyle admonishes readers "of romance" to enjoy the "beatific vision" of nature
while it lasts, for "it is the last provided for Thee. Too soon . . .
shall thy beatific vision . . . melt away; and only oxen and sheep
be grazing in its place."[28] "As to Nature," Carlyle suggests in his
marvelous description of the "Characteristics" of his age, we
fortunately have not been "entrusted" with "insight." It is good,
according to Carlyle, that we are "unconscious of her vital action,"
for only her "film" hides from us her "roots," her "basis of darkness
. . . Death and Night."[29]

Swinburne, in harmony with Carlyle's skepticism, was critical of
Wordsworth's vision of "a motion and a spirit" and Blake's "insane
cosmogony." He was, on the other hand, in accord with Arnold's
assessment of the life on "earth, and air, and sea" as "toil
perpetually, / And struggles, pants, and moans."[30] That is not to
say, of course, that Swinburne was blind to the influence of
Wordsworth and his nature poetry on Arnold, for Swinburne
laments the "influence of that . . . perverse theorist" and "incomplete man" on the work of *all* of his contemporaries, especially
Arnold, but adds, scripturally, that although the "incalculable
power" of Wordsworth's metaphysic of happy harmony "could not
but be," that same metaphysic, that same influence, "could not but
pass over."[31]

For Arnold, certainly, the supposedly happy faith, the supposedly incalculable power, of Wordsworth's vision did indeed
"pass over." Responding to Wordsworth's instinctive sense of
correspondence between the mind and the natural world, Arnold
declares that "to say the instinct is universally mighty . . . is . . .
doubtful."[32] Turning away from Wordsworth's belief that divine
powers are manifest in nature, that nature is a guide and guardian
of man's moral being, Arnold turns to Goethe and, through
Goethe, to Homer. Goethe, Arnold writes, knew that earthly life is
not properly represented by "pantheism," "this kind of sentimen-

tality, eminently modern," for he had come to "learn every day more clearly" from "Homer" that "in our life here above ground we have, properly speaking, to enact Hell."[33]

The Victorian criticism of a supposedly saccharine belief in nature runs deeper than the declaration that the romantic faith is doubtful or sentimental. Swinburne, Arnold, and Hardy, at least, would suggest that the romantic vision implies a morality as meretricious as its epistemology is unsound. For if the natural world is, in Arnold's terms, a "hell" to be endured, then, in Swinburne's agnostic view ("I write not as a disciple of the dishevelled school, *romantique, à tous crins* ") that romantic "worship" or "service" of nature as described in "Tintern Abbey" (ll. 149–55) is a dogma built upon "moral fallacies," a "school" which effects an ethically reprehensible "spirit of compromise with the nature of things."[34] (Arnold, we remember, had declared that "man hath all which Nature hath, but more / And in the *more* lie all his hopes of good," and Hardy would later register his agreement by claiming that any "object or mark raised or made by man on a scene is worth ten times any such formed by unconscious Nature.")[35]

In his work entitled *Evolution and Ethics*, Thomas Henry Huxley proclaims that human advancement can continue only "until the evolution of our globe shall have entered so far upon its downward course that cosmic process resumes its sway, and, once more, the State of Nature prevails over the surface of our planet."[36] For William Thomson, Lord Kelvin, as for Huxley, nature is one with time (or, perhaps more accurately, nature's "process" is at one with the temporal process), and the two, taken together, are nothing less than civilization's mortal enemy. As Jerome Buckley has shown in *The Triumph of Time*, Kelvin's second law of thermodynamics is only one of many mid-nineteenth-century statements (some "poetic," some "scientific") about the inevitability of the triumph of nature—and, through nature, time—over man. The second law states that "Within a finite period of time, the earth must have been, and within a finite period to come, the earth must again be, unfit for habitation of man."[37] Science and art, from Sir William Thomson, Lord Kelvin's "Mathematical and Physical Papers"[38] to H. G. Wells's *The Time Machine*,[39] unite in this ultimately skeptical doctrine; indeed, Tennyson goes so far as to echo Sir Charles

Lyell's *Principles of Geology* when he speaks of his own new awareness of natural, temporal process:

The hills are shadows, and they flow
From form to form, and nothing stands;
They melt like mist, the solid lands,
Like clouds they shape themselves and go.[40]

For Blake time may have seemed an apparition, a "dream of Urizen," but Tennyson can only chronicle "all things creeping to a day of doom" and Arnold feels compelled to make "the attrition of private time the main subject of his poetry."[41] Perhaps for the young and foolish Teufelsdröckh "there *is* no Space and no Time,"[42] but for the elder Carlyle of *Heroes and Hero-Worship* there is no white radiance of eternity, as there was for Shelley, there is only "the illimitable, silent, never resting thing called Time, rolling, rushing on, swift, silent, like an all-embracing ocean-tide, on which we . . . swim like exhalations, like apparitions."[43] *We* are the apparitions; time is the reality; this is the unanimous consensus of the agonized agnostics. Thus it is that Swinburne's tone is somehow both elegiac and condescending when he speaks of Blake, who "beheld . . . Time and Space as they were eternally, not as they are seen upon earth; he saw nothing as man sees: his hopes and fears were alien from all men's; and upon him and his . . . the terrors of troubled time had no power."[44]

This may be the one common denominator of all anti- or post-romantic definitions of the romantic faith: that it "saw nothing as man sees," that it took plain realities "as they are seen on earth" and "beheld [them] eternally." We can hardly doubt that this is the way in which Victorian poets and men of letters explained that most unique and curious of phenomena, the belief in romantic love, that state of immortal, transcendental, perfect union described by writers as various as Goethe, Shelley, and Emily Brontë, that fusion which explicitly seeks, in G. Robert Stange's phrase, "the annihilation of time."[45]

For Shelley, as for Blake, an important step toward harmony with nature—that expanded state of consciousness outside of time in which the poet feels the selfhood of nature—is taken when the individual establishes communion with another individual through romantic love. In "Epipsychidion," the poet, after praying to the

Moon and Sun for "magnetic might," speaks to his beloved of a unity "Which points to heaven and cannot pass away":

> We shall become the same, we shall be one
> Spirit within two frames, oh! wherefore two?
> One passion in twin-hearts, which grow and grew,
> Till, like two meteors of expanding flame,
> Those spheres instinct with it become the same,
> Touch, mingle, are transfigured; ever still
> Burning, yet ever inconsumable. . . .

[ll. 573–81]

Carlyle has his youthful Teufelsdröckh speak of the perfect union of lover and beloved through perfectly Shelleyan (and, indirectly, perfectly Goethean) metaphors of electro-magnetic attraction, of fiery transubstantiation. It is in the coming together of

> The Like and Unlike, that such heavenly attraction, as between Negative and positive, first burns out into a flame. Is the pitifullest mortal Person, think you, indifferent to us? Is it not rather our heartfelt wish to be made one with him; to unite him to us . . . ? But how much more, in this case of the Like-Unlike! Here is conceded us the highest mystical possibility of such a union, the highest in our Earth; thus, in the conducting medium of Fantasy, flames forth that *fire*-development of the universal Spiritual Electricity, which, as unfolded between man and woman, we first emphatically denominate LOVE.

Carlyle even allows his persona to dream of this quintessential romantic "Feeling" in Wordsworthian images of natural harmony. Once "*Me* and *Thee* . . . flowed softly into one another," Teufelsdröckh says, "the burden was rolled from every heart; the barriers of Ceremony . . . had melted as into vapour," and "Life lay all harmonious."

"Nevertheless," Carlyle's cynical editor interrupts to tell us, "into a thought, nay into an Action, [Feeling] must be shaped; for . . . mere 'Children of Time'" cannot "abide by Feeling alone." When Teufelsdröckh tries to translate his romantic feelings into reality, his dreams of transcendental fusion are shattered by a "timely" and practical (if unromantic) decision—Blumine's engagement to "wed some richer" man.[46] (This is exactly the predicament of Brontë's Heathcliff, Tennyson's lover in "Locksley Hall," and Swinburne's persona in "The Triumph of Time.") Teufelsdröckh's eventual

abandonment of personal, romantic "feeling," a response characteristic of so many empty-handed romantics of post-romantic
fictions, is, in some sense, inseparable from, or at least parallel to,
the post-romantic artist's abandonment of "romantic" self-worship
for a more selfless immersion in the grim realities of the contingent
world. The hero who is also a romantic lover, after all, is a kind of
fictional manifestation of his romantic creator, the self-worshipping author who holds such "promiscuous" intercourse with the
world that it finally comes to be a "sphere" which is "instinct with"
—and "transfigured" by—himself. The speaker of Arthur Hugh
Clough's witty "ἐπί λάτμῳ," a parody of romantic love poetry, is
rejecting both romantic love as an ideal and the poetic pose
necessary to embrace such a self-centered and self-expansive ideal
when he cries out in frenzy:

> 'Twas the vapour of the perfume
> Of the presence that should be,
> That enwrapt me!
> O my Goddess, O my Queen!
> And I turn
> At thy feet to fall before thee;
> And thou wilt not . . .
> And I feel my arms that stay me,
> And I feel————
> O mine own, mine own, mine own,
> I am thine, and thou are mine![47]

A poem like Clough's "ἐπί λάτμῳ" (indeed, any parody, for
parody is fatally torn between indebtedness and scorn) is clearly a
poem that, like most of Clough's best works, grows out of a
dipsychus: a confusion of counteracting and unresolvable sensibilities. Fortunately, all mid-nineteenth-century meditations on
romantic love, that "Goddess" at whose "feet" the faithful "fell,"
are not so deeply divided by the extreme and irreconcilable
polarities instinct in Clough's parody. In a work such as *Wuthering
Heights*, the romantic thesis and its antithesis, rather than being
held in a static, explosive tension, are allowed to generate a
post-romantic synthesis. Brontë's novel opposes a Shelleyan understanding of love as epipsyche ("I *am* Heathcliff") with a skeptical
vision of the consequences, if not the possibilities, of such a love,
generating in the process a revised mode of loving which Hardy
would later refer to as loving-kindness ("the enemies were, thence-

forth, sworn allies. . . . Loving and desiring to esteem").[48] In Teufelsdröckh's rite of passage through affirmation, denial, and revision of romantic articles of faith, we cannot fail to hear Carlyle, through Teufelsdröckh, redefining love in similar terms. Once past his *Sturm und Drang*, the sadder but wiser protagonist enjoys a more subdued—and more generally charitable—feeling, more like brotherhood than sanctified, incestuous, or, indeed, self-copulative passion:

> With other eyes, too, could I now look upon my fellowman: with an infinite Love, an infinite Pity. Poor, wandering, way- ward man! Art thou not tried, and beaten with stripes, even as I am? Ever, whether thou bear the royal mantle or the beggar's gabardine, art thou not so weary, so heavy laden; and thy Bed of Rest is but a Grave. . . . Man, with his so mad Wants and so mean Endeavours, had become the dearer to me; and even for his sufferings and his sins, I now first named him Brother.[49]

As *Sartor Resartus* would seem to intimate, Victorian modifi- cations of the romantic ideal of love necessitate an alteration in the understanding of social intercourse. Once a civilization no longer believes that two individual lovers can become "one / Spirit within two frames," it can hardly hope, with Shelley's *Prometheus Unbound*, for the apotheosis of a society in which all men become "a chain of linked thought, / Of love and might to be divided not" (4: 394–95). In the minds of mid- to late-nineteenth-century ag- nostics, the hope for the kind of social reform envisioned by Shelley was just one more vague and indecisive romantic prayer for impossible community, just one more poetically mystified "Feel- ing," just one more dreamy self-indulgence which never could find fruition in "Action." Swinburne, in an essay on Blake and his "church of rebels," uses old romantic metaphors to point out, somewhat incredulously, that "severed from other men" he "con- ceived himself . . . strangely interwoven with them. The light of his spiritual weapons . . . was seen, he believed, and was heard in faint resonance and far reverberation among men who knew not what such sights and sounds might mean."[50]

If romantic social idealism could be reduced to dogma by seizing upon Shelley's statement that "A man, to be greatly good, must imagine intensively, . . . he must put himself in the place of others . . . their pains . . . must become his own,"[51] then, as A. Dwight

Culler has suggested, Arnold's poem entitled "The Sick King in Bokhara" can surely stand as the later, agnostic response to romantic liberalism, to faith in the sympathetic poetic imagination.[52] For, Culler argues, the writ by which Arnold's sick and ineffectual king lives and rules is the romantic text of negative capability, the "Shelleyan" social text which says that justice is not done until the king can "imagine" so "intensively" that the "pains . . . of others . . . become his own," and, most interestingly, the simultaneously *Christian* scripture of constant charity, "the holy book / Carried before him, as is right" (ll. 47–48) which turns the king into an ineffectual angel, a leader so broken down by "Feeling" that all "Action" is impossible. The sympathetic king can bury an executed criminal in a palace of art so imaginatively indulgent that a mere natural man ends up looking, to those whose gaze is not too intent, like a holy prince awaiting resurrection. But the king is a dying youth—a visionary "infant," to use Carlyle's description of Shelley—who admits that "Clear in these things I cannot see." The Vizier is older, and he is far more cynical than he who has held power. But his vision, though limited, is sharply focused on the here and now. And his ascendancy, though modestly unstated, is as certain as the sick sovereign's demise.

There is some danger in outlining the Victorians' reductive conceptions of the romantic sensibility. We can modify, we can revise, we can even turn topsy-turvy the literary assessment of those critics who have come before us, but we cannot fully escape the influence of their judgments. We are forever separated from the activities of the romantic sensibility, and that which separates us, that which colors or discolors our vision, is the post-romantic, the agnostic reaction. We may, for instance, claim that the Victorian retrospective was correct in letter but unfair in spirit, that the value of romanticism lies in its internalization of nature, in its idealization of quests for romantic or social love, we may argue that art *should* by-pass the "here and now," we may (in fact we must) claim that the post-romantic critique has so distorted the annals of literary history that it is our duty to undertake a proper revaluation. But the basic details of the post-romantic critique will be difficult to circumvent.

No less distinguished a critic than Northrop Frye has said that "The 'romantic' has in popular speech a reputation for taking a facile or rose-colored view of things," and when Frye continues his sentence, he makes no attempt to completely isolate himself from this reductive but pervasive popular presumption: "even great works of Romanticism sometimes show us a mental quest achieved without having passed through any real difficulties or dangers on the way."[53] Frederick Pottle has given us quite a marvelous understanding of the "Eye and the Object in the Poetry of Wordsworth" without ever attempting to depart from that old familiar claim that at least "a good many" of Wordsworth's poems "either have no basis" in experience or are so "manipulated that the 'subject' corresponds to nothing Wordsworth ever saw with the bodily eye."[54] Owen Barfield argues that romantic poets achieved "the liberation of images" precisely *through* "the rejection of original participation" in the world,[55] Paul de Man suggests that the power of the romantic imagination is a power "for consciousness to exist entirely by and for itself, independently of all relationship with the outside world,"[56] Misao Miyoshi describes the achievement of romanticism as "overcoming the world as given,"[57] and Harold Bloom pleads that "Romantic nature poetry, despite a long critical history of misrepresentation, was an anti-nature poetry."[58] Thus we can see, coupled with this new, appreciative propensity, the old, mid-nineteenth-century claims that romanticism was an escapist's religion ("rejection of original participation," "overcoming the world as given"), that it fostered self-indulgence, self-worship ("to exist by and for itself, independently of all relationship with the outside world"), and that it was, in Swinburne's terms, colored by contact but not born of contact with nature ("Romantic nature poetry was anti-nature poetry"). Indeed, our own analyses, however new in theory or evaluation, are often strikingly derivative in observation. Georges Poulet claims that escape from time, "possessing life in an instant," is the "fundamental desire of the romantic,"[59] and Frye, after commenting that the romantic poet saw "society as held together by its creative power, incarnate in himself," concludes that "Romanticism finds it difficult to absorb the social perspective, and . . . often tend[s] to by-pass the more realistic tragic, ironic, and comic themes."[60]

This doesn't necessarily mean that some limited degree of objectivity is impossible—only that, given the nature of history and the necessity to create individual identity, it is extremely difficult. Certainly, the post-romantic explanation of romanticism *is* a reduction or distortion, and no matter how much we are trained in the distortion, we do occasionally deny its validity. Frye confronts our all too common dismissal of Shelley with the insistent claim that "if the main body of Shelley's work had not been directly concerned with social, moral, religious, philosophical, political issues he would have lost most of his self-respect as a poet."[61] M. H. Abrams argues that "The Spirit of the Age" was one "thoroughly in touch with mundane reality."[62] Frye counters our derision of romanticism's pale ideal of love as spiritual mixture with the counterclaim that the "romantic redemption myths" describe a movement from faith in *"agape* or love of God" to "emphasis on an *eros,* or love rooted in the human sexual instinct,"[63] and Harold Bloom, Alfred Cobban, and M. H. Abrams all unite under one banner: the one announcing that the so-called romantic political liberalism was, in fact, a *conservative* movement, a strong and tradition-bound response to a rootless society grown sick on Cartesian dualism, Lockean selfhood, and, hence, an individualism as tyrannical as it was anarchic.[64]

Whether these analyses are ultimately convincing or unconvincing, one thing is clear. That pervasive understanding of the romantic "faith," an understanding in which writers such as Swinburne, Hardy, and Lawrence were indoctrinated (indeed, the understanding which they helped to *make* into agnostic doctrine), is a grossly oversimplified version of the truth, one which somewhat misleadingly describes modern literature as an heretical abandonment of a system of belief as monolithic as it was hopelessly naive. For we can hardly doubt the fact that, by seeing romanticism as a settled system, post-romantic critics—from Arnold to the present—have tended to underplay the romantic proclivity to self-doubt and to metaphysical as well as aesthetic crisis and change. Geoffrey Hartman tells us that Wordsworth felt the crisis and the ravagement of self-consciousness every bit as fully as did Mill, who makes Wordsworth into the harmonious psalmist of a happier time.[65] And if M. H. Abrams is correct, it might even be fair to add that the crisis experienced by romantic poets was far *more* "real" (that is to say it grew out of more palpable, even political, conditions) than the spiritual, intellectual, political turmoil suffered by later writers, such as Arnold or Swinburne, Hardy or Lawrence.[66]

Surely we cannot be fully satisfied with the Victorian claim that romantic poets were angels happily lost in their solipsistic heavens. As Bloom points out in "The Internalization of Quest Romance," the romantic "quest . . . to widen consciousness . . . is shadowed by a spirit that tends to narrow consciousness to an acute pre-occupation with self. This shadow of imagination is solipsism, what Shelley calls the Spirit of Solitude or *Alastor*, the avenging daimon. . . . "[67] And "Alastor," after all, is *not* the poem of a "self-seeking, self-worshipping" poet (to quote Carlyle) but, rather, a poem about what *happens* to the "self-seeking, self-worshipping" poet!

"Alastor" can show us yet other ways in which post-romantic criticism was as reductive as it was influential in its portrayal of a supposed faith. To be sure, Shelley tells us that the young poet pursued "Nature's most secret steps . . . like her shadow," but is not this feeling of oneness with nature the "trance" from which he awakes into "The cold white light of morning, the blue moon / Low in the west, the clear and garish hills" (ll. 192–94)? To be sure, the youth of "Alastor," in a fit of romantic love, and "yielding to the irresistible joy, / With frantic gesture and short breathless cry / Folded his frame" in the "dissolving arms" of a delightful phantom (ll. 185–87), but does the young poet ever really find his romantic bliss? Or isn't Shelley perfectly aware (as Clough would later pretend he was not) that the youth is romantically pursuing a self-generated vision?

Such a defense of romanticism could go on at great length. Wordsworth's "Elegiac Stanzas" on "Peele Castle" could easily be used to refute the claim that all romantics succeed, or even intend to succeed, in what Stange has called "the annihilation of time." (Coleridge, in the *Biographia Literaria*, remarked that "the sense of Before and After" gives "permanence and identity to the shadowy flux of Time.")[68] But one of the factors which renders rebuttal so unnecessary is a certain schizophrenic quality in agnostic criticism itself—a tendency to vacillate suddenly from attack to appreciation, from blame to praise, of the romantic forebears. Arnold lauds Wordsworth for "the joy offered to us in the simple primary affections and duties,"[69] and Swinburne remarks that "as the poet of suffering, and of sympathy with suffering, his station is un-equalled. . . . "[70] Swinburne has said of Shelley that "his topics were not Hours of Idleness, and Hints from Horace, and the Waltz, they were the redemption of the world by the martyrdom of righteousness, and the regeneration of mankind through 'Gentleness, Virtue, Wisdom, and Endurance'."[71] Admittedly, Shelley is still framed and mounted as a holy martyr, even a savior, but the savior is a savior of the living, of the "here and now," and the commentary is more nearly apostolic than agnostic. Even poor, martyred Keats, whom Arnold once characterized as "wanting" in "character and self-control" and later as a "merely sensuous man," finds some appreciation in the very camp of the philistines, for it is none other than Arnold himself who argues that "Keats felt that place must be found for 'the ardours rather than the pleasures of song.'"[72]

Such admissions are by no means limited to the canon of Victorian prose, for similar acts of contrition, devotion, even zeal, are performed, implicitly, in the artistic works of most post-romantic writers. Arnold's admiration of Wordsworth and Keats, if not set forth in prose, could just as easily be discovered in his verse. Let us think about those familiar lines from "Stanzas in Memory of the Author of *Obermann*": "Away the dreams that but deceive . . . I in the world must live . . . and so, farewell / Farewell!' Keats, as early as "Sleep and Poetry," had bidden a similar adieu to the joys of pure vision:

> And can I ever bid these joys farewell?
> Yes, I must pass them for a nobler life,
> Where I may find the agonies, the strife
> Of human hearts. . . .
>
> [ll. 122–25]

Wordsworth, in his "Elegiac Stanzas Suggested by a Picture of Peele Castle," had cried out a similar farewell:

> Farewell, farewell the heart that lives alone,
> Housed in a dream, at distance from the Kind!
> Such happiness, wherever it be known,
> Is to be pitied; for 'tis surely blind.
>
> But welcome fortitude, and patient cheer,
> And frequent sights of what is to be borne. . . .
>
> [ll. 53–58]

The list could be prolonged. Tennyson's "Mariana" contains evidence of a double allegiance to Keats's "Isabella" and Shelley's "Alastor." Hardy's numerous compost-heap poems, such as

"Transformations," may be agnostic agonies, but they clearly have their roots in Wordsworth's Lucy ("No motion has she now, no force; / She neither hears nor sees: / Rolled round in earth's diurnal course, / With rocks, and stones, and trees"). Mid-nineteenth-century poets do not *always* antithetically revise poems of one or more predecessors, or, just as often, what they have been conditioned to see as the general sensibility of a predecessor or predecessors. Sometimes they simply attempt to validate their own sensibility by grounding it in the one which is previous to them.

It is worth digressing far enough to admit, at this point, that in this study I am taking a pluralistic, if not an anarchic, view of the nature of poetic influence. As later interpretations of several poems will no doubt prove, I have been intrigued by Harold Bloom's recent, genealogical approach to the problem;[73] I believe that his antithetical criticism is a perfect way of charting the relationships between certain poems by certain poets. I believe that there are other revisionary authors or works, however, which respond not to anything in any specific text but, rather, to the literary past—or some particular agent of that past—as it or he had been popularly perceived and portrayed. These acts of adolescent revolt, of course, are more patently unfair than those which Bloom describes. Carlyle tells Emerson that "the actual well seen is the ideal" as if no one had ever said it before; it is a statement made implicitly, of course, by Wordsworth, Shelley, and Keats in countless poems. When Thomas Hardy scoffs, early in *Tess of the D'Urbervilles*, at the "profound" poet who would have us rest secure in "Nature's holy plan," he is hardly taking to task the real William Wordsworth—who wrote *The Ruined Cottage* as well as "Lines Written in Early Spring." The Wordsworth who did nothing but roll in the grass with the One is, of course, a Wordsworth invented by Victorian criticism. But he is also the Wordsworth with whom Hardy argues vociferously in *Tess*. As for all the Victorian poems that are more interested in copying the past than revising it, these more grateful works remind us that post-romantic voices are obviously caught in a confused time between times, a period of uncertain loyalties, a situation described by Carlyle as a "Center of Indifference," by Arnold's "Stanzas from the Grande Chartreuse" as being "between two worlds, one dead, / The other powerless to be born" (ll. 85–86).

It is a time between times in a double, and thus doubly uncertain and anxious, sense. For, although the death of Christian faith is occasionally used by post-romantic writers as a metaphor for the death of romantic faith (and, conversely, elegies to the romantic sensibility often are thinly veiled agonies over the loss of Christian faith), the truth of the matter is that most Victorian lyrics of loss are either perfectly hazy or perfectly bifocal in their perception of their own visionary failure. Whether the supposedly harmonious and redemptive vision lost to the author of "Stanzas from the Grande Chartreuse" or "Dover Beach" or "In Utrumque Paratus" is romanticism or Christianity is just ambiguous enough to suggest that one faith has collapsed after the other and that now, although both continue to influence the present, neither remains tenable or valid. That double loss is surely what Arnold is referring to when, in the first *Obermann* poem, he speaks of that horrible time when, bathing on the shore, "Buried a wave beneath" we feel "The second wave" succeed "before / We have had time to breathe" (ll. 74–76). The "restless fool" made famous by Arnold's best-known sonnet is a "Preacher" whose *credo* is "harmony with Nature." Hardy's ineffectual Clym Yeobright is called, alternately, a "romantic" and a "preacher." As for the New Cyrenaicism Pater describes in the ninth chapter of *Marius the Epicurean* ("Be perfect in regard to the here and now"), it seems at once a hastily conceived replacement for high romanticism and Pauline Christianity.

Post-romantic writers, whether a Swinburne or a Lawrence, a Mill or a Hardy, can only know or hope to know that, in Arnold's words, they inhabit "a pause in which the turn to a new mode of spiritual progress is being accomplished."[74] Such a necessarily agnostic moment, however, is obviously as pregnant as it is agonizing, and even those writers who fail to adopt the nearly pervasive symbol of the phoenix for their own life, art, and historical age (that terrifying but hopeful phoenix age when, in Carlyle's terms, the ashes of the old are blown out, but organic filaments of the new spin themselves) sense that they occupy a critical moment of death and resurrection. Consequently, most of them describe the present as a Gethsemane, the future as a heavenly but *human* city. John Stuart Mill says in his *Autobiography* that a "transitional period commences, of weak convictions, paralyzed intellects, and growing laxity of principle, which cannot terminate until a renovation has been effected in the basis of . . . belief leading to the elevation of some faith, whether religious or merely human, which [man] can really believe."[75] Speaking at Oxford on the modern element in literature, Arnold speaks of a time of ripeness, a time which may bring about "a significant, a highly developed, a culminating epoch, on the one hand,—a commensurate, an adequate literature, on the other," and thus, in concert, the "intellectual deliverance" of "an age."[76] Carlyle, like Mill, uses the thinking of Saint-Simonians to suggest that a new "organic" period in the collective life of man may be incipient, and, in an essay on Diderot, seems to speak of the historical past and, by indirection, of a future time between times when, "Instead of here and there a stone falling out, here and there a handful of dust, whole masses tumble down, whole clouds and whirlwinds of dust: torches too are applied, and the rotten easily takes fire: so, what with flame-whirlwind, what with dust-whirlwind, and the crash of falling towers, the concern grows eminently interesting; and our assiduous craftsmen can encourage one another with *Vivats*, and cries of *Speed the work*."[77] Swinburne would hasten to add that as new masons of stone and of state hasten to build a new community and *credo*, so new artists must rise, like a "phoenix," from the ash-heap of the literary past, "birds of alien feather" to those tired and derivative fowl that presently rise "chuckling and crowing from the dunghill" of a dying aesthetic, a dying faith.[78]

Thus, just as "religion" and romanticism are linked, both as twin losses to be mourned and as dead, twin tyrants to be scorned, so the phoenix of the coming age must create and elevate not only (in Arnold's words) "spiritual . . . modes" but also "an adequate literature," a new and integrated "basis of belief" (in Mill's terminology) which might be "religious or merely human." Why? Because, to quote Carlyle, "for the last three quarters of a century, that same Pericardial Nervous Tissue (as we named it) of Religion, where lies the Life-essence of Society, has been . . . quite rent into shreds," and now, as "the Phoenix is fanning her funeral pyre . . . sparks" are "flying."[79] They are sparks which herald (in the words of Browning's *annunciatum*) not only a new faith, but also a new artistry, not only a new "doctrine," but also a new "poet," "fresh and living swathe" for a post-Christian, post-romantic, even post-agnostic world, a world yet powerless to be born.

> "But there is no Religion?" reiterates the Professor. "Fool! I tell thee, there is. Hast thou well considered all that lies in this immeasurable froth-ocean we name LITERATURE? Fragments of

a genuine Church-Homiletic lie scattered there, which Time will assort: nay fractions even of a *Liturgy*.[80]

If there is an irony for us in this claim it is that, for the Carlylean Professor, as for so many of his Victorian contemporaries, the divided self, together with the ambivalence of the age, requires that from the rubble of one demolished religion man will build another, that following the destruction of one Church he will assemble a new one, complete with scripture and liturgy, from the immeasurable chaos of his literature.

The Agnostic Agony

Swinburne's Poetry of Loss

2

If Swinburne is the supreme liminal poet in the English language, it is because his life, as well as the life of his age, encountered old borderlines and new horizons on every front. There was hardly an article of faith—in class structure, in material progress, in science or the function of art—that did not have to face loud and angry encounters with some strong article of doubt which had developed sometimes outside of, but just as often within, the very temple of "the dead and doubtful gods." It is little wonder that Swinburne was unable to maintain a consistent or definitive attitude towards those two faiths most crucial to his own development, Christianity and romanticism.

As a young man at Eton, Swinburne was enchanted by Shelley; one need only peruse "The Temple of Janus," the poem he composed during his first year at Oxford, to realize the depth of his early devotion. By 1865, however, adoration must have turned to skepticism, for Swinburne claims that even Shelley's great works are "spoilt" by "doctrinaire views."[1] Perhaps a clue to Swinburne's movement away from his predecessor can be found in a letter he wrote to William Michael Rossetti, a letter in which he reminds his friend that he, like Shelley before him, had been an "afflictive phenomenon" to his father. He goes on to say, in this discussion of himself, Shelley, and their respective genetic parents, that the filial bond is ultimately one of "irreparable, total, and inevitable isolation" between those at first "closest in mind and thought," that sons undertake an "inevitable" passage from proximity to "separation," from "separation to [that] antagonism of spirit . . . where attraction finally ends [and] repulsion gradually begins."[2]

Wordsworth, no less than Shelley, was half attractive, half repulsive, to Swinburne, who wrote democratic manifestos such as "The Eve of Revolution" even as he satirized Wordsworth for being *"un misérable du peuple"* and who wrote pantheistic ecstasies like "A Nympholept" even as he assailed Wordsworth for his "pantheism."[3] As for Christianity, Swinburne's ambivalent attitudes towards that old faith (as well as towards romanticism, with which he associates its "doctrinaire" views) can perhaps best be found in an 1875 letter to E. C. Stedman. He tells Stedman that he is a "kind of Christian (of the church of Blake and Shelley)." He then loudly decries natural religion, proclaiming that God cannot be known "by other than apocalyptic means" but later adding, in what seems a curious turn of argument, that Blake and Shelley were *not* poets of "supernatural revelation" but, rather, were discoverers of "human perfection." He ends by exclaiming that he is "in no sense a Theist" and declares himself, instead, a exponent of "clarified nihilism."[4]

It is hardly surprising to learn that Swinburne's art, like his life, is transitional to a degree. In *Atalanta in Calydon*, his first successful work, Swinburne compresses into seventy-five powerful lines the transitions in sensibility which connect Wordsworth's ebullient celebrations of man's unity with nature and Thomas Hardy's eventual, despairing concurrence. The Chorus begins by celebrating spring, a season which seems no less than a corollary of the citizens' "winter-long hopes" for an end to trouble and strife. And yet the lyrical longing for a new season of innocence is muted. Swinburne puns on the word "traces" so that the last residues of the winter become ominous reminders both of that season's inescapable reins and of the ever-present "tracks" of the beast. Nature, which speaks to man of a promised resurrection, speaks with a deceptive lisp. When the choral ode reveals that the "brown bright nightingale" is only *half* assuaged for Itylus, the attempt to transcend past and present through projection collapses into a lethargic list of all the painful impediments to vision:

When the hounds of spring are on winter's traces,
    The mother of months in meadow or plain
Fills the shadows and windy places

With lisp of leaves and ripple of rain;
And the brown bright nightingale amorous
Is half assuaged for Itylus,
For the Thracian ships and the foreign faces,
  The tongueless vigil, and all the pain.

Again, the Chorus attempts to triumph over despair, to connect
nature's moods with man's own hopes and dreams:

. . . winter's rains and ruins are over,
  And all the season of snows and sins;
The days dividing lover and lover,
  The light that loses, the night that wins;
And time remembered is grief forgotten,
And frosts are slain and flowers begotten. . . . [5]

But as the Chorus continues its attempted romantic ode to spring,
an ode which echoes the fourth act of *Prometheus Unbound* ("the
hounds of spring"), *Laon and Cythna* and "The Witch of Atlas"
("The Mother of Months"), and the majestic last movement of
"Adonais" ("frosts are slain and flowers begotten"), images of
natural, political, and moral harmony gradually give way to
images of wild, perverse, destructive power. As "the faint fresh
flame . . . flushes / From leaf to flower and flower to fruit," the
poet more and more blatantly reminds his audience, through the
Chorus, that in the closure of nature's sadistic system, renewed life,
the promised springtime resurrection, must necessarily rape—
"trammel," "crush," and "feed on" the "root" of—something
weaker:

The full streams feed on flower of rushes,
  Ripe grasses trammel a travelling foot . . .
And the hoofed heel of a satyr crushes
  The chestnut-husk at the chestnut-root.
                                                    [4:250]

Althaea knows, even better than the Chorus, that spring is all
too short and that the "fire" that bursts through the veins of man
and nature can hardly be a source of hope. It is only a happier
manifestation of natural process, that Phoenix-like fire that simultaneously creates and consumes not only vegetative and animal
nature but also the happiness and the hopes, the dreams and the
prayers, harbored by the spirits of men:

Night, a black hound, follows the white fawn day,
Swifter than dreams the white flown feet of sleep;
Will ye pray back the night with any prayers?
And though the spring put back a little while
Winter, and snows that plague all men for sin,
And the iron time of cursing, yet I know
Spring shall be ruined with the rain, and storm
Eat up like fire the ashen autumn days.
. . . .
Look, ye say well, and know not what ye say;
For all my sleep is turned into a fire,
And all my dreams to stuff that kindles it.

[4:251–52]

Althaea's speech, in diction, tone, and idea, echoes the Chorus's
speech to Panthea in Act 4, lines 73–76 of Shelley's *Prometheus
Unbound* (Shelley had written, "Once the hungry hours were
hounds / Which chased the day like a bleeding deer, / And it
limped and struggled with many wounds / Through the nightly
dells of the desert year"). But Swinburne's belated response is
perfectly post-Shelleyan, post-romantic, post-pantheistic. For
Shelley's Chorus refers to a state of disharmony which existed
before the romantic, apocalyptic marriage of reason and imagination, action and feeling, spirit and flesh, self and nature, lover and
beloved, individual and society, and heaven and hell—the very
marriage dramatized, indeed accomplished, by his own dramatic
structure. But Swinburne's lines describe quite the opposite—the
immanent *division* of all harmonious unions, a division that will be
even more excruciatingly painful *because* the belated Chorus of
Atalanta has been romanticized by the Chorus of *Prometheus*. As a
result, men, in the face of that fact which Goethe and Arnold
learned all too well (that life in nature is not to be "sentimental-
ized," rather, is a "Hell to be endured"), continue to hold to that
crazy old mystical metaphysic of meaningful, fortuitous, even
millennial interfluences of Promethean "dreams" and natural
"fires."

Swinburne thus suggests, through the shifting, dialectical presen-
tations of Althaea and the Chorus, that the nature which spring
revives may be more accurately described as a monstrous conflagration than as an apocalyptic flame, let alone a baptismal font, a
spiritually assuaging and renewing "ripple of rain" (4:249). And

just as Carlyle used images of gigantic size and complete indifference to describe natural process in the crisis chapters of *Sartor Resartus* ("one huge, dead, immeasurable steam-engine"), so Swinburne similarly describes the size and malign indifference of nature and nature's forces when he has Althaea refer to nature's power as that of a "boar," "the blind bulk of the immeasurable beast" (4:293, 292)

> That mars with tooth and tusk and fiery feet
> Green pasturage and the grace of standing corn
> And meadow and marsh with springs and unblown leaves,
> Flocks and swift herds and all that bite sweet grass. . . .
>
> [4:253]

The goddess Artemis is another metaphorical figure Swinburne uses to describe those immeasurable, indifferent powers of nature. Speaking of Artemis, Althaea says that "She" would

> . . . hurt us where she healed us; and hath lit
> Fire where the old fire went out, and where the wind
> Slackened, hath blown on us with deadlier air.
>
> [4:254]

Earth's "spring" is "Barren," the poet explodes in "Anactoria," for the same powers which create life also destroy it:

> Her spring of leaves is barren, and her fruit
> Ashes; her boughs are burdened, and her root
> Fibrous and gnarled with poison; underneath
> Serpents have gnawn it through with tortuous teeth
> Made sharp upon the bones of all the dead,
> And wild birds rend her branches overhead.
>
> [1:64]

The corresponding fruit of the romantic poet's faith or belief in his own powers is similarly ruined by this knowledge of the violence, division, even opposition of all natural forces. Just as Hardy would fear that poetic complaints about an indifferent, omnipotent, "Immanent Will" were fruitless, since his own act of writing was necessarily a manifestation of the Will in action, Swinburne suggests in his aptly named poem "The Triumph of Time" that his own tortured attempts to bring love and poetry to fruition in a cruel and barren world are "ruined at root." Poetry becomes "ruined rhyme," and love, which Swinburne calls "this fruit of my heart," "will not grow again" (1:36, 34).

Time does, indeed, ruin all of life at root for Swinburne. Far from being a repressive illusion, a self-constricting dream of Urizen which the imagination can pierce and transcend, time is, in Swinburne's early poetry, an inescapable facet of nature's unholy plan. It is an integral part of that larger, natural law which is symbolized in *Atalanta* by the burning brand—the law which the dying Meleager comes to understand when he says that

> . . . this death was mixed with all my life,
> Mine end with my beginning: and this law,
> This only, slays me. . . .
>
> [4:331]

Jerome Buckley, in *The Triumph of Time*, not only places Swinburne perfectly within the contexts of a changing attitude toward the supposedly romantic definition of time, but also defines Swinburne's *oeuvre* as an agnostic, thus paradoxical, psaltery. He writes that "Swinburne on occasion yearned for a life 'that casts off time as a robe,' but his most characteristic . . . poem remains the moving, rhapsodic 'Triumph of Time,' which hymns the irreversible passing of love":[6]

> It is not much that a man can save
>   On the sands of life, in the straits of time,
> Who swims in sight of the great third wave
>   That never a swimmer shall cross or climb.
>
> [1:36]

Carlyle had advised Emerson in 1836 that there is no escape, no vacation, "no rest" from monotony and defeat, for "all [is] spectral, for all [is] part of the Kingdom of Time,'"[7] and his advice was by no means lost on a somewhat later generation of nineteenth-century English poets. No one knew better than Swinburne that nothing could be salvaged "On the sands of life, in the straits of time," and for Swinburne, as for Carlyle and Arnold, the supposedly transcendent powers of romantic love were no exception. In one of his very early *Poems and Ballads* entitled "Stage Love," he writes that "Time dies and is not slain; / . . . love grows and laughs and cries and wanes again" (1:118), and in his more persuasive hymn to "Dolores, Our Lady of Pain," he cries out that

> Time turns the old days to derision,
>   Our loves into corpses or wives;
> And marriage and death and division
>   Make barren our lives.
>
> [1:159]

Swinburne makes clear in poems as various as "Before Parting," *Atalanta*, "Laus Veneris," "The Triumph of Time," and "Hermaphroditus" that it is the romantic ideal of love, the ideal of love in "the old days," that he sees turned "to derision," to "death and division" by the matter-of-fact massacres of "Time." In "Laus Veneris," as in the others, he defines love as the attempt by a dualistic visionary to blend with another being into one indivisible identity. The speaker seeks a consummation with Venus, his "soul's body" (1:12), so complete that "till the thunder in the trumpet be, / Soul may divide from body, but not we / One from another" (1:26).

Just as Swinburne allows us to see the sinister and brutal side of nature even as the Chorus attempts to sing a hymn to spring, so, in "Laus Veneris," he similarly allows a celebration of romantic love to give evidence of his own deep doubts about love's transcendent powers. "Ah, with blind lips I felt for you, and found / About my neck your hands and hair enwound," the lover cries out:

> The hands that stifle and the hair that stings,
> I felt them fasten sharply without sound.
> Yea, for my sin I had great store of bliss. . . .

If the hiss of sibilance is effective communication of the serpentine nature of the speaker's "bliss," then the harsh images which connect and unify the outer and inner landscapes of "Laus Veneris" are equally powerful in conveying the sinister, not stellar, fieriness of love's consummation. The "day" of "Love," the lover of Venus tells us, "Stunned me like lights upon some wizard way, / And ate like fire mine eyes and mine eyesight,"

> . . . till before us rose and fell
> White cursed hills, like outer skirts of hell
>   Seen where men's eyes look through the day to night,
> Like a jagged shell's lips, harsh, untunable. . . .
>
> [1:22–23]

These lines would seem to recall both the fifth book of Wordsworth's *Prelude* (where the poet hears, from the "soothing" lips of a visionary "shell," a "loud prophetic blast of harmony") and the tortured vision of the first and second books of Tennyson's *Maud* (a vision of a landscape where hills and hollows are "lips . . . dabbled with blood," where even a "lovely shell" "vexes" the "ear" with memories of soul's division). They suggest that for Swinburne, as for Tennyson, Hardy, and Lawrence, the supposedly visionary harmony of lovers in romantic love is (to break down the synesthesia) a "light" which begins as a new dawn but which eventually blinds the lovers' eyes, a sound which begins as perfect harmony but which becomes, ultimately, an "untunable" dissonance, and a seeming union which produces, finally, only the "grief" and "Sharp words" of "soul's division" in a "hell" of pain (1:23, 4:255).

Much as Hardy will suggest in *Far from the Madding Crowd* and as Lawrence will argue some forty years later in *Women in Love*, Swinburne's Sappho reveals, in "Anactoria," that the "romantic" desire to achieve perfect union with another human being leads to the martyr's pleasure on one hand, but to physical collision and pain—the revised fate of romantic lovers—on the other:

> . . . O that I
> Durst crush thee out of life with love, and die,
> Die of thy pain and my delight, and be
> Mixed with thy blood and molten into thee!
> Would I not plague thee dying overmuch?
> Would I not hurt thee perfectly? not touch
> Thy pores of sense with torture, and make bright
> Thine eyes with bloodlike tears and grievous light?
>
> [1:61]

Morse Peckham thinks that Swinburne was the first writer to attack the notion of romantic love.[8] Firsts are difficult phenomena to locate, but it would certainly be safe to agree with Peckham in spirit and with John Rosenberg in fact when Rosenberg says, in his introduction to an edition of Swinburne's poetry, that Swinburne is "the poet of love's impossibility."[9] When Swinburne sings of love (and of romantic love poetry) in "Before Parting," it is only to lay to rest the impossible dream of a previous age:

> A month or twain to live on honeycomb
> Is pleasant; but one tires of scented time,

Cold sweet recurrence of accepted rhyme,
And that strong purple under juice and foam
Where the wine's heart has burst. . . .

The association here of a "sweet" or "honeyed" hope for lasting
romantic union and the "accepted rhyme" of an old poetry is clear,
and although Keats seems to be the once "strong," now "bitter"
(1:184) eucharist in this poem and in "Laus Veneris" (where Venus
"smells of all the sunburnt south, / Strange spice and flower,
strange savour of crushed fruit, / And perfume" [1:25]), Shelley is
held no less responsible in "Hermaphroditus" and, especially, in
"The Triumph of Time," for our sweet but ultimately painful
"honeycomb" faith that, had we only found love,

We had stood as the sure stars stand, and moved
    As the moon moves, loving the world; and seen
Grief collapse as a thing disproved,
    Death consume as a thing unclean.
Twain halves of a perfect heart, made fast
Soul to soul. . . .

                                                        [1:35]

Although the disillusioned lover of Swinburne's "A Match" longs
to begin, with his beloved, a new quest for "Love," this would be a
quest with a difference, for

We'd hunt down love together,
Pluck out his flying-feather, . . .
    And find his mouth a rein. . . .

                                                        [1:105]

To Swinburne, the romantic hope for a love through which
"flesh and spirit are molten in sunder" and two may become "One
splendid spirit" (1:46, 35) had been a hope for finding something
heavenly, something godly (in the terms of "A Match," a god both
airborne and unbridled), a hope which had as its ultimate extension
the possibility that, through perfect communion with a beloved as
through perfect communion with nature, the self could rise above
the vicissitudes of time as a transcendent deity. The autobiographical voice of "The Triumph of Time" still clings, though precariously to be sure, to the romantic faith that

We, drinking love at the furthest springs,
    Covered with love as a covering tree,

We had grown as gods, as the gods above,
Filled from the heart to the lips with love,
Held fast in his hands, clothed warm with his wings,
   O love, my love, had you loved but me!

[1:35]

But this hope is perfectly compromised, for it is framed in and controlled by the time it seeks to transcend. The idea that love could have precluded the triumph of time is a projection utterly emptied out by the coincident fact that time's triumph is that which has forever *prevented* the union. Beyond that, these lines compromise romantic hope by making it a hope anterior to Miltonic language, a language which reminds that the hope that love could, "as a covering tree," hide lovers from time and change and make them "as the gods above" is a deceptive fantasy with tragic consequences, a cold-hearted Satan masquerading as warm-winged Love, a "bliss" with a serpentine tail. Swinburne associates romantic expectation with the tragic presumption incited by Satan; he also suggests that the speaker's present hellish torment derives from the romantic hope that, like a Keatsian version of Milton's Adam, he would awaken from his dream of love to find it fact. Not unlike his contemporaries, then, the young Swinburne is coming to feel that faith in attainable states of transcendence is often the source of our pain. In "The Triumph of Time" we see the lover making the "gate" to the heaven of romantic love fiendishly "strait" (1:39); in "Anactoria" Swinburne shows us, through Sappho, that the fruitless lust for complete union with the beloved not only makes the ardent worshipper suffer cruelly but also become "Cruel," for

. . . love makes all that love him well
As wise as heaven and crueller than hell.
Me hath love made more bitter toward thee
Than death toward man; but were I made as he
Who hath made all things to break them one by one,
If my feet trod upon the stars and sun
And souls of men as his have always trod,
God knows I might be crueller than God.

[1:61–62]

If Swinburne is skeptical about the outcome of man's devotion to a romantic quest for union with external nature or, through love, with external human nature in the form of a beloved, then he is equally dubious about the "romantic" hope that the isolating forces of selfishness will ever break down and flow gently into a new and harmonious social brotherhood. Indeed, through allusions to Helen of Troy and Cleopatra, "Laus Veneris" suggests that love's explosive fire is not only the occasional cause of social combustion but may even stand as a synecdoche for social strife. In any case, love is a devastating energy. As *Atalanta* reminds us, the birth of the goddess of love required that Chronos's genitals be torn from his body and cast upon the sea. Love, the Chorus cries, is "an evil blossom . . . born / Of sea-foam and the frothing of blood" (4:273). It is, quite literally, the bastard child of time and nature's "mixture." Walking arm in arm with death, love is indistinguishable from another power which controls society named "Fate." Addressing "Love and Fate," the Chorus asks:

> Wilt thou turn thee not yet nor have pity,
> But abide with despair and desire
>   And the crying of armies undone,
>   Lamentation of one with another
>   And breaking of city by city;
> The dividing of friend against friend,
>   The severing of brother and brother . . . ?
>   [4:277]

And how do the men and women of Calydon face this inevitable fact of fated chaos, of "the severing of brother from brother"? Often, with the paradoxical, romantic dream of social meliorism, a faith that the inspired word of the hero-lover (Meleager) can bring order where there is disorder, social bonding where there is only "crying . . . Lamentation . . . breaking . . . dividing . . . severing." It is the supposed romantic faith in the Promethean power of love, social brotherhood and poetry that Althaea voices when she counters Meleager's growing anxiety with the encouragement that

> Speech too bears fruit, being worthy; and air blows down
> Things poisonous, and high-seated violences,
> And with charmed words and songs have men put out
> Wild evil, and the fire of tyrannies.
>   [4:263]

It is impossible to reconcile Althaea's failing hope and the contradicting skepticism voiced by the Chorus concerning the ultimate "Fate" of man and society. When Swinburne wrote

Atalanta in Calydon, he was, to a great extent, caught in a middle time between faith and skepticism, and this fact no doubt has something to do with his choice of the dramatic or monodramatic form. The poet need not commit himself either to dogma or to heresy so long as he can clone his divided self into a series of soliloquies (as in *Poems and Ballads*, first series) or into dramatically opposed characters (as in *Atalanta*).

This heart's division is evident in Swinburne's poetry in oxymorons like "Adorable, detestable" (4:307), a phrase used to describe the coolly perfect Atalanta, but it also compels Swinburne to create larger oxymoronic structures, too. There is a pair of monodramas entitled "A Ballad of Life" and "A Ballad of Death." There are the unresolvable conflicts of *Atalanta in Calydon*, a work in which a writer torn between dreams and despair creates a world in which every love is balanced by a loathing, every triumph by a catastrophe. Exactly like Althaea's son, *Atalanta* is a *corpus* brought into being by a divided soul. Indeed, Swinburne might describe the world of his poem with the very words Althaea uses when she calls Meleager "a fire enkindled of mine hands / And of mine hands extinguished" (*Atalanta*, 4:316):

> . . . the fire I lit
> I burn with fire to quench it; yea, with flame
> I burn up even the dust and ash thereof.
>
> [4:314]

And yet the burning brand, that unforgettable emblem of death mixed with life, of springtime flame and tragic conflagration, is not an emblem original to Swinburne. A similar brand, after all, burned brightly but menacingly in the cave of Shelley's muse of visionary poetry, the Witch of Atlas. But in Shelley's cavern, although the "blazing . . . brand" consumed "many a piece / Of sandal wood, rare gums, and cinnamon," the Witch, "broidering the pictured poesy / Of some high tale"

> . . . beheld it not, for in her hand
> She held a woof that dimmed the burning brand.
>
> [xxvi–xxvii]

Tennyson's Lady of Shalott had not found it so easy to look away, and by 1865, at the time of the writing of *Poems and Ballads*, Swinburne, like Hardy, can only demonstrate that the world is a place where man

> . . . weaves, and is clothed with derision;
>   Sows, and he shall not reap. . . .

[4:260]

He has come face to face with the same crisis that Arnold wrestles with in *Empedocles on Etna*, that Teufelsdröckh faces in "The Everlasting No," and that the young Hardy confronts in his first successful poem, "Hap" (1865):

> If but some vengeful god would call to me
> From up the sky, and laugh: "Thou suffering thing,
> Know that thy sorrow is my ecstasy,
> That thy love's loss is my hate's profiting!"
>
> Then would I bear it, clench myself, and die,
> Steeled by the sense of ire unmerited;
> Half-eased in that a Powerfuller than I
> Had willed and meted me the tears I shed.
>
> But not so. How arrives it joy lies slain,
> And why unblooms the best hope ever sown?

[ll. 1–10]

Hardy's poem is a poem of questions, not of answers, and the same could be said of Swinburne's early works, especially of *Atalanta in Calydon* (1865) and *Poems and Ballads* (1866). I have been careful to use words like "increasingly agnostic" or terms such as "anti-romantic" in order to avoid any suggestion that the young Swinburne begins his poetic career as a sure-footed satyr, an autonomously agnostic and solidly post-romantic poet. Swinburne's earliest works meriting accolades are, in fact, so divided between faith and heresy, indebtedness and scorn, that their predominant imagery is that of people and things caught between one thing or place or time and another.

Atalanta opens, literally and figuratively, between the moon and the sun, since the time of day is dawn and the chief huntsman's opening speech begins as an invocation to Artemis and becomes, suddenly, an invocation to Apollo. The first choral ode describes the transition from winter to spring, but Althaea quickly counters the description with a reminder that no sooner does winter turn to spring than summer, once again, turns to autumn. As the poem develops its images, we soon realize that Calydon is a world caught between seasons, between "night" and "day," "hound" and "fawn"

(4:249–51), "pain" and "pleasure," "strength" and impotence
(4:258), "sow[ing]" and "reap[ing]," "desire" and "death," that it
lies paralyzed in an utterly divided and divisive place and time
"Between a sleep and a sleep" (4:259–60).

Depictions of interspace are so abundant in *Poems and Ballads*
(1866) that the following list comprises no more than a quarter of
such images and includes only those in which the poet actually uses
the word "between":

between the sundawn and the sun
between the nightfall and the light

["Laus Veneris"]

between the remote sea-gates

["Hymn to Proserpine"]

Between white arms and bosom
Between the bud and blossom
Between your throat and chin

["Before Dawn"]

I sing with sighing between.
My days . . . lie between death's day and birth

["April"]

What shall be said between us here
    Among the downs, between the trees . . . ?

["Félise"]

Between the dawn and the daytime

["An Interlude"]

. . . red moons wane to white
'Twixt grey seamed stems of apple trees

["August"]

. . . this child is grown
Within me between bone and bone

["Masque of
Queen Bersabe"]

Lying asleep between the strokes of night

["Love and Sleep"]

My lady has her house
Between two bowers

["Madonna Mia"]

The only accurate description of the place and time described by
"A Ballad of Life" and "A Ballad of Death," the very first (and very
fine) lyrics of *Poems and Ballads*, would tell us that the lyrics
describe nothing more or less than the indescribable: a place
between all places, a time between all times, a feeling between all

definable emotions. "A Ballad of Life" (1:1) opens "In midst" of "a place of wind and flowers," the time is the time of "dreams," between dusk and dawn, consciousness and unconsciousness. "Lust," "Shame," and "Fear" are present somewhere in this border between "trees" and "grass," but they are entranced, bereft of their powers, neither living nor dead. "In midst" of this utterly middle place stands "A Lady," but even her centrality is not definitive. The unidentified lady's smile is perfectly ambiguous, for "her mouth . . . / Seemed sad with glad things gone." When the poet says that "She held a little cithern by the strings" and that the instrument was "strung with subtle-coloured hair / Of some dead lute-player / That in dead years had done delicious things," we feel that we have found *something* final, something as decisive as death, but indeed we have not, for the lute can still play and the dead song can be revived.

These poems do not yield easily to explication, but the "dead lute player" that "in dead years had done delicious things" is surely akin to the mad lutanist of "Kubla Khan," the frenzied romantic in search of the "milk of paradise," the artist who had become an almost stock image for those dreamy-eyed youths supposed to be the poets and priests of "delicious" but "dead years." The strings of the abandoned lute, moreover, strings such as tenderness and charity, pleasure and love, are the old ideals of the dead romantic singer. We know that these were hymnal strings, strings which once accompanied the songs of the faithful, for when the Lady revives their long vanished harmonies, the realities of Lust and Fear and Shame are, suddenly and temporarily, "transfigure[d]," resurrected from "grey old miseries" of the flesh and blood into holy images of freshness and hope:

> . . . those three following men
> Became as men raised up among the dead;
> Great glad mouths open and fair cheeks made red
>   With child's blood come again.

> Then I said: Now assuredly I see
>   My lady is perfect, and transfigureth
>   All sin and sorrow and death,
> Making them fair as her own eyelids be. . . .

The "lady" would seem to be the romantic muse who allowed poets like Blake (in Swinburne's opinion) to see realities "not as they are seen upon earth," who enabled them to see "nothing as man sees."[10] For what happens to reality, to lust and shame, fear and pain, "dust and rust," is something that happens to the Lady's eyes as the old song of dead years is played, something magical that happens when the mundane is seen through the rose-colored glasses (Frye's term) of romantic "vision." As lust comes to look like love, indeed as all the "men's faces" are made "perfect," the speaker sees that they are being made "fair as her own eyelids be."

Shelley, in his "Epipsychidion," had written of a lovely lady in whose—and because of whose—gaze raw reality is so transfigured. The "Seraph of Heaven! too gentle to be human" addressed in the opening lines of that poem had been one whose presence could at once metamorphose experience and the poems that capture it in song. "All shapes look glorious which thou gazest on!" Shelley claims:

> Ay, even the dim words which obscure thee now
> Flash, lightning-like, with unaccustomed glow. . . .
>
> [ll. 32–34]

Swinburne's romantic faith is wearing, however, and he would make clear the degree to which such fires of transfiguring inspiration can be dangerous to the poet so inspired. In *William Blake*, the lengthy critical work he was beginning to write even as "A Ballad of Life" was being published, Swinburne considers the rather pathetic fate of a man who could not "be cured of illusion," of an "inexplicable" poet who could evidently imagine a "perfect" world but could not "make himself comprehensible." Blake, according to Swinburne, was a man for whom his own "art" came to embody "all faith, all virtue, all . . . religious necessity," a poet whose "creed was about this: as long as a man believes all things he may do any thing; scepticism (not sin) is alone damnable, being the one thing purely barren and negative." Here was a "pure fanatic" who would ask—if Swinburne is correct—"will any one prove or disprove for me the things I hold by warrant of imaginative knowledge? things impossible to discover, to analyse, to attest, to undervalue, to certify, or to doubt?"

In the essay on Blake, Swinburne associates this profound faith in the power of the romantic will to make its own reality with a childish, if lovely, belief in an attainable "land of dreams." He first quotes, in part, Blake's poem by that title:

"O, what Land is the Land of Dreams?
What are its Mountains & what are its Streams?
O Father, I saw my Mother there,
Among the Lillies by waters fair."

. . . .

Dear child, I also by pleasant Streams
Have wandered all Night in the Land of Dreams;
But though calm & warm the waters wide,
I could not get to the other side.

Then, having taken the liberty to equate, implicitly, the sentiments
of the speakers with those of their poet, he goes on to pronounce,
with firmness and brevity, "We may say of Blake that he," for one,
"never got back from that other side."[11]

It is important to realize that Swinburne, too, has been long
nurtured by that maternal sensibility which leads to "the other
side" of reality; ample evidence is the fact that in order to question
the romantic dream poem, the poem which helps us to see things
"not as they are seen on earth," he must annex yet another
romantic dream poem which finds "in dreams a place of wind and
flowers." Keats's prescient and autumnal lyric, "La Belle Dame
Sans Merci," is clearly an adumbration of Swinburne's dream-
verging-on-nightmare. She whose "beauty" is "fervent as the fiery
moon" recalls the "Full beautiful . . . faery" of Keats's ballad;
when Swinburne tells us that his beloved lady is "clothed like
summer," we may remember that it was Keats's knight-at-arms
who, for such a one, "made a garland for her head, / And bracelets
too" of "fragrant" flowers. The "wild" muse who presided over the
earlier poem sang "A faery song" in "language strange" and thus
transported her knight into a state of "dream," the eventual loss of
which made reality look all too "wither'd" and "cold," made the
dreamer feel "moist" with "fever." Swinburne's lady, too, makes
her poet "swoon," makes his "blood burn," and sings with "sweet
mouth a song in a strange tongue," a song which brings "extreme
sad delight."

The echoes of Keats's sad glad ballad do not make "A Ballad of
Life" into "A Ballad of Death." That "latest dream," to quote
Keats's pale loiterer, has not yet been dreamed. But they do insure
that the tone of Swinburne's ballad is not one of celebration. To be
sure, the speaker of the poem is not unaffected by the transfigura-

tion to which he is witness. He does, after all, produce "A Ballad of Life," and it certainly seems a visionary poem written under the influence of the romantic muse. Here the influence ends, however, for although the visionary ballad itself may be "kiss[ed] . . . with soft laughter on th[e] eyes" by its *belle dame*, the balladist is definitely not, and while "A Ballad of Life" flies "Forth" with "roses in both arms," the latter-day singer awakes, suddenly and abruptly, on the post-romantic scenario. He finds himself in a cold, grey landscape where transfiguring vision is no longer possible and where the poem that Keats left him to write, the heretical reply to "A Ballad of Life," is the only song that can be sung.

"A Ballad of Death" (1:4) is that absolute denial of the romantic "Ballad of Life," and thus it forms a terrible polarity for the skeptic caught in that middle place, that anything-but-restful center of indifference which lies between two sensibilities. The dark and funereal second poem is an agnostic declaration of the death of the divine romantic lady whose powers give life to "A Ballad of Life," a fact which Swinburne confirms through the use of a biblical motif, specifically the biblical motif (from Psalm 137) which had been annexed by English romantic poets as a central icon, namely, the image of the aeolean harp:

> O Love's lute heard about the lands of death,
> Left hanged upon the trees that were therein;
> O Love and Time and Sin,
> Three singing mouths that mourn now underbreath,
> Three lovers, each one evil spoken of;
> O smitten lips wherethrough this voice of mine
> Came softer with her praise;
> Abide a little for our lady's love.
> The kisses of her mouth were more than wine,
> And more than peace the passage of her days.

Swinburne's use of the lute image is subtle and complex, but his meaning (though Swinburne, like Shelley, almost defies paraphrase) seems to be something like this: the lutes of the "dead lute player" which transfigured Lust, Shame, and Fear in the past (and in that belated "Ballad of Life" that momentarily resurrected the "dead days" of the past) have been abandoned by their dead and departed romantic player, hung on trees, and thus left the instrument of the wind and the only available accompaniment for the post-romantic poet. The romantic lute is now truly an aeolean harp, but the breath of the mere wind is not so inspired as were the fingers of the romantic singer, and the heavenly strings that once transfigured reality in song and underscored the praises of a heavenly romantic muse now only intone the raw realities of "Love and Time and Sin."

Swinburne critics have long suggested that the dead goddess whose "kisses . . . were more than wine," the muse whose "days" brought a bliss more profound "than peace," is Venus. A dead or dying Venus does appear and speak to the poet, but she begs him to

> . . . Arise, lift up thine eyes and see
> If any glad thing be or any good
> Now the best thing is taken forth of us;
> Even she to whom all praise
> Was as one flower . . . of many and glorious,
> One day found gracious among many days.

The two, then, are not the same. The corpse who had seemed alive to the momentarily inspired poet of "A Ballad of Life" is "she whose *handmaiden* is Love" (italics mine), the spirit of intellectual love or imagination whose constant inspiration Swinburne has vainly sought. She is the dead goddess whom the transitional poet must praise and, at the same time, abandon, for "A Ballad of Death" is a poem of agnostic cleavage ("My tears ran down . . . to the place . . . where her parted breast-flowers . . . are cloven apart," to "the tender interspace" where precious "leaves grown thereof were things to kiss / Ere their fine gold was tarnished at the heart"). In this lyric, the singer's cleavage from his "lady" is a cleavage from a time of faith, a time "found gracious among many days,"

> . . . in the days when God did good to me . . .
> In the good days when God kept sight of us. . . .

"A Ballad of Life" had been "kissed" by a last, brief sputter and spark of romantic inspiration, but its poet had lived on unblessed (yet another division in a poem instinct with divisions). He survived "the good days when God kept sight of us" to write a second schizophrenic ballad where although "flowers" exist they are all "poppies," where there are "sheaves" but they are all "rusted," where although the "rain" comes it makes life "Rain-rotten," and where "grass" grows but "fades ere any of it be mown." This second ballad means to "Seek out Death's face ere the light altereth, / And say 'My master that was thrall to Love / Is become thrall to Death.'"

These last lines of "A Ballad of Death" are telling, for they show us that the "interspace" in which the young poet is caught is not the mid-point of positive transition but, rather, that death-in-life which produces only contradictions in terms, namely, a philosophy which is nihilistic and a poetry whose primary meanings are confusion. In "A Leave-taking" (1:52) the poet, caught at a real and symbolic shoreline, promises to become decisive, "to go seaward as the great winds go," but the transition from shore to sea is even less satisfying than the rather similar seaward movement described by Arnold in "The Forsaken Merman." For the sea, in Swinburne's poem, offers no alternative to the drab or painful visions of the land, rather, it offers only "drowning," an end to all poetic perspectives.

The poem, from first line to last, is fraught with polarities and ambiguities. Does the world (symbolized by the land) look barren *because* the poet has not achieved romantic union with his beloved or has the romantic quest failed because of the barrenness of the world? Or is it that even if the universe *were* an all-harmonious place *she* "would not hear" or "see," "know" or "weep," "care" or "love"? Furthermore, if the doubts raised by this utterly ambiguous (and nonetheless lovely) lyric could be reduced to one overriding indecision, it might be framed by an unresolved question something like this: which is more desolate, more meaningless, to sing of pain and loss or not to sing at all?

Poems founded on such a question can only be poems of eternally unaccomplished suicide, that is, of masochism, of singing about those subjects too painful to sing about, and "Itylus" (1:54), perhaps Swinburne's greatest early lyric, is certainly such a poem. The poet and the poem are caught precisely between "land and sea," "A Ballad of Life" and "A Ballad of Death," between the respective songs of the swallow and the nightingale, the singer who transcends Lust and Shame and Fear by escaping "to the sun and the south" and the younger sister, the sadder voice who can only chronicle the real world of suffering, "the place of the slaying of Itylus," the "small slain body, the flowerlike face,"

> The hands that cling and the feet that follow,
>   The voice of the child's blood crying yet. . . .

The lines of the poem are, to be sure, spoken by this latter poet, this nightingale who marvels at her sister's ability to forget—let alone transfigure or transcend—lust, fear, shame, and death. And in that sense, of course, Swinburne might seem to be closer to the post-romantic than to the "romantic" position. But "Itylus" remains, for the most part, a poem about utter motionlessness ("For where thou fliest I shall not follow, / Till life forget and death remember, / Till thou remember and I forget") and "heart's division" ("Thy heart is light as a leaf of a tree; / But mine goes forth among sea-gulfs hollow"). It is a poem about non-resolution, for resolution would entail *either* the nightingale's choice to be like her sister, to escape, to transcend reality through the wings of transfiguring song *or* the nightingale's acceptance of the mundane world of suffering and pain. Neither resolution occurs. In fact, one of the strange things about the poem is that the suffering nightingale never calls for her sister's silence and at times even suggests that her light-hearted escapism is exactly as tempting as it is fraudulent ("Could I forget or thou remember, / Couldst thou remember and I forget").

This hermaphroditic dichotomy between fraudulence and pain is reminiscent of the dichotomy instinct in Arnold's early poetry: Mycerinus is living somewhere between true revelry (which is no longer possible) and acceptance of the world's harsh fate (which is impossible to bear); in "Isolation. To Marguerite" the poet envies those innocents who dream that two human hearts may become one and yet knows that loneliness, however unbearable, is the soul's true state. In "The Sick King of Bokhara" we are presented with a noble but unrealistic king and a practical but rather unfeeling vizier; *Empedocles* introduces a poet who does not live in the world and a stoic who cannot tolerate the world in which he lives; and neither poem allows us any real, conclusive sense of Arnold's position within the terribly unsatisfying dialectic.

The inconclusive conclusion, the agonizing *nexus* of Swinburne's early lyrics, is precisely the origin of one of his favorite images, for necrophilia, like hermaphroditism, communicates the poet's paralyzing inability to be one thing or the other, either to believe in the viability of the past or to break away from the past for the even more grisly visage of the future. In "The Leper," the speaker kisses the corpse of his leprous lover, an act which allows him to embrace a dead ideal even while admitting its (and insuring his own) demise, a perfect denial of both past and future. In recalling "Laus Veneris," a poem in which lover and beloved exist in a hazy twilight ("Asleep or waking is it?") "between the sundawn and the sun," it is interesting to remember that the lover who speaks in the poem, although he has been called by Christ to walk into a new era of a new faith, strays out of the procession and returns to kiss the dying goddess of the old spiritual (and aesthetic) order:

> . . . for her neck,
> Kissed over close, wears yet a purple speck
>   Wherein the pained blood falters and goes out. . . .
>
> But though my lips shut sucking on the place,
> There is no vein at work upon her face;
>   Her eyelids are so peaceable, no doubt
> Deep sleep has warmed her blood through all its ways.
>
> Lo, this is she that was the world's delight;
> The old grey years were parcels of her might. . . .
>   [1:11]

The lover of Venus is, in his own words, caught "between the iron sides of death" (1:17), for to live he will have to stop kissing dead or dying deities of the past, but to abandon them for the drab new god of the future is such a repulsive thought to him that his only choice is to die, "To have known love, . . . / And afterward be cast out of God's sight" (1:26).

There are other lyrics in *Poems and Ballads* similarly caught in the rather isolating position of being elegies to the past and diatribes against the future. "St. Dorothy" is a poem which, by describing the fierce persecution of a religious virgin, convinces us both that the fleshly agnostics may be correct in seeing the virgin's faith as a hopelessly innocent vision and that Dorothy's vision, absurd and childlike as it may be, is (if we are to make sense of the poem's *dénouement*) a noble, even ethically compelling force. "Dolores" catalogues the sorrows and sins of Dolores, "which are seventy times seven" and which include, among other things, the vicissitudes of nature ("Fierce midnights and famishing morrows"), the divisive "loves that complete and control / All the joys of the flesh," and "all the sorrows / That wear out the soul" (1:154). On one hand this catalogue of sorrows convinces us that Dolores is a more likely candidate for "Notre Dame" than is Mary, with her infinite virtues and her mere seven sorrows. But, on the other hand, is she a mother to whom we want to pray, in whom we want to trust? The poem, like many of Swinburne's early lyrics, having described the inadequacy of of the past and the insufferability of the future, can only collapse into a quiet prayer for annihilation:

> What ails us to fear overmeasure,
>   To praise thee with timorous breath . . . ?
> We shall change as the things that we cherish,
>   Shall fade as they faded before,
> As foam upon water shall perish,
>   As sand upon shore.

[1:168]

It is this kind of tonal, rhetorical, and structural collapse, a collapse which follows upon unresolvable dialectics of equally unacceptable images, emotions, philosophies, theologies, and aesthetics, which gives Swinburne's poetry that peculiarly beautiful place of decomposition, that "Garden of Proserpine" (1:169) where faith and doubt, beauty and ugliness, tears and laughter, hopes and despondencies, romantic faith and Victorian heresy, all dissolve in a place "where the world is quiet," a place called into being by the agonized poet's desire for nothingness:

> From too much love of living,
> From hope and fear set free,
> We thank with brief thanksgiving
> Whatever gods may be
> That no life lives for ever;
> That dead men rise up never;
> That even the weariest river
> Winds somewhere safe to sea.

[1:171]

These lines subtly revise the fourth act of *Prometheus Unbound*, where Shelley celebrates the fact that "Man" is

> . . . one harmonious soul of many a soul,
> Whose nature is its own divine control,
> Where all things flow to all, as rivers to the sea. . . .

[ll. 400–403]

Swinburne's world is one of utter division, not harmony, so he poetically corrects Shelley by refashioning the image of effluence into an image not of control, interdependence, and energetic unity, but of isolation, impotence, sleep, dissolution. In doing so, he denies the propriety of Shelley's optimistic misreading of Ecclesiastes 9 (where "All things come alike to all" described human unity more in terms of catastrophe, disappointment, suffering than in terms of divine potentiality) and reemphasizes the feeling of endurance, fatigue, and loss which pervades that most striking scriptural text.

The emotional, aesthetic undoing of "The Garden of Proserpine," out of unfruitful argument, into a prayer for sleep, can also be found at the conclusion of Swinburne's "Hymn to Proserpine" (1:67), a hymn torn between faith in a goddess whose time has forever passed and faith in a new religion with new gods, "merciful, clothed with pity, the young compassionate Gods" whose "new device" and whose new "days are bare" for the speaker. But before his song collapses "beyond the extreme sea-wall" where "Waste water washes," the singer of the "Hymn to Proserpine" reveals to us that he is not all that different from "The Leper," or from Venus's lover in "Laus Veneris," for he, like all of these men, would rather court the dead (for the leper, it is "the service God forbids") than embrace the present. This preference, this position, moreover, makes these lovers spiritual brothers to nearly all of the speakers of all of Swinburne's early lyrics, for to so stray out of the public way is to be a martyr, and martyrdom is the one identity which all the speakers of all of Swinburne's early poems have in common.

In "The Triumph of Time," the lover caught between two views of love (one of transubstantiating romantic union, the other of degrading marriages of convenience), between two visions of nature (one of harmonious spring, one of divisive, destructive autumn), and two conceptions of the self (one as divinity, the other as meaningless fragment) knows that the old romantic visions are as obsolete ("ruined") as the newer, colder, more cynical understandings are painful ("icy"). It is this agonizing vacillation between an impossible romantic dream of the heart ("We had grown as gods") and an unbearable observation by the mind "of the sound of the sorrow of years" (1:40) which makes this great poem, spiritually and aesthetically, as unresolved as the act of martyrdom itself. How *does* the poem end? (It is a question seldom asked about poetry.) With a series of rhetorical questions:

Rest, and be glad of the gods; but I,
    How shall I praise them or how take rest?

Come life, come death, not a word be said;
Should I lose you living, and vex you dead?

I never shall tell you on earth; and in heaven,
    If I cry to you then, will you hear or know?

It is an ending as tentative as it is appropriate to a poem whose images (light and dark, spring and fall, sea and land) and whose themes (fecundity or barrenness, faith or faithlessness, ruined dreams or icy realities) offer perfect dichotomies of unavailable and unacceptable choices. For just as these polarized images and themes can resolve, respectively, only in landscapes of undisturbed sleep and in prayers for annihilation, so such a poetic structure can only resolve in the perfect ambiguity—the question which is not a question, the question for which no answer is possible:

. . . O sweet,
Had you felt, lying under the palms of your feet,
The heart of my heart, beating harder with pleasure
    To feel you tread it to dust and death—

Ah, had I not taken my life up and given
    All that life gives and the years let go,
The wine and honey, the balm and leaven,
    The dreams reared high and the hopes brought low?
                                                                [1:46]

In one sense or another, all of Swinburne's early poems end, in tone if not in punctuation, with some kind of unanswerable or at least unanswered question—one need only think for a moment about "A Leave-taking," "Laus Veneris," or "Faustine" to see that this is so. The same may be said of *Atalanta in Calydon*, the great poetic drama published one year before, but composed simultaneously with, the first group of *Poems and Ballads*.

Atalanta, like the shorter lyrics, ends in explosive fireworks of utter and irreconcilable divisions that have been growing ever wider since nature's inception of the dramatic action. Most of these schisms are obvious and many have been so critically belabored that a handful of examples should suffice. The Chorus is torn between describing the world as it really is and "dreaming" or "praying" that soon the natural, romantic, and social disorder will be "assuaged." (Even the choral definition of God vacillates from "high" good [4:253] to "supreme evil" [4:287] to a perfectly

oxymoronic "resolution" of these definitions ["good with bad,"
4:298].) Althaea's speeches are similarly divided, even from the
beginning, between honeyed lines of an obsolete scripture (4:265–
68) and unbearably painful descriptions of the world as it is (4:251).
Besides being torn between faith and doubt in the gods, Althaea is
torn between two kinds of love—one for her son, the other for
those brothers who have been slain by her son—and it is this inner
conflict which brings about both Meleager's death and her own
spiritual death. Meleager's tragic actions are similarly controlled by
diametrically opposed passions and loyalties. All these divisions,
plus some others, catalyze those tragic reactions that form the
terrible climax of the drama, a climax without release, a "resolution" characterized not by tragic recognitions, communications,
and catharsis, but rather by deafness, inarticulateness, and departure.

The tragedy of *Atalanta* is that tragedy which cannot be
resolved, that catastrophe which results when romantic and religious dreams are exploded by reality and when reality, in turn,
cannot be borne, when fancy and fact explode each other in one
fire, leaving the characters' "speech flicker[ing] like a blown-out
flame," leaving their stammering author in the analogous position
of ending his work, in action, tone, and punctuation, with only
questions. Does death bring Meleager release from consciousness,
or only "wail[ing] by impassable streams" (4:324)? Does he,
through his last speech, earn his mother's forgiveness? From
Atalanta, his coldly quiet beloved, does Meleager earn "honour"
and the consummative "kiss" for which he pleads? Is Atalanta good
or evil, human or divine? Will the slaying of the boar usher in a
better, more harmonious age for nature, for lovers, for Calydonian
society? Have the gods ever really existed, or have "gods" been
merely the names man has given to his own irresponsible, evil
propensities? Who are the "lords" with which the Chorus, in its
final speech, says man must constantly "contend"—supernatural
forces or man's own destructive romantic dreams?

> Who shall contend with his lords
>   Or cross them or do them wrong?
> Who shall bind them as with cords?
>   Who shall tame them as with song?
> Who shall smite them as with swords?
>   For the hands of their kingdom are strong.

Crisis and Transition

Swinburne's Songs before Sunrise

3

If there is any deep-seated relationship between epistemology and expression (a matter on which linguists, Marxists, structuralists, and phenomenologists can almost agree), then we would have to conclude that something happened to Swinburne's vision of the world between *Poems and Ballads* (1866) and *Songs before Sunrise* (1871). Gone are the fierce dichotomies of images, actions, and beliefs (reconcilable only through hermaphroditism, necrophilia, or other unstable couplings); gone also are those larger poetic structures which would suddenly disintegrate in unfinished thoughts and actions, in unanswered, often poorly posed, questions, in inconsolable cries of anguish, or in prayers for annihilation and sleep.

In their place is a relatively stoical, even relatively political poetry. Its gospel—that man must live an ethical, finite life in an indifferent natural world—is advanced through a controlled, synthetic poetic structure and, consequently, a voice capable of resolving ambiguities through confident declarations. That is not to say, of course, that the *Songs before Sunrise* foresee "the final end of war or suffering or struggle." As Jerome McGann points out, the volume is "not" the work of "a meliorist."[1] Swinburne from 1870 on is neither a full-fledged nor half-hearted member of that congregation in which the adolescent poet had admitted membership. "The church of Blake and Shelley" is one whose dogma Swinburne had come to dismiss as a crazy old vision "spoilt" by "'progress of the species' . . . feelings."[2]

To be sure, a writer works out of essentially the same perceptions and beliefs, just as he draws upon the same basic vocabulary and expresses himself through the same linguistic structures, throughout his career. So the objection might be raised, at this point, that many of the stoical revisions of what mid-nineteenth-century authors somewhat reductively called romanticism or the romantic faith are, to some degree, present in poems which antedate the *Songs before Sunrise*. In "Anactoria," after all, Sappho had spoken about the certainty of oblivion in the line "Thee too the years shall cover" (Hardy's favorite) and had gone on to tell her lover,

. . . thou shalt be
As the rose born of one same blood with thee,
As a song sung, as a word said, and fall
Flower-wise, and be not any more at all,
Nor any memory of thee anywhere; . . .

. . . like those herds of his
Who laugh and live a little, and their kiss
Contents them, and their loves are swift and sweet,
And sure death grasps and gains them with slow feet,
Love they or hate they, strive or bow their knees. . . .
                                                    [1:63, 65]

Here is a view of self and time, of nature and love, which parallels Carlyle's post-romantic declaration that "soon . . . shall thy beatific vision . . . melt away; and only oxen and sheep be grazing in its place."[3] And the lines clearly anticipate Hardy's (or Lawrence's) myriad poems on simple love and slow decay midst nature's dumb, indifferent compost-heap. "Anactoria" must, nevertheless, be distinguished from the more comfortable, post-romantic assertions of mature Hardy, of Lawrence, or even of the more maturely agnostic Swinburne whom we encounter in *Songs before Sunrise*. However much the poem may suggest that the self is insignificant, that nature is void of redemptive moral harmonies, that the temporal process is inevitable, and that all love is therefore "swift and sweet," we must remember that these are facts with which the "herds" are "content," facts which the speaker finds unbearable, truths against which the poet of the poem rebels in an agonized claim that, through art, at least, some small degree of immortality can be attained:

. . . he hath his will of these.
Yea, but albeit he slay me, hating me—
Albeit he hide me in the deep dear sea . . .
Of me the high God hath not all his will.

Lo, earth may labour, men live long and die,
Years change and stars, and the high God devise
New things, and old things wane before his eyes . . .
But having made me, me he shall not slay.
Nor slay nor satiate, like those herds of his. . . .

[1:65]

It is true that in "Laus Veneris" the poet-lover anticipates Hardy's
startling ode to purely organic immortality (wittily entitled "Transformations"):

Ah yet would God this flesh of mine might be
Where air might wash and long leaves cover me . . .
Ah yet would God that stems and roots were bred
Out of my weary body and my head. . . .

[1:13]

And it is equally true that the even more autobiographical voice in
"The Triumph of Time" longs for a similar burial, without hope of
finding either a burning fountain or a Christian resurrection:

I wish we were dead together to-day,
Lost sight of, hidden away out of sight,
Clasped and clothed in the cloven clay,
Out of the world's way, out of the light. . . .

[1:37]

But the longing for decay in "Laus Veneris" is an entirely negative
longing, a plea for nothingness which results from the simultaneous
inability to keep old ideals alive or to live in a world without them,
and the wish for double burial in "The Triumph of Time" is really
more of a romantic longing (Heathcliff, after all, wished the same
wish) than a stoical post-romantic reconciliation with the timeless
clay of the dumb, indifferent earth. The speaker himself dismisses
his longings for romantic interment with his beloved some two
stanzas later by referring to them as "sick dreams"!

"Sick dreams," those lovely remains of a romantic faith which
bring paralysis to the necrophiliac Swinburne of *Atalanta* (1865)
and of *Poems and Ballads* (1866) and block his progress into what
Arnold had called "a culminating epoch,"[4] a "turn to a new mode

of spiritual progress,"[5] have little place in *Songs before Sunrise*. Swinburne can hardly be recalling anyone but himself when he says, of the youthful singer whose gradually liberated career is chronicled by the "Prelude" to the volume,

Then he stood up, and trod to dust
Fear and desire, mistrust and trust,
   And dreams of bitter sleep and sweet,
   And bound for sandals on his feet
Knowledge and patience of what must
   And what things may be, in the heat
And cold of years that rot and rust
   And alter; and his spirit's meat
Was freedom, and his staff was wrought
Of strength, and his cloak was woven of thought.

                     [2:3–4]

Knowledge, patience, freedom, strength, thought—they are nothing less than the polar opposites of the dreaming, restlessness, spiritual tyranny, ineffectuality, and feeling which form the terms of the post-romantic, post-Christian definition both of romanticism and of the Christian faith. The youth of the "Prelude," moreover, is none other than the poet, the Swinburne who has only recently escaped that paralyzing "fellowship forlorn" that had locked him into spiritual necrophilia and that had turned the potentially fruitful dialectics of his poems into sterile wishes that he "had . . . not been born":

Nor holds he fellowship forlorn
   With souls that pray and hope and hate,
And doubt they had better not been born,
   And fain would lure or scare off fate . . .
He builds not half of doubts and half
Of dreams his own soul's cenotaph. . . .

                     [2:5]

The structural paralysis and the funereal tone of Swinburne's early works resulted from precisely this problem—the poet "built" his works "half of doubts and half / Of dreams," and he ended up with nothing less, but nothing more, than an exquisite aesthetic "cenotaph." (Arnold, in his *Empedocles*—a work that Swinburne read many times and adored as often[6]—also had spoken of the vague, unrealizable "longing of our youth" as "hopes entombed"

[I.ii.370].) Elsewhere in the "Prelude" to *Songs before Sunrise* Swinburne speaks of this disabling polarity of unresolved and unresolvable "doubt" and "dreams" as "twin-born faith and disbelief / Who share the seasons to devour" (2:3–4). Thus "dreams" and "faith" are implicitly merged, and romantic melancholia, as well as the spiritual doubts which Swinburne believes to be inherent in any formal belief in God, are doubly dismissed as the agonies of "devouring" faiths.

Faiths which speak always of divinity, perfection, apocalypse, and transubstantiation, according to the "Prelude" to *Songs before Sunrise*, keep man from bearing—and from improving in limited ways and to limited degrees—the "actual earth," the "here and now." "What has he whose will sees clear," the poet asks, "To do with doubt and faith and fear, / Swift hopes and slow despondencies?"

> His soul is even with the sun
> Whose spirit and whose eye are one,
>   Who seeks not stars by day, nor light
>   And heavy heat of day by night.
> Him can no God cast down, whom none
>   Can lift in hope beyond the height
> Of fate and nature and things done
>   By the calm rule of might and right
> That bids men be and bear and do,
> And die beneath blind skies or blue.
>
> [2:4]

The young poet writing in 1865 had suspected, even in his most tortured, agnostic pieces, the existence of a mysterious but real, omnipotent power. "We know not if he care for anything," Swinburne had complained in his poem "To Victor Hugo" (1:149). But the poet composing the "Prelude" or "To Walt Whitman in America" in 1870 believes that God-as-conscious-presence is just another God of man's "romantic" dream- or wish-fulfillment. He is, Swinburne argues, the "God of [a] grievous people" created in man's own image, "After the likeness of [his] race," a vision made necessary by humankind's "blind helpless eyeless face" (2:81).

The time has come, the new priest of the "Hymn of Man" sings out, when this "grievous" "God of your making" (2:95) should grow sick and die of human neglect. It is God, not man, the hymnist sings, who is "servant with Change for lord," and the lord of Change in this later hymn is none other than the collective "Man" on whose breath the terrible old deity may be "driven as a wind at their will" (2:95, 98). In the gospels, Jesus feared that his Father had forsaken him; in Swinburne's vision of man's agnostic future, it is even more certain that Christ will be forsaken by his Creator, for the poet sees man's only salvation as coming through (to quote John Stuart Mill's phrase) a "human" faith, "a renovation . . . in the basis of belief." "Set not thine hand unto" the "Worm-eaten . . . cross" of the old faith, the poet pleads "Before a Crucifix,"

> Let not thy tree of freedom be
> Regrafted from that rotting tree.
>
> [2:85–86]

The "tree" from which mankind is to graft his new-found faith is not the eidelon of the pale Galilean's sacrifice. It is perhaps distantly related to the "elm tree bright against the west" of "Thyrsis," an Arnoldian symbol of distant but attainable truth and integrity; it is even more nearly akin to that symbol of organic birth, growth, and death, that "Life Tree" which Carlyle had recently resurrected from Norse mythology. The tree from which man's revisionary *credo* is to be taken is, in Swinburne's cosmography, a symbolic tree of life, a tree bearing the post-Christian, post-romantic knowledge that nature speaks no divine messages and is not a transparency through which the eternal can be glimpsed, that time, since it is inescapable, is to be used responsibly, and that bonds of love and society, though poor and fragile tools, are, at the same time, the only tools by which man can, at least temporarily, better the human condition.

Swinburne (somewhat paradoxically) gives voice to this tree of true, earthly knowledge in "Hertha" so that his latter day "goddess" can define herself ("The life tree am I; / In the buds of your lives is the sap of my leaves"),

> Mother, not maker,
>   Born, and not made;
> Though her children forsake her,
>   Allured or afraid,
> Praying prayers to the God of their fashion, she stirs not for all
>   that have prayed.
>
> [2:76, 74]

"Hertha," the un-goddess of the world, is the source of life ("mother") but is not a personal, creative god ("not maker"). Therefore, she answers no visionary's prayer ("she stirs not for all that have prayed") and yields her secrets neither to the saints nor to the Shelleys, neither to Moses nor to Wordsworth. She asks of men who have "communed in spirit" with "the winds," "the sea," "the wilderness," and "the night"—have "spoken" as "brethren" with "the sun and the mountains"—"What is here, does thou know it? / What was, hast thou known?" And then she answers her own question, saying that neither "Prophet nor poet," neither "spirit nor flesh can make answer" (2:74).

There is just enough of the new, didactic voice of Swinburne in this supposedly more pluralistic Mother ("All forms of all faces, / All works of all hands") for Hertha to pointedly advise us with respect to all her many opinions. But, all in all, she is an acceptable fabrication, a tolerable self-contradiction. Hertha at once allows Swinburne to work within a tradition (for surely she traces her line of descent back to those speaking Earth-spirits of romantic fictions as various as Blake's *The Four Zoas*, Shelley's *Prometheus Unbound*, and Emerson's "Brahma") and, at the same time, allows him to deny the very bases of what he believed to be central to that unfortunate tradition of "faith"—faith in man's ultimate ability to transcend time and trees and dirt, faith in a divine power of love, faith in social meliorism, in revelation and millennial transfiguration.

"Hertha" can be shown to be, among other things, a specific response to and revision of Shelley's "Alastor." When she denies that, in the "wilderness," "from the sea," on "the mountains," through the winds' "counsel" or communion "with night," man has gained any real "knowledge of me," she reminds us pointedly of the pathetic failures of the young "Poet" of "Alastor," who "left / His cold fireside ... / To seek strange truths" in a "tangled wilderness," who fruitlessly sought "Knowledge and truth" in the voice, the "woven sounds of streams and breezes," of an utterly elusive demon or spirit (11. 74–78, 155–58). It was Shelley and his poet, after all, who had "watched" the "motions of the forests and the sea," who had listened attentively to "murmurs of the air," the windy "breath" of an elusive "Great Parent," always searching for "the haunt / Of every gentle wind whose breath can teach / The wilds to love tranquility" (11. 45–47, 586–88). It was the young poet of "Alastor" who had, "in lone and silent hours, / When night makes a weird sound of its own stillness, / Like an inspired and desperate alchemist," tried to perform "Such magic as compels the charmed night / To render up" her "charge." And, when the youthful poet's quest had ended in death, it was that surviving lyricist, the sadder and wiser Shelley in "Alastor," who had continued to insist that "sea and mountain ... and wilderness," the "shapes / Of this phantasmal scene," had "to thee / Been purest ministers" (ll. 29–36, 693–98).

Wordsworth's marvelous lines in Book VI of *The Prelude*, where he describes the crossing of the Alps, are no less present in, no less important to, "Hertha." Hertha presides "On the world's mountain-ranges / And stream-riven heights"; her "tongue is the wind's tongue and language of storm clouds" (ll. 128–30). And Wordsworth, it will be remembered, had followed "a rough stream's edge," a "stony channel" of a "stream" which seemed "Conspicuous invitation to ascend / A lofty mountain" (ll. 569–82). Having crossed the Alps, he had "Entered a narrow chasm," witnessed the "giddy prospect of the raving stream," and heard "Winds thwarting winds, bewildered and forlorn" (ll. 621–28). It was at this point that the poet had his vision of "Tumult and peace, the darkness and the light," the "workings of one mind, the features / Of the same face, blossoms upon one tree;"

> Characters of the great Apocalypse,
> The types and symbols of Eternity,
> Of first, and last, and midst, and without end.
>
> [ll. 635–40]

The "features" of Hertha's "face" might seem to reflect just such a prophecy of eternal unities:

> All forms of all faces,
>   All works of all hands . . .
> All death and all life, and all reigns and
>   all ruins, drop through me as sands.
>
> [ll. 131–32, 135]

The "blossoms" of her "tree," moreover, seem equally Wordsworthian "types and symbols of Eternity":

> The storm-winds of ages
>   Blow through me and cease . . .

> Ere the breath of them roughen my tresses,
>> ere one of my blossoms increase.
> . . . .
>> In the spring-coloured hours
>>> When my mind was as May's,
>> There brake forth of me flowers
>>> By centuries of days,
> Strong blossoms with perfume of manhood,
>> shot out from my spirit as rays.
>
> [11. 121–25, 146–50]

Swinburne's poem, however, is not a poem of revelation or apocalypse. A poet on the "heights" does not see, reflect upon, and somehow understand Hertha's face, her blossoms, her tumult and peace, darkness and light, rather, he, as a man, *is* the blossom on her face, her tumult and her peace, her darkness and light. Wordsworth (and by Wordsworth I mean both the poet of *The Prelude* and the less complicated Wordsworth of Victorian myth) speaks of the mind's power to see into the life of things; in Swinburne, silent man is told to know himself, for, in Arnold's words, "so much, not more, he can" ("To George Cruikshank").

Hertha, because of her bastardly relationship to romantic ancestors, thus effectively rephrases the ideas and reworks the motifs of the "Prelude" to *Songs before Sunrise*, the "Prelude" to the new poetry and the new poet who " . . . hath given himself to time, whose fold / Shuts in the mortal flock that lives / On its plain pasture's heat and cold / And the equal year's alternatives" (2:5). She offers nothing less than a manifesto to the post-romantic poet who "takes cheer / With the actual earth's equalities, / Air, light, and night, hills, winds, and streams, / And seeks not strength from strengthless dreams" (2:4), the new poet, finally, who can effectively communicate one most important truth, namely, that there is but

> A little time that we may fill
> Or with such good works or such ill
>> As loose the bonds or make them strong
> Wherein all manhood suffers wrong.
>
> [2:9]

In "The Eve of Revolution," Swinburne expands upon this theme of responsible, social action (the agnostic's revision of "good works") and, just as in "Hertha," he effectively uses the romantic tradition to signal his own incipient departure. The poem initially

flaunts its revisionary debt to Shelley's "Ode to the West Wind."
"Down the wild wind of vision," the poet says, "Dreams" are
"caught and whirled,"

> Dead leaves of sleep, thicker than autumn leaves,
>> Shadows of storm-shaped things,
>> Flights of dim tribes of kings,
> The reaping men that reap men for their sheaves. . . .

The speaker suddenly hears "A voice more instant than the winds
are clear,"

> Say to my spirit, "Take
> Thy trumpet too, and make
> A rallying music in the void night's ear . . .
> Till, as through sleep false life knows true life near,
> Thou know the morning through the night,
> And through the thunder silence, and through
> darkness light."

[2:10–11]

Late in the poem, however, "The Eve of Revolution" seeks to
become a very different poem from "Ode to the West Wind" or
from Shelley's drama of gradual psychic revolution, *Prometheus
Unbound*. For Swinburne's poem is not an ode about or dramatization of some mythical, even mystical marriage of love and reason
which will, someday soon, revolutionize social existence. To be
sure, this ode on "The Eve of Revolution" does, on one level, seek
to continue in what Swinburne might have called the romantic
business of dreaming "Dreams" which, as they are "whirled"
"Down the wild wind of vision" (2:10), induce a liberating psychic
change in the collective Imagination of mankind ("O multitudinous
bosom. . . . / O many-minded . . . Asia"). And yet, even while
"The Eve of Revolution" works out of this romantic tradition, it
also seeks transformations far more immediate and concrete,
namely, to actually sever bonds of iron as well as imaginatively
melt away those cloudier spiritual or psychic bonds,

> . . . to break *and* melt in sunder
> All clouds *and* chains that in one bondage bind
> Eyes, hands, *and* spirits, forged by fear and wonder
> *And* sleek fierce fraud with hidden knife behind. . . .

[2:15, italics mine]

Swinburne, running perfectly counter to Shelley's "Preface" to *Prometheus Unbound, does* "dedicate" his poetic compositions "to the direct enforcement of reform." Whereas "Didactic poetry is" an "abhorrence" to the Shelley of the "Preface," it is not to Swinburne during this, his middle period. (In 1865 Swinburne had called Shelley's poems "doctrinaire"; they, of course, are not, but Swinburne needed to say so in order to assert the uniqueness of his own early poems which, *mutatis mutandis,* were about as free of "doctrine" as Shelley's.) If his poetry could be an effective force in freeing "hands" as well as "spirits" from "chains" as well as from "clouds," from "fraud" and "knife" as well as from "fear and wonder," then, Swinburne feels, he could "give himself to time," take "cheer with the actual earth's equalities," seek "not strength from strengthless dreams," and "fill" a "little time . . . with such good works . . . / As loose the bonds . . . / Wherein all manhood suffers wrong" (2:9). He could, furthermore, accomplish that youthful ambition of being "less of [a] Shelley," of writing "something that would do good and might endure."[7]

But if it is not just "Alastor" that Swinburne would supersede in "Hertha," neither is it only the Shelley of *Prometheus* and of "Ode to the West Wind" that Swinburne would correct in "The Eve of Revolution." *Songs before Sunrise* was published three years after *William Blake* (1868), an essay which, in turn, came out two years after the publication of *Poems and Ballads.* The study of Blake, in fact, might be seen as the first real evidence of Swinburne's imminent departure from the romantic mode, for in that piece he refers to Blake as a "perfect" man "beautifully unfit for walking in the way of other men" and, upon examining a "likeness" of his predecessor, says that Blake's "is not the face of a man who could ever be cured of illusions; here all the medicines of reason and experience must have been spent in pure waste." He does not deny the fact that his poet of innocence was prophet to a world on the eve of revolution, but he does assail the ineffectuality of Blake's prophecies. As for the "poor men" who needed to hear a voice, Swinburne says, "their new prophet had not one point they could lay hold of, not one organ or channel of expression by which to make himself comprehensible to such as they were." Even Shelley, "mysterious" a convert to Blake's "church of rebels" as he was, "was less made up of mist and fire." Blake's poetic "maze of cloudy colour," Swinburne claims, was "incomprehensible." His practical sense, if it ever existed, had been "possessed by" some "fury and fervour" of a "belief" which "sane men" could not grasp, a "devil" of a "faith" as "inexplicable" as it was "absolute and hard, like a pure fanatic's."

To a certain extent, of course, such an assessment misses the mark, a fact of which Swinburne himself was half aware, as he reveals when he praises the "quality of actual life" which permeates "every shred of [Blake's] work," or when he lauds his elder for being a "simple poetic genius."[8] And yet, in the *Songs before Sunrise*, there is evidence not only that Swinburne is reacting against the ineffectual William Blake of *William Blake* but also that there is a degree of truth in the "likeness" Swinburne has etched in that important critical work. For when Swinburne, in a poem like "The Eve of Revolution," seeks to write lyrics which may liberate men from real knives and bars as opposed to those "chains" of "mind" that are "forged by fear and wonder," he is specifically responding to poems like Blake's "London," in which the poet is incited to utterance by "mind forg'd manacles" that leave "Marks of weakness, marks of woe." Swinburne would go beyond the sentiment Blake expresses in one of his *Songs of Experience*, the sentiment Shelley would make into romantic doctrine:

CAN I see another's woe,
And not be in sorrow too?

Like Blake, Swinburne would change the "world" through "Art" ("To God"). Unlike Blake, he is not sure that the "Arts," once "Renew[ed]," will "restore" the world through "mental Charms" alone. Blake may have felt that

GREAT things are done when Men & Mountains meet.
This is not done by Jostling in the Street.
                                    [from the Rossetti manuscript]

Swinburne, on the eve of his own revolutions, is not so sure. Whether his own poems ever incited a single "Jostling in the Street" is open to question. That he hoped they would is not.

The poet of "The Eve of Revolution" realizes that the "Light . . . to break and melt in sunder" man's chains is not some heavenly light instinct in the nature of things ("It is not heaven that lights / Thee" [2:23]) but rather "the heavenlier light" of that "repossessing day" when "the souls of men" assert their "all-renovating right" to "Freedom" (2:25). Now Swinburne can comfortably address time and nature, change and death, much as the maturing Teufelsdröckh had stoically addressed these spectres in "The Everlasting Yea":

> O time, O change and death,
> Whose now not hateful breath
> But gives the music swifter feet to move
> Through sharp remeasuring tones
> Of refluent antiphones. . . .
>
> [2:24]

And his revisionary, antiphonic poetry of "remeasuring" and "refluen[ce]" can emerge from the shadows of early spring into the daylight of fruitful summer:

> I set the trumpet to my lips and blow.
> The night is broken northward; the pale plains
> And footless fields of sun-forgotten snow
> Feel through their creviced lips and iron veins
> Such quick breath labour and such clean blood flow
> As summer-stricken spring feels in her pains
> When dying May bears June. . . .
>
> [2:14]

The spiritual and philosophical emergence of Swinburne from, in Hillis Miller's terms, the "precarious equilibrium" of Victorian poetry[9] (or, to use Thomas Carlyle's special construction, a "centre of indifference,") brings static images of dawn and spring to fruition in sunny, summer landscapes. It also pushes the poet up and out of those seductive shorelines which promised sleep by drowning and into a new, reversed direction of "leave-taking," away from shorelines and towards images of land, not sea. In "The Eve of Revolution," the emergence from "hours" of paralysis "Wherethrough we row like slaves" (2:16) leads the poet from water to "the green Rhineland" (2:17), to the great crowned hill of "republican" Athens, whose "armed head" stands above the "sea-sounds of a thousand caves" as symbol of the "sunward and the fair / Daylight of time and man" (2:17–18), on to "Milton's land" of "streams and waters that bear witness still / To the earth her sons were made of" (2:19–20), and finally to oppressed Italy, "the world's wonder, the world's care, / Free in her heart ere quite her hands be free":

O too much loved, what shall we say of thee?
What shall we make of our heart's burning fire,
The passion in our lives that fain would be
    Made each a brand to pile into the pyre
That shall burn up thy foemen, and set free
    The flame whence thy sun-shadowing wings aspire?

[2:22]

The brand, a symbol of irretrievable loss in *Atalanta in Calydon*,
is thus transformed in *Songs before Sunrise* into a Carlylean torch
of liberation,[10] just as age and disease and aristocracy, the lovely
old triumvirate which earned the loyalty and love of necromantic
Swinburne in *Poems and Ballads*, have become a threatening,
repressive trio—a trinity to be pulled down, incinerated, and
replaced—in the later volume of *Songs*. In "Super Flumina
Babylonis," the "angel of Italy's resurrection" characterizes the
present, national crisis as a time of old and dying kings, kings in
whom people should put no trust, "For the life of them vanishes
and is no more seen, / Nor no more known." In "The Halt Before
Rome," Swinburne recalls smouldering Italy's near-emergence from
a "weary funereal season, / In that heart-stricken grief-ridden time"
(1867) as a time when

The weight of a king and the worth,
With anger and sorrowful mirth,
We weighed in the balance of earth,
And light was his word as a treason,
    And heavy his crown as a crime.

Banners of kings shall ye follow
    None, and have thrones on your side
None; ye shall gather and grow
Silently, row upon row,
Chosen of Freedom to go
Gladly where darkness may swallow,
    Gladly where death may divide.

[2:47]

Man's primary duty, according to the *Songs before Sunrise*, is to
work for freedom and brotherhood, a society built upon loving-
kindness, in spite of the latter-day knowledge that bonds of love
built by man's effort will not outlast the vicissitudes of nature and
of time, and that the builders themselves may be "swallowed" by

"darkness," "divided" by death. How does a poet teach such a worldly lesson, especially a poet nurtured on the faith that nature affords glimpses into the life of things, that the grinding, temporal process is mere illusion, and that romantic and social bonds are as implicitly divine as they are inherently melioristic? First, by doing the one thing which the poet raised on "romanticism" finds most painful—by (to quote Hardy's "In Tenebris") agnostically admitting that "if way to the Better there be, it exacts a full look at the Worst," by heeding Arnold's sonnet "To George Cruikshank" ("Know thou the worst!"), by doing what Swinburne does in his own "Tenebrae" of *Songs before Sunrise*, that is, moving *towards* an optimistic projection into the future only by moving *through*, stanza by stanza, all the horrors which free man must accept or overcome: "passionate years," "years unassuaged of desire," "song beaten and broken," "dust and the dead," "spirits athirst unsloken," "things unspeakable spoken," "tears unendurable shed" (2:88–89).

It is this process of "moving through" which makes "Prelude" and "The Eve of Revolution," "Hertha" and "Hymn of Man," "Tenebrae" and "Christmas Antiphones" what they are—developing, emerging, linear arguments which, stanza by stanza, move the naïve poet, audience, even national consciousness out of seeming ambiguities, difficult dialectics, and paralyzing crises into synthetic revisions, resolutions, conclusions. "Hertha" begins by defining reality, proceeds to describe man's vision of God, and ends up instructing man that his present reality is all the God he has or needs to have. "Prelude" begins "Between the green bud and the red" where "Youth . . . sang by Time, and shed . . . tears" (2:3). However, as Youth and "Prelude" move, hand in hand, through this educating temporal process ("Between the bud and the blown flower / Youth talked with joy and grief"), the speaking poet is able to convince the younger poet in his poem, not to mention himself and his reader, that time, which had seemed a devouring ogre in youth and an interminable process of education in adolescence is, in maturity, our one opportunity for meaningful action ("A little time we gain from time / To set our seasons in some chime" [2:8]).

This structure of emergence, in most of the *Songs before Sunrise*, moves poet, speaker, and reader from transcendental expectation to mundane reality to redefinition of divinity-as-mundane. It is also, as we have seen, inseparable from the structure of the image systems in Swinburne's mature poems, systems in which shorelines, twilights, and springs, respectively, move out of their dialectical ambiguities and into the resolutions of day, land, and summer. In "Christmas Antiphones," however, this very same structure of simultaneous narrative and spiritual emergence is accompanied by an image system founded upon dialectic and emergence which is somewhat unusual (for Swinburne) and entirely appropriate. "Christmas Antiphones" is structured in three parts: the first, entitled "In Church," is addressed to the "Very light of light," the "perfect day" "whose eyes are skies / Love-lit" with "Light above all love," "Light not born with morn / Or her fires above" (2:126–29); the second and antithetical movement of the poem is called "Outside Church," and it describes the harsh light of the world, a light made even more unbearable by the romantic victim's "In Church" longing for a "perfect day":

> Man beneath the sun,
> What for us hath God?

> We whose right to light
> Heaven's high noon denies,
> Whom the blind beams smite . . .
> And but burn our eyes,

> With what dreams of beams
> Shall we build up day,
> At what sourceless streams
> Seek to drink in dreams
> Ere they pass away?

[2:130, 132]

If the poem ended here, Swinburne would be right back where he was in 1865–66, writing poems in which reality disintegrates vision, reality is less bearable than vision's atrocious distortion, and the speaker, faced with an impossible choice between fraudulence and unbearable pain, leaves his questions unanswered and prays for annihilation. But "Christmas Antiphones" has a third movement, a movement out of the paralyzing questions of the agnostic agony, the vacillations "in" and "outside" of and back "in church" again, a movement neither inside nor outside but, rather, "Beyond Church." It is a new realm where, to be sure, "No man's might of sight" and "No man's hand hath might / To put back that light" for which Christian visionaries of old prayed, "Kneeling with void hands" (2:135). Furthermore, it is a place where the abandoned lyre, though left an aeolean harp to be played by the harmonized inspirations of Wordsworthian, Coleridgean, Shelleyan winds, only gives sound to the tunelessness of creation:

> No desire brings fire
>   Down from heaven by prayer,
> Though man's vain desire
> Hang faith's wind-struck lyre
>   Out in tuneless air.
>
> [2:135]

It is, admittedly, a place where "All the range of change / Hath its bounds," including "death" and "sin" (2:135); but it is also a place where, unconstrained either by perfectibilian faith or by the agnostic agony which follows a faith's demise,

> Man shall do for you,
>   Men the sons of man,
> What no God would do
> That they sought unto
>   While the blind years ran.
>
> [2:133]

Thus, "Christmas Antiphones," although it offers an interesting imagistical departure from Swinburne's more usual poems of lands, seas, and interstitial gardens, is nevertheless a perfect paradigm of the poetry of Swinburne's middle period. For, like "Hertha" and "Prelude," the "Hymn of Man" and "The Halt Before Rome," "Christmas Antiphones" moves, in image, narrative structure, tone, and philosophy, from a painful thesis of failed idealism to an equally painful antithesis, namely, cruel reality, and, finally, beyond good and evil, toward that new scripture, that new mythus that Arnold, Mill, Pater, and Browning were all seeking, of which Carlyle was speaking when, in a letter to his "romantic" American friend, Ralph Waldo Emerson, he scolded: "You call Goethe *actual*, not *ideal*, . . . is not the whole truth rather this: the actual well-seen *is* the ideal?"[11]

Matthew Arnold had made a somewhat similar proclamation through the voice of Empedocles when his otherwise unworldly and despondent philosopher announced that

> Harsh Gods and hostile Fates
> Are dreams! This only *is*—
> Is everywhere; sustains the wise, the foolish elf.[12]

The recognition that God and Fate are dreams obstructing the activities which human wisdom, unshackled, would demand, is the subject of *Erechtheus* (1876), a drama which symbolically reenacts and resolves a conflict in Swinburne's sensibility—a conflict which the poet foresees in the collective human psyche—a clash which can only be resolved by the simple act of realizing first that God and Fate are dreams ("In Church"), then that the natural world is neither good nor evil, melioristic nor millennial ("Outside of Church"), and ultimately that, in Arnold's words, "This only *is*— / Is everywhere," or, in Carlyle's phrase, "the actual well-seen *is* the ideal" ("Beyond Church").

Briefly stated, the work dramatizes a battle between the citizenry of Athens and the army of Eumolpus, son of Poseidon. Erechtheus, King of Athens, and his Queen, Praxithea, learn from an oracle that their daughter Chthonia must be sacrificed if Athens is to defeat her enemy from the sea. When Chthonia hears of the necessity of her death, she freely agrees to die. Upon her sacrifice, Athena reveals that Athens has defeated Eumolpus's forces, though not without losing Erechtheus in the battle. In a close examination of this simple plot, the ambiguities which have long caused the work to be dismissed are all apparent. W. R. Rutland[13] has complained that the reader cannot determine whether Athens is at war with the natural sea, with the immortal, powerful gods of the sea, or with the mortals from Thrace, who simply arrive by sea.

His confusion is natural. When the play opens on the morning of the great battle, Erechtheus speaks both of the gods and of the Thracian forces who seem to be fighting for them, but then he begins to refer to the antagonists as the "Thracian foam," which will soon "Break its broad strength of billowy-beating war / Here" (4:342). The city of wisdom is apparently at war with the gods, but is Poseidon's army really that of gods and men, or is it literally the "billowy power" of the waves, the destructive forces of time and nature? Erechtheus fears that the opponents will, after "this day's ebb of their spent wave of strife / Sweep" Athens

> . . . to sea, wash it on wreck, and leave
> A costless thing contemned; and in our stead,

> Where these walls were and sounding streets of men,
> Make wide a waste for tongueless water-herds
> And spoil of ravening fishes; that no more
> Should men say, Here was Athens.
>
> [4:342]

The Chorus admonishes Athens's citizenry to prevent the "blind wave" from "breach[ing] . . . thy wall scarce built" (4:346), for "A noise is arisen against us of waters, / A sound as of battle come up from the sea" (4:345–46).

The vagueness which surrounds this seemingly central event of the play is surpassed only by the haziness shrouding the sacrifice of Chthonia. What does this human sacrifice have to do with a conflict between the fragile city of Athens and the malign sea which surrounds it? Why does Chthonia accept her unmerited fate without a single syllable of demur? Is she a human being? Swinburne creates, then he multiplies, confusions such as these, but the ambiguities which result are a far cry from those uncertainties that lie at the very heart and form the very structure of the 1866 *Poems and Ballads* volume. The uncertainties which the poet builds into *Erechtheus*, rather, are surrounded by authorial knowledge, are precisely controlled and purposeful ambiguities which play an important symbolic role in leading the reader, even as the author had been led, out from the confusions of false hopes and dreams and into an emergent revison of all past, perfectibilian faiths.

Associating the attackers with the soldiers from Thrace, the waves of the sea, and the capricious cruelty of the gods, Swinburne demonstrates that *Erechtheus* is less a dramatization of a military conflict than of a psychic or spiritual conflict, namely, that of the self's simultaneous confrontation with the world of death and the death of an old, unworldly faith. On the morning of the battle, the Athenian elders admit that "all men" hope to see "Death at last" as "a harbour,"

> . . . yet they flee from it,
>   Set sails to the storm-wind and again to sea;
> Yet for all their labour no whit further shall they be from it,
>   Nor longer but wearier shall their life's work be.
>
> [4:369]

The site of the battle in *Erechtheus* is the sea's edge (that site of Swinburne's youthful, psychic agony), the place where "the sea-

marks . . . divide" the "kingdoms to Ocean and Earth assigned"
(4:344). The at once supernatural, Thracian, and "billowy" attackers (4:342) create a powerful wind which blows like a "bride-
song" on "the blast of [its] breath"—a song none other than "a song
. . . of death" (4:393). When the psyche or soul of man confronts
the inevitability of time's "march" and the awesome blast of death's
song, a crisis of belief results, an inner conflict which Swinburne
symbolizes by the great battle in *Erechtheus*, a battle that "makes
cold our trust in comfort of the Gods" (4:359) and annihilates man's
belief in a beneficent nature whose basis is both moral and divine.
The "wave of war," Praxithea tells us, "takes the sun / Out of our
eyes, darkening the day" (4:359).

By associating a spiritual crisis and a crisis of sensibility with a
battle between Athens and the sea, the Thracian army, and the
gods, Swinburne increases and varies the possible number of tones,
reverberations, and dissonant reactions which can be generated by
the subject of the self confronting both its own death and the death
of its faith in a beneficent environment and benevolent deity.
Erechtheus forces us to contemplate spiritual paradoxes and prods
us to enter intellectual conflict with questions such as these: Why
does man's isolated, intelligent nature perish in the trammel of
nature's apparently mindless but immortal powers? When man is
faced with the fact of mortality, what justification can be advanced
for his petty but fatal conflicts with his fellows? If intelligent or
moral forces exist in or beyond the natural world, if the "light of
day" has sources in a higher, "light above all lights," then why must
suffering and death be realities? Finally, could man's fearful and
agonized confrontation with the "cruelty" of nature and with the
idea of death be a product of his innocent and "romantic" (in the
most reductive possible sense of that word) belief in the attain-
ability of transcendence, perfection, divine wholeness, and a white
radiance of eternity?

This understanding of the poet's symbolic use of conflict, in turn,
proves Chthonia's sacrifice to be an equally symbolic act in a
drama which seeks to enact a moment in the life of the collective
human self. For Chthonia, understood in purely symbolic terms,
represents that choice always available to man of defeating the
cruel power of the gods by recognizing that the cosmos is a
mysterious but amoral cycle of composition and decomposition,
that "perfection" and "transcendence" and "divinity" are human

terms of limited meaning, that morality and goodness can be found in man and man alone, and that the only immortality available in the universe is that offered by nature's mindless compost heap. That is to say, if *Erechtheus* describes a spiritual conflict, then Chthonia literally and figuratively puts an end to that conflict by embracing a death which she conceives to be an entrance only into nature's continuity of flux. She is, in this sense, Swinburne's answer to that elegiac paradox (coming to terms with death) faced by poets from Moschus to Shelley (in his romantic translation of Moschus), for she transforms the lament that Bion "sleeps both sound and long a sleep that is without end"[14] into a paean.

A digression seems imperative here. I have been arguing, generally, that ambiguities inherent in *Erechtheus* eventually give rise to clear and consistent meanings, whereas those found in earlier works produce, at best, rich patterns of contradiction. To see how this could be so, it is necessary to take a careful look at some lines of Swinburne's poetry, for it is there that the most basic ambiguities are found and there that they enrich or confuse poetic meaning. A brief comparison of Swinburne's first and second great tragedies may suggest some of the ways in which local differences in stylistic ambiguity extend (naturally) to larger structures of meaning.

Althaea, just before killing her son and resigning herself to silence, cries out to the Chorus that the "gods laugh at us," that "Fate's are we." In the latter clause, she poses an implicit question which Swinburne leaves unresolved throughout this great, early work. Althaea would suggest that all of us belong to Fate, but her audience, which cannot hear a punctuation mark and which has not heard any verb indicating possession or control (i.e., "Fate holds our future," "Fate guides our actions"), may well entertain a different interpretation, namely, "We are Fates." To be sure, Althaea's next expression might indicate, to her keenest listeners, that her initial word contained an apostrophe ("Yet fate is ours"). And, admittedly, her audience is a fiction anyway, a fictional Chorus within a poem meant to be read, not performed aloud. Nevertheless Swinburne's inversion of conventional syntax makes it nearly as impossible for a reader to initially comprehend the possessive as it would be for a listener to hear an apostrophe. We are invited, almost compelled, to reread. If we do, we are forced to contemplate two opposite possibilities and to realize that only a tiny mark precludes an interpretation which some members of the

Chorus, fictional or not, could doubtless assume to be their Queen's meaning.

As we move on through Althaea's monologue, moreover, we soon realize that the notion thwarted but not entirely repressed by an apostrophe—that we humans are our own and only Fates—is not one foreign to the speaker. "Fate is ours," Althaea says, then "Fate is . . . mine for ever;"

> he is my son,
> My bedfellow, my brother. You strong gods,
> Give place unto me; I am as any of you,
> To give life and to take life.
>
> [4:314]

But Althaea's feeling that she *is* a strong god, an omnipotent giver and taker of life, cannot be fully maintained. We sense her continuing suspicion that "Fate's are we" in the ambiguous declaration that "Fate is . . . my son, / My bedfellow, my brother." For while the statement might seem to imply that she is a Fate amongst friends and family ("We are Fates"), the fact is that the rash actions of Althaea's brothers, the passionate response of her son, and the pathetic ineffectuality of Oeneus, her bedfellow, may be said to have led Althaea to the threshold both of murder and spiritual death. Thus, her son, husband, and brothers make up the sum of determining actions beyond her control. When the Queen proceeds to exhort the "earth" ("Thou hast made man and unmade; thou whose mouth / Looks red from the eaten fruits of thine own womb") to "Behold me with what lips upon what food / I feed," we are left with an hermaphroditic fusion of opposite, or at least uneasily reconciled, meanings that are instinct to the poem. Has the determining, destructive force in *Atalanta* been Althaea's character? It is her passionate, possessive nature that first makes Meleager overly defensive of Atalanta and later prompts her to filicide. But does that mean that Althaea, who often blames God and Fate, is what she so deplores? Does the fact that she, like the earth, consumes the fruit of her own womb mean that she is a Fate of rivaling power or merely a small and pitiful agent of horrible, all-consuming external energies? Swinburne poses, but he does not quite resolve, such questions. Or, if he does, he pairs unreconcilable answers.

The ambiguities which abound in *Erechtheus*, on the other hand,

are resolvable, and important meanings emerge from their resolution. The Chorus of this later play, on the eve of the awful battle
with watery warriors and in response to the King's speech on his
daughter's fate, wonders who could be "mother" but "Night"—and
who could be "father" but "Death"—of a "sorrow" that rends
without mercy a family and city. Addressing "Night," the Chorus
says that "From [thy] slumberless bed"

> Hast thou brought forth a wild and insatiable child, an
>   unbearable birth.
> Fierce are the fangs of his wrath, and the pangs that they give;
> None is there, none that may bear them, not one that would
>   live.
>
> [4:354]

The insatiable, fierce-fanged sorrow born to Night would seem to
be death, for Death is He whose pangs none may survive. And yet
"Death" is the *father* of this sorrow, the mother being "Night."
What kind of father fathers himself? And why does the poet, after
identifying the parents of the child, continue to play with images of
childbirth ("his . . . pangs . . . / None . . . may bear"; "an insatiable child, an unbearable birth")? Can the "birth" be "unbearable" if "Night" has "brought [it] forth"? If the poet means simply
that we mortals find death unbearable—if Death indeed is the name
of the insatiable child—then why doesn't he say "unendurable"?

The problems are suggestive and surmountable. Death can have
Death for a father just as the Son of God can be "God incarnate
with us." There is Death the abstraction, and then there is that Son
of Death gone forth to war against Athens. *Erechtheus*, as we shall
see later, is rife with allusions to and revisions of the Gospels. This
is, after all, a play about an historical era which dawns on the day
that man, through an intercessor who is *not* God incarnate,
triumphs over fear of death. The "insatiable child," therefore, is at
once Death and also, in a subtle sense, Chthonia, the child who will
swallow up Death forever in victory. Thus the phrase "unbearable
birth" expands to encompass several meanings. The pangs borne
easily enough by "Night" bring forth a child, whose pangs are
unbearable to man, named Death. The "pangs" of Praxithea's
delivery are not so bearable; they bring forth the death of a child, a
child whose death, nonetheless, shall be death to the child named

"Death." There may be one more meaning to be derived from the speech of the Chorus. Chthonia, a savior, is not only an "unbearable birth" because she was born to die before anguished parents. Swinburne may also mean that whereas Christ was a "bearable" savior, that is to say he was literally "born a savior" because of his divine paternity and a heavenly mission, Chthonia is not. She must, through accumulated circumstance and wisdom, become a redeemer; her mother, unlike Mary, is not able to "bear" the "death" of "Death." Chthonia is a match for her foe because she, like Death and unlike the paler Christ, is an "unbearable" force.

Chthonia's decision to sacrifice her own life, her willed death into the organic and mineral nature of her "mother . . . Earth" (4:383), gives mankind "A stay to fetter the foot of the sea" (4:364), just as Teufelsdröckh's acceptance of time, suffering, and death allowed him to name the "Earth" his "Mother" and prepared society for its "metamorphoses" into the future.[15] The "doom that seals [Chthonia] deathless till the springs of time run dry" (4:375) thus both symbolizes and dramatizes a crucial, epistemological choice. It is a choice that moves man out of the spiritual twilight that accompanies the loss of any consoling faith and into the light of a humanized *ethos*, a society that, though neither perfect nor millennial, is established in liberty, wisdom, and justice. As G. B. Tennyson suggests of Carlyle's early work, Swinburne's *Erechtheus* can also be said to "ask [its] readers . . . to effect an inner change, a change of heart. Only then will [man] realize that *he* is . . . the *imago Dei*."[16]

The "characters" of the play—Chthonia, Praxithea, and the King —are no more and no less than eidolons of what Swinburne sees to be man's psychic tendencies, inner forces, and it is perfectly emblematic that not one of the speaking characters, save Athena herself, is ever named in the actual verse. For *Erechtheus* dramatizes not the details of individual human tragedies but the poet, and human society, in the act of finding an utterly humanized, demystified scripture. The drama explores that moment of psychic stasis followed by revolutionary choice, that time between times, when fear and confusion reign and when the tragic divisiveness of life is most acute. In Teufelsdröckhian terms, it is the moment in which the Phoenix of history lies in an ashen heap, but a heap in which "Creation and Destruction" are "proceed[ing] together . . . as ashes of the Old are blown out" and as "organic filaments of the new spin themselves."[17] It is a moment in the life of the individual and collective human self which Lawrence would later write about when asking the reader:

> Are you willing to be sponged out, erased, cancelled, made
>   nothing?
> Are you willing to be made nothing? dipped into oblivion?
>
> If not, you will never really change.
>
> The phoenix renews her youth
>   only when she is burnt, burnt alive, burnt
> down to hot and flocculent ash.[18]

Erechtheus describes this very moment of spiritual crisis, a trying time when the men and women of Athens, the citizens of the free city of wisdom, "Lie in the lap of the unknown hour" (4:368). Like (and unlike) Jesus, who "lifted up his eyes to the heavens" and said "Father, the hour is come" (John 17:1), an elder of Swinburne's Chorus speaks of his "fear of the hour that is on me" (4:392). It is altogether appropriate, therefore, that this moment in which the poet and all of mankind must choose between submission and insurrection should be dramatized by Swinburne at the "dew of dawn" (4:342). The morning of Chthonia's sacrifice and of Erechtheus's battle with the gods is a long, dark dawn when "the sun's self" seems "stricken in heaven, and cast out of his course as a blind man astray" (4:392), a daybreak which ironically parallels, if it does not quite parody, the "darkness over all the land . . . from the sixth hour . . . unto the ninth hour" on the morning of Christ's crucifixion (Matthew 27:45).

Swinburne suggests that the "dark" moment of our "dread" (4:397) in which mankind seeks to annihilate his expectations of spiritual immortality, to accept the cycles of life and death in nature, and to embrace wholeheartedly the ideals of spiritual and political freedom is a shadowy time of great fear between symbolic hours of darkness and light. A member of the Chorus nervously asks:

> What cloud upon heaven is arisen, what shadow, what
>   sound, . . .
> That scatters from wings unbeholden the weight of its darkness
>   around?

> For the sense of my spirit is broken, and blinded its eye,
>   As the soul of a sick man ready to die. . . .
>
> [4:392]

Such an anxious hour of spiritual crisis, however, is obviously as pregnant as it is dreadful, and the fearful citizens of Athens are perfectly aware of the fact that they stand upon the brink of a "new dawn." The Chorus, at one point, calls the "rose-red" morning forth from the "bride-bed of dawn" (4:394), and the King addresses the earth and says,

> . . . Lo, I stand
> Here on this brow's crown of the city's head
> That crowns its lovely body, till death's hour
> Waste it; but now the dew of dawn and birth
> Is fresh upon it from thy womb. . . .
>
> [4:341–42]

In addition to being a drama of that fearful moment between darkness and light, Swinburne also suggests that this same moment of spiritual convulsion takes place somewhere between what he might call the Kingdom of the Cruel Sea (Poseidon) and the Terrestrial, Human Republic of Liberty (Athena). "Now the stakes of war are set, / For land or sea to win" (4:367), the Herald of Eumolpus says, and Erechtheus responds by saying that "waves of inland and the main make war / As men that mix and grapple" (4:368). The symbolic Thracian forces are intimately associated, through image, both with the sea ("the broad strength" of "the Thracian foam") and with the cruelty of man's belief in and acceptance of forces greater than those of the human self. The Herald of Eumolpus declares that his master, son of blustering Poseidon, "swears to raze from eyeshot of the sun / This city named not of his father's name" (4:367). When Erechtheus, King of the Land, contrarily asserts that Poseidon's forces shall soon be impotent, the Herald of the Sea asks "Shall Gods bear bit and bridle, fool, of men?" (4:365).

The choice between eternally wearing the "bit and bridle" of the gods or bridling those same man-created "gods" of "faith" and "belief" and millennial fate through acceptance of man's isolation and his consequent duty to be responsible and selfless is not only a choice between darkness and light and between the cruelty of the

sea and the peace of the Terrestrial Republic; it is also a choice
between spiritual sterility and fertility for mankind—a choice
imagistically suggested by Swinburne's symbolic midseasonal
description of the equally symbolic landscape of the Athenian
Republic:

> For the season is full now of death or of birth,
> To bring forth life, or an end of all. . . .
>
> [4:399]

Following the lead of Shelley's *Prometheus*, Swinburne anticipates
Hardy's *Tess* and Lawrence's *The Rainbow* by making the change
of hours, seasons, and landscapes symptomatic of a change in
sensibility. Halfway between night and incipient day, sea and land,
and the sterility of winter and the rich fecundity of emergent
summer, the moment of man's inner battle for liberty is taking
place when the land is "Green yet and faint in its first blade,
unblown / With yellow hope of harvest" (4:367).

Chthonia, who later in the drama will become a symbol of both
natural and spiritual fertility and harvest through death, describes
her own mental and spiritual condition just before death in
metaphors which are strikingly similar to those used to describe the
land's "faint" "green" condition. Chthonia offers thanks that she
may

> . . . give this poor girl's blood of mine
> Scarce yet sun-warmed with summer, this thin life
> Still green with flowerless growth of seedling days,
> To build again my city. . . .
>
> [4:376]

This moving address by Chthonia to the Chorus suggests yet
another way in which *Erechtheus* dramatizes a time between times.
The drama not only unfolds at a symbolic dawn, along a symbolic
shore, and between the symbolic times of "seedling days" and
"yellow hope of harvest"; it also takes place at a moment when
man is spiritually "old" and "hoar of head" but on the brink of a
spiritual rejuvenation that Swinburne symbolizes through the
young virgin. It is no coincidence that the Italian present was
symbolized by sick, old, dying kings in "Super Flumina Babylonis"
("For the life of them vanishes and is no more seen, / Nor no more
known" [2:38]) or that the free Italy of the future was symbolized

as a young woman in "The Halt before Rome." The elders of the Chorus are men of "grey-grown sorrow" (4:364), tyrannized by the blast both of age and the cruel gods, in whose powers they firmly believe. Like the elders, King Erechtheus is also a man living in the time of the old reigns of faith, belief, and omnipotence. "No desire of man's," Erechtheus thinks, "Shall stand as doth a God's will" (4:343). Erechtheus is willing to do battle with the sea, but he clearly believes in the omnipotence, let alone the existence, of the gods:

. . . the soul runs reinless on sheer death
Whose grief or joy takes part against the Gods.
And what they will is more than our desire,
And their desire is more than what we will.

[4:343]

Swinburne's main symbol of the Old Man, Erechtheus, freely admits that his wife and daughter, who as women are symbols of the new man, are wiser than himself. "O woman," he says, "thou hast shamed my heart with thine / To show so strong a patience" (4:353). When this King of the closing era of man's bad faith dies, moreover, the poet seems to suggest that with his death the last strife ever to be caused by the gods is over. As Chthonia had predicted, "their strength" is now "quenched and made idle," and the "foam of their mouths" has been put in "bridle" (4:385). The gods without substance have just claimed their last victim in the King, who is said by Athena's herald to be "slain of no man but a God" (4:406). As Jerome McGann points out, "the death of Erechtheus and the birth of Athens are made inseparable, even, in some sense (however we explain it), identical."[19] Thus, with Chthonia's "voluntary," "patient," and "self-sacrificing death," and with the King's death at the hands of the gods in whom he believes, "the whole clear land is purged of war" (4:406).

Singing its own song before sunrise, the Chorus realizes that, in the wake of this battle for a new "glory of day" (4:397), there is "no help from on high" (4:398). In its place, however, there emerges that human wisdom which provides man with "a wide sea-wall, that shatters the besieging sea" (4:384) and which will serve as far better guidance than that provided by a "god," or, rather, by *belief* in a god. Praxithea had predicted this fruition of wisdom earlier, upon presenting her daughter to the citizenry for sacrifice:

Give ear, O all ye people, that my word
May pierce your hearts through, and the stroke that cleaves
Be fruitful to them; so shall all that hear
Grow great at heart with child of thought most high
And bring forth seed in season; this my child,
This flower of this my body, this sweet life,
This fair live youth I give you, to be slain. . . .

[4:380]

Because of "green," "spouseless" Chthonia's acceptance of death, "Sweet land" is "reconciled with sea" (4:411), Athena tells her city at play's end, and in "one spirit and single-hearted strength," men, "wind and sea shall keep / Peace" (4:410). "Joy out of woe / May arise . . . out of tempest and snow" (4:399), she adds, and human wisdom, once thought to be a deity dwelling on an imagined mountain off-limits to man, now has a real presence in the realm of everyday human affairs, as is suggested by Athena's lengthy speech at the end of what is, in every other respect, a notably traditional Greek drama. Athena's presence, moreover, in no way suggests that the gods still exist for men, for now she is a symbol only of man's limited but useful mental, spiritual, and social resources. As McGann points out, she "is no longer an Olympian, but a Republican goddess. She is to her Athenians what Hertha is to man in general."[20] When Athena speaks, her language and her bearing remind the reader significantly of the dead Chthonia. In fact, a careful rereading will show that throughout the drama Swinburne, just as he has carefully confused superficial elements of the action, has purposely blurred Chthonia's image with Athena's, as when he has the Chorus of elders say of the former:

From the empire of her eyes
Light takes life and darkness flies;
From the harvest of her hands
Wealth strikes root in prosperous lands;
Wisdom of her word is made;
At her strength is strength afraid. . . .

[4:373]

But it is not only Athena that Chthonia is made to resemble. As an anti-type of Eve whose wisdom is far greater than that of either Erechtheus or the Chorus of elders, Chthonia remains innocent to her death, is never banished from the voiceless, vegetative cycles of

Earth, which is her only paradise, and gives to mankind the fruit of the tree of knowledge—wisdom to act which is free from all dictates of "the gods." In giving to man this anti-deific wisdom, Chthonia, who is almost the incarnation of that "oracular" voice of "self-sufficience" which Swinburne had celebrated in an essay on Arnold's poetry, saves the soul of man from insufficiency and its despair. Through her quintessential enactment of the post-romantic hero or heroine's one ideal, that of dutiful, unself-conscious, self-sacrifice, Chthonia not only prefigures Hardy characters like Gabriel Oak, Diggory Venn, and Giles Winterborne, but she also becomes an effective, *negative* image of a much more ancient self-sacrificing hero. Addressing both her mother and the Earth, she both prays a kind of modulated Gethsemane prayer and, at the same time, echoes Isaiah 53:

> . . . for all the world
> Thou brought'st me forth a saviour, who shall save
> Athens; for none but I from none but thee
> Shall take this death for garland;
> . . . the dry wild vine
> Scoffed at and cursed of all men that was I
> Shall shed them wine to make the world's heart warm,
> That all eyes seeing may lighten, and all ears
> Hear and be kindled; such a draught to drink
> Shall be the blood that bids this dust bring forth,
> The chaliced life here spilt on this mine earth. . . .
>
> [4:377–78]

An anti-Eve and, ultimately, an anti-Christ, Chthonia buys for mankind, with her death, salvation from the cruelty of God.

New Words

Swinburne and the Poetry of Thomas Hardy

4

Like Matthew Arnold, whose "Resignation" and whose "Strayed Reveller" prove an attachment to not one but two romantic predecessors, Thomas Hardy, as a young man, was equally attracted to Shelley and to Wordsworth. He had christened his fledgling career with unpublished poems like the one in which an ancestor describes his rustic family's cottage life in language and in images so ancestral that the poem is hardly more than *Prelude pastiche*:

> Our house stood quite alone, and those tall firs
> And beeches were not planted. Snakes and efts
> Swarmed in the summer days, and nightly bats
> Would fly about our bedrooms. Heathcroppers
> Lived on the hills, and were our only friends;
> So wild it was when we first settled there.[1]

In his strange, covert autobiography, Hardy warmly recalls an evening when, as a nine-year-old boy traveling with his mother, he was lucky enough to spend a night in London at a "coaching inn," "The Cross Keys, St. John Street":

> It was the inn at which Shelley and Mary Godwin had been accustomed to meet at weekends not two-score years before, and was at this time unaltered from its state during the lovers' romantic experiences there—the oval stone staircase, the skylight, and the hotel entrance being untouched. As Mrs. Hardy and her little boy took a room rather high up the staircase for economy, and the poet had probably done so for the same

reason, there is a possibility that it may have been the same as that occupied by our most marvellous lyrist.[2]

We know that Hardy, some years later, visited Swinburne at Putney and that, "owing to a conversation with Swinburne," he traveled "a day or two later" to the church "where Shelley and Mary Godwin were married, and saw the register, with the signatures. . . . The church was almost unaltered since the poet and Mary had knelt there."[3] In a passage even more bizarre and more revealing in its reverence, Hardy recalls a very special Sunday afternoon on which he fulfilled an ambition to meet "Sir Percy Shelley (the son of Percy Bysshe) and Lady Shelley":

> . . . the meeting was as shadowy and remote as were those
> previous occasions when he had impinged upon the penumbra
> of the poet he loved—that time of his sleeping at the Cross-Keys,
> St. John Street, and that of the visits he paid to Old St. Pancras
> Churchyard. He was to enter that faint penumbra twice more,
> once when he stood beside Shelley's dust in the English cemetery
> at Rome, and last when by Mary Shelley's grave at Budmouth.[4]

Hardy, for all his devotion, learned early that the poet of one era can only "impinge upon" a past era, a previous sensibility. Like Swinburne, he realized that to live in "the faint penumbra" of a predecessor or his faith is to live in a shadow world of the dead, where only the ghosts of reality can be embraced. Consequently, Hardy began writing new poems, poems that were in every way as dark and melancholy as "The Triumph of Time" and that raised just as many questions about the romantic world-view as had "Itylus" or "Anactoria," poems that allowed the poet to make the transition from romantic *pastiche* to post-romantic assertion.

During what Evelyn Hardy calls the "formative years" of 1865–67, Hardy developed his strong, almost passionate attachment to Swinburne's poetry.[5] The stirring *Atalanta in Calydon* had appeared in 1865, and the even more passionate accents of the *Poems and Ballads* had been published the following year. In 1897, upon reading Swinburne's translation of a line by Sappho, Hardy wrote to the elder poet to tell him that a certain phrase "carried me back to the buoyant time of thirty years ago, when I used to read your early works walking along the crowded London streets to my imminent risk of being knocked down."[6] Later, in his witty elegy on Swinburne, Hardy describes the effect of Swinburne's early poems as a "garland of red roses" dropped "about the hood of some smug nun," and in the next stanza of "A Singer Asleep," narrows his vision from "Victoria's formal middle time" to a view of Thomas Hardy, architect, walking to work near Hyde Park in 1865. Even more wittily now, because of a tone of sophisticated self-deprecation, he describes their effect upon himself in the very accents of Keats discovering Chapman's Homer with a "wild surmise." Instead of the Isthmus of Panama, we have a terraced street in London, but, *mutatatis mutandis*, the idea is the same. Hardy recalls

> that far morning of a summer day
> When, down a terraced street whose pavements lay
> Glassing the sunshine into my bent eyes,
> I walked and read with quick glad surprise
> New words, in classic guise.[7]

It is, of course, true that while working in 1860 for the Dorsetshire architect, John Hicks, the sixteen-year-old apprentice captured the attention and affection of William Barnes, whose home was adjacent to the office in which Hardy labored. However, Hardy did not write any real ballads during the years of his association with the beloved dialect poet and balladeer; the impact of the folk ballad and its various themes and forms manifests itself to a significant degree only in the poems that Hardy composed well after 1870. Still more interesting is the fact that Swinburne had begun, albeit subtly, to revitalize the ballad as early as 1866. In his first volume of *Poems and Ballads*, he had anticipated his own, not to mention Hardy's, later ballad improvisations on death, worms, and post-mortem sufferings in poems like "A Ballad of Burdens." Here, the speaker's burden is exactly that which will later oppress Hardy's *personae* in "Friends Beyond" or "Wessex Heights," namely, "the burden of dead faces," for "Out of sight" and "out of love, beyond the reach of hands":

> They walk and weep about the barren lands
> Where no seed is nor any garner stands. . . .
>
> [1:27]

Another lyric, entitled "After Death," is a macabre ballad that, like Hardy's "Ah, Are You Digging On My Grave?" deals with the suffering of the dead when they learn that life goes on without them. In Hardy's later lyric, the conversation will be between a dead woman and a living dog; in Swinburne's poem, it is between a dead man growing "grave's mould" "in his mouth" and "The four boards of the coffin lid" (1:279), but the idea is similar enough.

This is not to suggest, of course, that William Barnes was anything less than a strong influence upon young Thomas Hardy. What Barnes taught Hardy about ballad composition, however, did not come to full fruition until Swinburne had shown Hardy that the ballad could be an effective vehicle for communicating the rather stoical revision of a "melioristic" faith. For "Swinburne's ballads," unlike those of Barnes, "aim for us to hear the murmur 'of a nearer voice below' the ancient music, as if the present were somehow more ancient than one ever knew and the past its mere future." In "Swinburne's ballads," Jerome McGann points out, it is "as if the antique voices . . . and the aesthetic voices of nineteenth-century England were somehow in league, contemporaries in a land and of a time more like ours here than anything in history."[8]

The importance of Swinburne's poetry to Thomas Hardy has always been underestimated and, in nearly all cases, utterly ignored. Only McGann, in his very recent study of Swinburne, mentions the extent of this influence, and he goes no further than to say that "Hardy worshipped Swinburne, as well he might, since his own poetry owed a profound debt to the older man's work."[9] A very brief and incomplete indication of the enduring importance of Swinburne to Hardy may at least place this matter of influence in proper perspective. Hardy recalls, in the (auto)biography, the pleasure he felt upon learning that the poet whom he so greatly admired was an occasional visitor to the offices of the Reform League—a suite of rooms located one floor below the room of the young architect-poet. Although he lacked the nerve to attempt a meeting with Swinburne, he took equal pleasure in knowing that Swinburne, like himself, frequented the Newton House (later the Cannibal Club) for meals. He lost little time in taking the trouble, he happily admits, to learn that he was living "within half a mile of Swinburne,"[10] and even in matters of recreation Hardy proudly owned up to the proximities of their tastes. Recalling the buoyant years between 1867 and 1870 in *The Early Life* volume of the autobiography, he writes, "Being—like Swinburne—a swimmer, he would lie a long time on his back on the surface of the waves, rising and falling with the tide in the warmth of the morning sun."[11]

Years later, having actually met and corresponded with the elder poet, he received one of his few admiring responses to *Jude the Obscure* from his first poetic muse, the aging satyr of Putney, to whom he felt spiritually close and with whom he felt the shared pain of constant public outrage. "The tragedy," Swinburne wrote, "is equally beautiful and terrible in its pathos. The beauty, the terror, and the truth, are all yours and yours alone. . . . I think it would hardly be seemly to enlarge on all that I admire in your work—or on half of it. . . . If you prefer to be—or to remain— [the most tragic of authors] no doubt you may; for Balzac is dead, and there has been no such tragedy in fiction—on anything like the same lines—since he died."[12]

Although Hardy humbly wrote to a friend to say that "Swinburne writes, too enthusiastically for me to quote with modesty,"[13] Swinburne's spiritual and aesthetic identification with his younger admirer was apparently genuine. In 1897, Hardy wrote to his poetic mentor in reference to *The Well-Beloved*. "I must thank you," he wrote, "for your kind note about my fantastical little tale, which, if it can make, in its better parts, any faint claim to imaginative feeling, will owe something of such feeling to you, for I often thought of lines of yours during the writing; and indeed, was not able to resist the quotation of your words now and then. And this reminds me that one day . . . I . . . stumbled upon your 'Thee, too, the years shall cover,' and all my spirit for poetic pains died out of me. Those few words, present, I think, the finest drama of Death and Oblivion, so to speak, in our tongue."[14]

Hardy visited with Swinburne at Putney in 1899,[15] and then revisited him in order to recommend that he "make his headquarters on the Holy Isle" (Lindisfarne), "an idea which Swinburne was much attracted by."[16] Swinburne, some years later, he relates, spoke with amusement of a scathing review of late-Victorian literature which, for Hardy, contained a blasphemous epigram and a flattering comparison: "Swinburne planteth, Hardy watereth, and Satan giveth the increase." Indeed, Hardy and Swinburne always felt a certain hellish fraternity in this matter of their joint, eternal damnation at the hands of pristine critics. On the occasion of one reunion, Hardy recalls, "we laughed and condoled with each other on having been the two most abused of living writers,"[17] and later, when Swinburne was dead and buried, Hardy would write that "since Swinburne's death there was no living English writer

who had been so abused" as he himself had been.[18] On the day of
the elder poet's death, Hardy claims to have meditated upon some
of Swinburne's thoughts about Shelley, Newman, Carlyle, Time,
and Man,[19] and "In March," Hardy later wrote of himself, the poet
"visited Swinburne's grave at Bonchurch, and composed the poem
entitled 'A Singer Asleep.' It is remembered by a friend who accompanied him on this expedition how that windy March day had a
poetry of its own, how primroses clustered in the hedges, and noisy
rooks wheeled in the air over the little churchyard. Hardy gathered
a spray of ivy and laid it on the grave of that brother-poet of whom
he never spoke save in words of admiration and affection."[20]

The poems that Hardy composed during the years 1865–67 and
combined with a group of later lyrics in order to form *Wessex
Poems* (1898) are clearly Swinburnian in their tendency toward
deifying abstraction ("Fate," "Love, "Crass Casualty," "Change,"
"Great Dame Nature," and "Dicing, Mechanic, Sportsman Time"),
in their tone ("sorrow is my ecstasy," "joy lies slain," "Hope . . .
unblooms," "Time for gladness casts a moan"), in their obsessively
precise metrical, or more accurately diametrical, sound patterns
("For winning love we win the risk of losing, / And losing love is as
one's life were riven"), in their "Sapphic" stanza forms, in their
plaintive protest against time's ruination of the life-tree at root, and
in their implicit denial of transcendental possibilities.

In a poem entitled "Amabel" (1865), the earliest Wessex poem for
which a date of composition has been established, Hardy's speaker
looks upon the "ruined hues" of his once beloved Amabel and
muses upon the fate of utter annihilation that time brings to the self
and to love. "I felt that I could creep / To some housetop, and
weep," the speaker says, "That Time the tyrant fell / Ruled
Amabel!"

> I said (the while I sighed
> That love like ours had died),
> "Fond things I'll no more tell
>   To Amabel,
>
> "But leave her to her fate,
> And fling across the gate,
> 'Till the Last Trump, farewell,
>   O Amabel!' "

[ll. 21–32]

The poem turns away from romantic love poems like "She Was a Phantom of Delight," and it echoes, in its diction, Poe's "Annabel Lee" as well as the more somber tones of "The Bells." But "Amabel" also bears the mark of the young Swinburne, "that brother poet," not only in the masochistic cruelty of its speaker (I said the while I sighed; I'll leave her to her fate) but also in its deep epistemological ambivalence. Is the poem's last phrase, "'Till the Last Trump, farewell," hopeful? Does it speak of faith in a holy order of things which will, at the Last Trumpet, reunite joyous lovers in a heaven of happiness? Or does the phrase suggest a hellish, malign order in which man holds all the low cards, in which "Time the tyrant . . . / Rule[s]" and always plays the "Last Trump"? The phrase, like so many found in *Poems and Ballads* ("winter's traces," "Fate's are we"), allows for, and perhaps insists on, two interpretations.

There is yet another ambiguity in "Amabel," for even as the poet seems to be talking about his beautiful beloved, he makes us wonder just who or what she is. It takes only a little imagination to suspect that Amabel may be nature, another of the poet's earlier ideals, another young man's fancy now lost to Time:

I looked upon her gown,
Once rose, now earthen brown;
The change was like the knell
Of Amabel.

[ll. 5–8]

Once we have allowed this reading, however, there are still more difficulties to contend with. The poet says he "marked the ruined hues" and "custom-straitened-views" of his beloved

And asked, "Can there indwell
My Amabel?"

But has nature really lost her soul, have her landscapes—her "views"—really been ruined? Or is it that the speaker's vision has been lost, his "views" been "custom-straitened"?

One thing is sure. Hardy's early poems, like Swinburne's, exist in a world so bleak and faded that its inhabitants have to occasionally suspect that it is rife with hounds of "Time and Fate, Gods without pity." It is a place in which men and women who are all too human fail to achieve or maintain either their high ideals or some transcendental state of being, in any case, their "Amabels." In

"Hap," a poem written in the year Swinburne published *Poems and Ballads*, Hardy wrestles doggedly with the Swinburnian tendency to allegorize—or theologize—visionary failure, ruined hope. The first half of the poem almost succeeds in proclaiming (as both Swinburne and Hardy would later proclaim) that man's sense of suffering ("Fate") *may* be the unwarranted paranoia which results from the romantic desire to give nature meaning, to believe love to be eternal, to transcend or escape the grinding temporal process, and to define the self as a divine entity deserving of eternal happiness:

> If but some vengeful god would call to me
> From up the sky, and laugh: "Thou suffering thing,
> Know that thy sorrow is my ecstasy,
> That thy love's loss is my hate's profiting!"
>
> Then would I bear it, and clench myself, and die,
> Steeled by the sense of ire unmerited;
> Half-eased, too, that a Powerfuller than I
> Had willed and meted me the tears I shed.
>
> But not so.

The structural disintegration manifested in this very abrupt halt in syntax three words into the third stanza signals an extremely important, simultaneous break in the emotion and the logic of the speaker's soliloquy. The plaint has thus far verged towards an admission that there may well be nothing "Powerfuller than I," that the speaker's sorrows may not be anyone's ecstasies, that the term "vengeful god" could be a fanciful overreaction to nature's complete indifference, and thus that much suffering may even be "merited" rather than "fated." The conclusion of the poem, however, plunges into a despairing complaint against personified obstructions to the full attainment of the speaker's "hope" for "joy":

> . . . How arrives it joy lies slain,
> And why unblooms the best hope ever sown?
> —Crass Casualty obstructs the sun and rain,
> And dicing Time for gladness casts a moan. . . .
> These purblind Doomsters had as readily strown
> Blisses about my pilgrimage as pain.
>
> [ll. 10–15]

The poem, which moves from hypothesis (*if* there were vengeful gods) to plan (*then* I would die) to denial of hypothesis (*but* there may be no vengeful gods), does not in fact culminate in any new hypothesis, any positive or synthetic revision of the poet's understanding of himself or his environment. Rather, with the three-word denial of the vengeful gods' existence ("But not so") the rhetoric of the poem breaks down, just as so many early Swinburne poems disintegrated rhetorically, first into an unanswered, unanswerable question ("How arrives it joy lies slain, / And why unblooms the best hope ever sown?"), then into a perfectly hermaphroditic conclusion that, on one hand, almost belligerently confirms the death of an old belief (in intelligent deities) but, on the other hand, is not at all ready to accept the bleak new knowledge that the cosmos is without an intelligent plan or a divine direction. Hence, the last stanza is built upon the most unsatisfying, even perverse, of all possible resolutions or unifications, namely, the contradiction in terms. We find ourselves in a universe supposedly without "vengeful gods" but where we are, nevertheless, asked to believe that "Crass Casualty" actively *"obstructs"* the sun, that "Time for *gladness* casts a moan," and that these absolutely blind and indifferent forces could have just "as readily strown / Blisses about my pilgrimage as pain"!

In "Neutral Tones," the intensely powerful lyric written one year after "Hap" (and one year after the publication of Swinburne's "An Interlude," a poem strikingly similar to "Neutral Tones" in style and in subject), this same logical, spiritual, and structural breakdown is evident. The speaker reveals that in the past, while actually experiencing a rift with a loved one, he noticed that the whole cosmos *seemed to* participate (but wasn't *necessarily* participating) in his personal tragedy. "That winter day," the voice recalls, "the sun was white, *as though* chidden of God," fallen "leaves" from "an ash" were "grey" on "the starving sod," and his beloved's dying smile "swept thereby / *Like* an ominous bird a-wing" (italics mine). In the final stanza of the poem, however, the tentative feeling that God and nature might or might not be participating in the speaker's tragedy—a feeling subtly communicated through the comparative but not equivocating conventions of simile and pathetic fallacy—suddenly gives way to what seems to be the time-taught conviction that, indeed, the self, nature, and love *are*, in fact, "God-curst":

Since then, keen lessons that love deceives,
And wrings with wrong, have shaped to me

> Your face, and the God-curst sun, and a tree,
>   And a pond edged with grayish leaves.

>   [ll. 13–16]

The last stanza of the poem, like the last stanza of "Hap" or of
Swinburne's *Atalanta in Calydon*, remains utterly and gorgeously
unclear. On the surface of things, it would seem that the ambiguities (inherent in the similes and pathetic fallacies) of the opening
stanzas have been resolved by "keen lessons." But what is that
resolution? What are those lessons? The sun once looked "as
though" it were "chidden of God," now it looks decidedly "God-
curst," but is Hardy proclaiming that time and experience teach this
inevitable truth, confirm this horribly accurate suspicion (as most
critics have suggested), or is Hardy, through the narrator, proving
to us that we imaginatively project or envision controlling forces in
our lives according to the mere circumstances of our chance
existence? Has the fact that the speaker has been wronged and
deceived gradually caused him to change simile into equation, quite
literally caused him to revise the scenes of his own past? Could it be
that what we call the "truth" of any given situation is something
"shaped" by every single happenstance before, and after, the fact?

The answer to these questions, the meaning of "Neutral Tones,"
is not so clear as Hardy critics have heretofore assumed. The poem
resolves none of the ambiguities surrounding that situation which is
the subject of the reverie. It only suggests that later situations may
have shaped a bleak vision of the past event. Then it ends by
rhetorically collapsing into an almost insanely fragmented list of
disconnected images which make up the time-shaped vision:

> Your face, and the God-curst sun, and a tree,
>   And a pond edged with grayish leaves.

The terrible tension which has given the poem its force is a
Swinburnian division of attitudes toward human responsibility
(who was responsible, or need anyone ever feel responsible, for
human suffering?), toward the world (is nature malign, indifferent,
or merely another victim?), toward God (is God a malign fate, or is
He the imaginative explanation for our own failure?), and toward
the very nature of experience (does memory have lessons, or is it
merely the mind's way of confirming present suspicions?). It is
almost as if this tension were, as it was for Swinburne, too painful,
perhaps too impossible, to resolve save through a few morbid,

disconnected images and a fleeting, final suggestion that all such questions, all such divisions, are part of a larger, divine disharmony.

Like the Chorus in Swinburne's *Atalanta*, which blames "hearts' division" upon "God," and like Matthew Arnold, who laments in the early 1850's that "A God" "renders vain . . . deep desire" and orders the "severance" of lovers ("To Marguerite, Continued"), the speaking voice of Hardy's earliest poems is clearly a disappointed young romantic who, out of need to blame someone or something for the failure of life to live up to an inherited (and somewhat garbled) prophecy, creates or "shapes" a divisive poetic world fraught with guilty, cursing, and accursed "Gods" or "Fates." In a poem entitled "At a Bridal" and subtitled "Nature's Indifference" (1866), nature is personified, if not deified as she is by Swinburne through Artemis, only to be accused of spoiling human life by refusing to honor the ideal of perfect and immortal unity and harmony through romantic love.

The distraught speaker of the poem, sounding ever so much like Swinburne in "The Triumph of Time," like Tennyson's antagonizing protagonist in *Maud*, and like Carlyle's Teufelsdröckh in "The Sorrows of Young Teufelsdröckh," complains that time has allowed his beloved to "compound," "mingle," and become "corporate" with another man. Yet even though the married woman has "paced forth, to wait maternity," the speaker's "mind" is still "held" by "A dream of other offspring," namely, those "Compounded of us twain as Love designed; / Rare forms, that corporate now will never be!" (ll. 2–4). He knows that his faith in Love's design has been invalidated, and yet, like Swinburne's early speakers, he persists in dreaming of "rare forms," in doing homage to dead ideals, anyway. The result is a poetry which verges on incoherence:

> Should I, too, wed as slave to Mode's decree,
> And each thus found apart, of false desire,
> A stolid line, whom no high aims will fire
> As had fired ours could ever have mingled we?

[ll. 5–8]

It is at this point that, goaded by an intense displeasure he can apparently neither articulate nor alleviate, the speaker personifies "Nature," who, he says, "does not care" about thwarted romantic dreams, forms, or compounds. This "Great Dame," at once indifferent and cruel, oblivious of and malign to the speaker, is just another example of those contradictions in terms which emanate from the mind of one who has recently lost the faith. Not unlike the early poems of Swinburne and Arnold, Hardy's early lyrics scream out against the meaningless chaos of the cosmos, renounce old visions of cosmic harmony, and at the same time posit some kind of Power Not Ourselves (Arnold's phrase) which makes creation an orderly disorder, the work of a Something malign in its idiocy. And yet, exactly as in the cosmic denunciations of Swinburne (in *Atalanta* or "The Triumph of Time") and the early plaints of Arnold (through "Mycerinus," for instance), the interesting thing about Hardy's early poems of the cosmic curse is their implicit, antithetical movement, namely, the speaker's cautious, acquiescent withdrawal from participation in life which seems, paradoxically, to go hand in hand with the energetic and ever-defiant verbal bullying.

Hardy's poetry, like that of his contemporaries and immediate precursors, combines strong, dogmatic protest with the desire to withdraw from whatever action or quest has been undertaken, to drown in a kind of existential nothingness. A sonnet written in 1866 and entitled "In Vision I Roamed," begins as a quest of the "spirit" through "the flashing Firmament," becomes, suddenly, a complaint against the "ghast heights of sky," a "monstrous dome," and ends, finally, by shrinking back from contemplation of a "Universe taciturn and drear" into a modest statement about the mere and relative sadness of a man left behind by a lover. In other poems of this early, 1865–67 group, of course, it is the universe of love itself, the fiery firmament of romantic love as Hardy conceived it, which the poet sets out in quest of and which he reviles in strong, didactic language of revulsion and disgust even as he quietly removes himself from the scene at hand. In "Revulsion" (1866), for instance, the speaker says,

> Though I waste watches framing words to fetter
> Some spirit to my own in clasp and kiss,
> Out of the night there looms a sense 'twere better
> To fail obtaining whom one fails to miss.

> For winning love we win the risk of losing,
> And losing love is as one's life were riven;
> It cuts like contumely and keen ill-using
> To cede what was superfluously given.

> Let me then no more feel the fateful thrilling
> That devastates the love-worn wooer's frame,
> The hot ado of fevered hopes, the chilling
> That agonizes disappointed aim!
> So may I live no junctive law fulfilling,
> And my heart's table bear no woman's name.

In Hardy's first poems, whether in "Revulsion" or "Hap," "Amabel" or "At a Lunar Eclipse," human lives seem to be of utterly negligible import or significance when weighed against the overpowering, crushing indifference of "Nature" or "Love," "Time" or the "Flashing Firmament." These are poems, finally, not about resolution and independence, certainly not about the alpine power of the human mind that dwells apart in its tranquility, but, rather, about human powerlessness. What power these poems contain and convey as poems, therefore, must reside in jarring paradoxes, in self-exploding structures, in dialectics of tone and content, in unresolvable thoughts and feelings. That is to say, the power of these poems lies in the utterly frustrated anger of a speaker like the jilted young woman of "She to Him" (1866), who, though aware that her whole life will be adequately summed up someday when her former lover sighs "Poor jade," nonetheless thinks it worth a little energy to lament and protest this life of ruin which "Sportsman Time," who "rears his brood to kill," will inevitably bring to pass. It is this poetic voice—a voice that can only affirm through denial—it is this poetic structure—a structure founded upon the opposition of wishes and facts, acts of defiance and acts of surrender—it is this tone or mood—latent with both acquiescence *and* anger—that gives Hardy's early poems the pathos of Swinburne's earliest *Poems and Ballads*, poems which ask countless times,

> Is it worth a tear, is it worth an hour,
>   To think of things that are well outworn?
> Of fruitless husk and fugitive flower,
>   The dream foregone and the deed forborne?
>   ["The Triumph of Time," ll. 9–12]

Sometimes subtle, sometimes even dramatic changes in Hardy's world-view, and in those poetic structures which embody a poet's sensibility, can be found in those verses that were composed in or after the year 1870. Hardy, following Swinburne's lead, later tried to explain away transitions by claiming that the excruciatingly painful lines written earlier in his career advance a "series of feelings or fancies . . . in widely differing moods" through "dramatic or impersonative" pieces, highly "imaginative writings" that convey "mere impressions of the moment, and not convictions or arguments."[21] In other words, Hardy, like Swinburne, apparently tried to put his past behind him by suggesting that his most agonized agnosticisms, his most maimed, incomplete, and in some way unsuccessful poems of dissent, were monodramas.[22]

In Hardy's case, the gradual disappearance from his early poetry of the themes of loss and acquiescence may well have been the result of certain biographical catalysts. In 1870, Hardy fell passionately in love with Emma Lavinia Gifford, the woman he married in 1874, and it was also during this period (1871–74) that he realized his ambition to become a published author. Beginning with *Desperate Remedies* (1871) and following up with *Under the Greenwood Tree* (1872), *A Pair of Blue Eyes* (1873), and *Far from the Madding Crowd* (1874), Hardy grew in writing ability almost as rapidly as in popularity and wealth. He planted, he watered, and Something (as Clough would have put it) gaveth increase.

Literary influences must have been at least as responsible as biographical facts for the transition in which Hardy moves out of a period of agonized, anti-romantic protest into a new period of post-romantic affirmation. To deny the influence of this clear and well-marked literary trend, or pattern of transition, upon Hardy's world-view and aesthetic would be particularly myopic in light of the fact that a similar pattern can be found in the work of Tennyson, Carlyle, Arnold, and Swinburne, work that Hardy read intimately and often, work that antedated his own poetry and fiction by anywhere from two (Swinburne) to thirty (Tennyson) years.

One of the immediately obvious transitions observable in the poetry of (or after) 1870 is a greater emphasis on "Chance" than on "Fate." To be sure, this "Chance"—or "Circumstance"—of the later poems often has such a deterministic ring as to seem *almost* synonymous with "Fate," but the tone of the poetry written after 1870 seems to indicate that the change in vocabulary is, indeed, symptomatic of real transition. In "Ditty," a poem Hardy composed in 1870 (the very year he met Emma Gifford), the speaker, like dozens of others since the disappointed lover of "Amabel" (1865), admits that "bond-servants of Chance / We are all," and that

> To feel I might have kissed—
>   Loved as true—
> Otherwhere, nor Mine have missed
>   My whole life through . . .
> Is a smart severe. . . .

[ll. 28–33]

What makes this poem so different from those earlier, agonized love-laments, such as "Revulsion," is the tone of the somewhat clumsy final stanza. Gone is the bitter, early Swinburnian rhetoric of complaint, gone is young Teufelsdröckh's will to cease loving or to cease living, gone, too, is that tendency of Hardy's earlier poems to disintegrate, in the final stanza, into disjointed images, contradictory claims, unanswered questions. In its place is a positive exclamation that comes close to declaring a new willingness to make the best of, perhaps even to celebrate, the accidental gifts of "unknowing" chance:

> I but found her in that, going
> On my errant path unknowing,
> I did not out-skirt the spot
> That no spot on earth excels,
>   —Where she dwells!

[ll. 41–45]

The speaker admits throughout his ditty that it is tempting to look upon the woman he has met by accident as the divine answer to prayer, as a portion of the loveliness which she has made more lovely. The temptation, strong as it is, is fairly well resisted by the speaker (who is inseparable from the poet). He exorcises the romantic exaggeration by forcing it into quotation marks and attributing it not to himself but, rather, to the outside world. Speaking of nature on a springtime day, he says that

> Upon that fabric fair
>   "Here is she!"
> Seems written everywhere
>   Unto me.

To be sure, we instantly attribute nature's one-line romantic poem to the observer, but when he so openly admits his own projection (*"Seems* written . . . / Unto me") and never allows it to become more than a projection (as did the speaker of "Neutral Tones") he proves himself the ultimate master of his fancy.

The poet of "Ditty," then, would resist not only the romantic notion that great romances are the rarefied designs of "Love" (the speaker of "At a Bridal" had been deluded by precisely that pathetic hope), but also the belief that the *inamorata* is some kind of metaphysical find, a route to transcendental bliss. When the poet comes to accept the fact that his lady "is nought, / Even as I, beyond the dells / Where she dwells," he is not just saying that he and his mate, like Wordsworth's Lucy, have dwelt among untrodden ways. He also means that their union is not one of phantoms—of men and women but spirits too. It is, rather, the marriage of beings who don't exist beyond the physical "dells" in which they dwell, not only the provincial environment by which they have been limited and determined, but also the temporal bodies which they can neither leave in life nor survive in death.

The tendency to accept the limitations of a physical reality and "Chance" too indifferent and erratic to be personified as God or Fate is even more noticeable in another "Wessex" poem that was composed after the initial 1865–67 group.[23] "The Temporary the All" (almost certainly composed during the early seventies) systematically ridicules transcendence-seeking idealism and states what Hardy gradually came to see as the facts about nature's indifference—not malign indifference or seeming indifference but real, dumb indifference. The phonetics and metrics of the poem, which imitate rather successfully Old English kennings, are unique in the Hardy canon, but the narrative structure of "The Temporary the All" is one which, to varying degrees, gives form to Hardy's poetry and fiction from the lyrics of 1870 onwards. A dreamer—a romantic persona distanced from the post-romantic philosophy and aesthetic of his or her omniscient "author"—is taught the danger of unrealistic fancies (faith in romantic love, nature's divine presence, social apocalypse) by the temporal process. In the meantime, the progressive, point-by-point stanza (or chapter) structure of the poem (or novel) teaches the very same lesson to the reader as he or she moves through a different time continuum, that is, the temporal process of reading.

In "The Temporary the All," the speaker recalls a time when "Change and Chancefulness . . . / Set me . . . near to one unchosen" (ll. 1–2). Once "Fused . . . in friendship" with the unchosen associate, however, the speaker soon looked beyond their union to the establishment of an Ideal Friendship with some perfectly kindred (and perfectly hypothetical) soul. He remembers the day when he "self-communed,"

> "Cherish him can I while the true one forthcome—
> Come the rich fulfiller of my prevision. . . . "

[ll. 5–6]

The former romantic recalls that, when a woman entered his life by "chance," she seemed "unformed to be all-eclipsing" but an acceptable diversion " 'till arise my forefelt / Wonder of women' " (ll. 10–12). Next, a series of shabby "tenements" fell far short of that Wordsworthian, "visioned hermitage" where he had longed to go with perfect friend and ideal lover in order to "transcend" life through some "high handiwork" that, he had hoped, " 'will . . . Truth and Light outshow' " (ll. 13–18). Chance, ultimately, brought the fulfillment of not one dream, and in the last stanza the experienced speaker (who speaks of the past and present, not the future; whose words are not enclosed in quotation marks; whose present experience frames his past innocence) can finally communicate, uninterrupted by the dreaming voices of his past, the fact that "Mistress, friend, place, aims to be bettered straightway" have never been bettered. Those experiences which drifted into life atomistically, on the winds of "Change and chancefulness," were "never transcended" (l. 24). The "intermissive aim" has become, in his present view, the only reasonable ambition for the artist on an "earth-track" (l. 19, l. 23). The "temporary" has come to be seen as identical with the "All"—in the speaker's mind, in Hardy's mind (these two, after all, seem to become one), and in the reader's understanding.

The poetic form of "The Temporary the All" is a structure of resolution exactly like those linear, synthetic structures of Swinburne's *Songs before Sunrise* and not all that different from that larger, more complex pattern of "The Two Voices," the poem in which Tennyson had emerged from his own agnostic agony by hearing out warring voices of faith and disbelief and then by achieving that liberating resolve to celebrate the simple mysteries of the here and now, symbolized at the end of the work by the image of an ordinary family on Sunday morning. In Hardy's poem of what Lawrence would later refer to as "Coming Through," the thesis (the romantic dream of divine states of existence) and the antithetical voice (the mundane fact about the barrenness of the quotidian) are resolved. They are synthesized by the post-romantic structure into that emergent philosophy that is "beyond church" and says that the mundane is all we have or need of the divine, that the temporary *is* the all of life.

With that affirmation, of course, the static, unchanging, romantic ideals that once seemed worthy of man's dreams gradually come to be the subjects of irony, occasionally even ridicule, in Hardy's mature verse. Like the young dreamer whose various dreams of transcendence are exploded, step by step, as time passes in "The Temporary the All," "The Ivy Wife," a vine seeking to grow into indivisible union with various dark and handsome trees, eventually finds and shows her quest for romantic unity to be a destructive quest as she moves in time from stanza to stanza, from beech to ash, being poisoned by the one, strangling the other. (Swinburne had already described romantic love through the metaphor of a strangling, poisoning serpent in "Laus Veneris," and both Swinburne's and Hardy's lyrics are imperiled by Shelley's "Alastor," a despairing romantic poem which nearly renders those post-romantic efforts redundant. In the precursor's poem "those that love" are compared to the "parasit[ic] plants" which like "restless serpents . . . twine their tendrils" about the "trunks" and "boughs" of grey-grown "beech" and "oak" [ll. 431–45].)

"The Ivy Wife" is an embarrassingly silly exercise in dogmatic poetry. What makes it interesting is not its aesthetic achievement but, rather, the fact that it is collected in *Wessex Poems* and thus juxtaposed with earlier lyrics in which sympathetic speakers long for perfect union with a beloved. (In "She to Him IV" [1866], a lover wishes in vain to be "fused" to another "by ecstasy.") The date of composition of "The Ivy Wife" is known to be some—perhaps many—years later than 1866, and the attitude of the poem toward romantic fusion is anything but that of intense longing.

For Hardy, evidently, the reverie has faded. The early romantic dream songs of poets such as Blake are now transposed into a minor key by Hardy (as they were by Shelley and Swinburne before him). In *Paradise Lost* Milton described an innocent Adam and Eve "le[ading] the vine / To wed her Elm; she spous'd about him twines / Her marriageable arms" (V, ll. 215–17). Blake had fashioned these lines into an image of romantic love:

Love and harmony combine,
And around our souls intwine,
While thy branches mix with mine,
And our roots together join.

["Song," from *Poetical Sketches*]

But Hardy suggests, through his own entwining "Ivy Wife," that lovers who would always be joining and mixing with another soul, always striving for perfect and harmonious unity with a beloved, are latter-day Satanic overreachers. Through their ascendant twinings they will eventually destroy their beloveds and, at the same time, be brought down by them (poisoned by impurities or weighted down by mere physical reality). Hardy's serpentine vine precipitates just such a double catastrophe when, clutching too close and reaching too high, she sets in motion a latter-day version of the Fall. "In my triumph," the Ivy-Wife says, as she recalls reaching from an ash for the heavens beyond,

I lost sight
Of afterhaps. Soon he,
Being bark-bound, flagged, snapped, fell outright,
And in his fall felled me!

[ll. 21–24]

Hardy seems to suggest that, like Satan, ascent-prone romantics bring down not only their intended victims but, in so doing, are themselves bruised, crushed, down-trodden, the agents of their own plunging doom.

In place of a romantic ideal of love as perfect unity, in place of the bitter complaint against life in a world where the old, romantic ideal is no longer tenable, the poems composed in or after 1870 resynthesize and redefine love as it occurs in two emergent, post-romantic forms. One of these definitions can be found in poems like "The Husband's View" or "The Dark-Eyed Gentleman," where love is stripped of all destructive or at least corrosive spiritual pretenses and is described as sexuality-without-shame. This tendency to define and to learn to accept love in what Hardy saw as its most unromantic, elemental form was one of the facets of his art that most influenced D. H. Lawrence. In "The Dark-Eyed Gentleman," a lusty woman of the earth sings out:

I pitched my day's leazing in Crimmercrock Lane,
To tie up my garter and jog on again,
When a dear dark-eyed gentleman passed there and said,
In a way that made all o' me colour rose-red,
    "What do I see—
    O pretty knee!"
And he came and tied up my garter for me.
. . . .
Yet now I've beside me a fine lissom lad,
And my slip's nigh forgot, and my days are not sad;
    . . . No sorrow brings he
    And thankful I be
That his daddy once tied up my garter for me!
                                        [ll. 1–7, 15–16, 19–21]

The other type of human love defined by Hardy's post-1870 poetry is that of brotherhood or, as he so often called it, borrowing directly from Swinburne, "loving-kindness."[24] This alternate mode of loving will be discussed at some length later in the chapter, for its importance to the post-romantic social ideals of humility, responsibility, and self-sacrifice is immense. Suffice it to say at this point that "The Burghers" offers a choice example of loving-kindness as it interacts with its counterpart, unabashed sexuality, bodily expression. This perfectly progressive and illustrative poem describes the initial, nearly homicidal rage felt by a husband who learns of his wife's passionate affair with a lover, the "sad thoughts" that follow the demise of his too-high expectations, the "drowse" of indifference the husband feels as his initial, self-righteous outrage passes, and finally the eventual decision to act out of kindness toward the lovers by freeing them from the prison both of social convention and of jealousy spawned of irrational idealism. (A veritable embodiment of Beyond-Church "Charity," a humanely revised God, this husband even decides to bestow upon the penniless adulterers their "daily bread.") The pattern of "The Burghers" becomes, for Hardy, a kind of paradigm of loving-kindness, one which he improvises upon several times in the course of his poetic and novelistic career, perhaps most persuasively, if not most purely, in *Jude the Obscure*.

It was Carlyle, of course, who had contributed the seminal

definitions of these two, post-romantic reductions of the supposedly ethereal romantic vision of love. In his treatise *On Heroes and
Hero-Worship*, he had turned to Novalis (as Hardy would later
turn) to find a new, revised, and reduced definition of heaven.
There he comes upon, and relates, an heretical revision of an old
Biblical passage. " 'There is but one Temple in the Universe,' says
the devout Novalis, 'and that temple is the Body of Man. . . . We
touch Heaven when we lay our hands on a human body.' "[25] "We
are the miracle of miracles," Carlyle hastens to add in this proto-
Lawrentian passage, and in *On Heroes and Hero-Worship*, as in all
his other works, he goes on to outline yet another plain and simple,
post-romantic ideal of love—that of caring, helpfulness, shared
troubles, and divided labors—the goal of human kindness which
Teufelsdröckh is groping to define when he begins, in the "Everlasting Yea" chapter of *Sartor Resartus*, to look upon his "fellow-
man with an infinite Love, an infinite Pity."[26]

Sexual energy or loving-kindness, each in its own way, replaces
romantic love as a desired relationship in the poems Hardy wrote
after 1870, especially between 1870 and 1890. This is not to say, of
course, that the concept of romantic love disappears but rather that
it, like the pathetic fallacy, like the enervated, solipsistic speaking
voice of the early poems, becomes a kind of straw man which the
poet frames, carefully controls, and continually cuts down in favor
of his newly evolved definitions and devices. The reason I have
preferred the term "post-romantic" to an equally ambiguous but
usable term such as "modern" is precisely because of the constant
presence of generalized romantic concepts in Hardy's works, as in
Swinburne's, and the extreme degree to which his mature poems
and fictions are rhetorical, imagistic, and structural metamorphoses of romanticism as he conceived it. In *Poems of the Past and
Present* (1901), Hardy includes a poem entitled "I Said to Love,"
which neither he nor J. O. Bailey includes in their respective lists of
poems composed during the 1860's, a poem which, by virtue of its
extreme similarity to "He Abjures Love" (1883), must have been
composed sometime during the early 1880's. In this lyric, the
speaker is clearly addressing that destructive, strangling, absurd
dream of romantic love which had often seemed as desirable as
elusive to the yearning, youthful, Swinburnian poet of the 1860's.
Once again, Hardy uses quotation marks and shifts in tense, this
time to safely distance himself from that attractive old deity who

had once promised "a heaven beneath the sun" (stanza 1), that holy
One who had, in fact, become a sadistic god to whom adoring
masochists prayed for inflicted agonies (stanza 2):

> I said to Love,
> "It is not now as in old days
> When men adored Thee and thy ways
>   All else above;
> Named thee the Boy, the Bright, the One
> Who spread a heaven beneath the sun,"
>   I said to Love.
>
> I said to him,
> "We now know more of thee than then;
> We were but weak in judgment when,
>   With hearts abrim,
> We clamoured thee that thou would'st please
> Inflict on us thine agonies,"
>   I said to him.

[ll. 1–14]

The presence of Swinburne's early poetry in Hardy is still occasionally detectable, but the role of that presence is now utterly
different. Hardy is now able to confront and deny what he believes
to be the romantic faith or expectation directly, as opposed to the
nervous confrontation implied by his earlier, agonized mimicry of
Swinburne's poems of protest. Swinburne, therefore, can now
become a stand-in for his own spiritual and poetic adolescence, a
youth "weak in judgment" who "clamoured" for "inflict[ed] . . .
agonies." Hardy thus represses his own moment of crisis, first by
transferring it to the youthful Swinburne of *Poems and Ballads*,
then by locking that Swinburne within the finality of quotation
marks and surrounding him with the mature rhetoric of the
beyond-all-that.

In another poem of the same vintage, Hardy reiterates his
address to those distorting, destructive fancies which led young
innocents, "weak in judgment . . . , / With hearts abrim," to see
"Love," in the "old days," as something more than sex, kindness, or
a combination of the two. In "He Abjures Love" (1883), the speaker
abandons the rose-colored vision which precedes "Love's . . .
fever-stricken . . . disquietings" and accepts a world of "common,"
"gray," "faulty . . . things beholden." "No more will now rate I,"
the speaker declares,

The common rare,
The midnight drizzle dew,
The gray hour golden,
The wind a yearning cry,
The faulty fair,
Things dreamt, of comelier hue
Than things beholden.

[ll. 31–41]

To be fair, both "He Abjures Love" and "I Said to Love" confess, subtly, some sadness in abandoning "things dreamt." The former asks, "after love what comes?" and answers, "A few sad hours"; the latter claims mankind is becoming too cynical, "too old in apathy," to worry that the race may be diminished with the passing of the "kindling coupling-vow" of a "cherubic" vision. More important, however, these lyrics demonstrate the fact that Hardy's attitude toward romantic love underwent a significant, if not quite dramatic, change between those early years of crisis, in which his various voices cry out in agony that real lovers, "of earth's poor average kind," are "blank" and "common" to each man who has a dream-vision of a beloved ("At Waking," 1869), and those later, transitional years in which he resolves to quit rating "Things dreamt, of comelier hue / Than things beholden" (1883). As is the case with the very similar transitions from agony to acceptance in the Swinburne canon, moreover, Hardy's changing attitudes towards self or love or nature or society or time are accompanied by parallel transitions in his attitudes toward all the others. Nature, for instance, is no longer even dreamed of as a realm of Intellectual Love or Beauty or moral order but, rather, is accepted as a meaningless cycle neither benevolent nor malign to man. (John Stuart Mill had recently argued that "conformity to nature has no connection with right and wrong.")[27] In one of the poems collected in *Wessex Poems* but composed well after the 1865–67 group, the poet admits that he would still like to believe that nature is really the "sweetness, / Radiance that"

. . . I thought thee
When I early sought thee,
Omen scouting,

that he wouldn't mind believing again that "Love alone had wrought thee— / Wrought thee for my pleasure," nay, even for his poetry:

Planned thee as a measure
  For expounding
  And resounding
Glad things that men treasure.

The trouble is, time will not allow a man to reenter his youth or its faiths; there is no going home again to the romantic world of the poet's infancy, and emergence, we learn from "Time" as the poem unfolds in time, is as inevitable as it is desirable:

But such readorning
Time forbids with scorning—
  Makes me see things
  Cease to be things
They were in my morning.

["To Outer Nature," ll. 1–20]

Once this realization, this inner change, has been brought about, the need to cry out in protest to nature for her failures (one of the catalysts of Swinburne's and Hardy's earliest poems) disappears. It is replaced by that conviction expressed in "The Lacking Sense" which had been expressed only a few years earlier in Swinburne's "Hertha" and *Erechtheus*, namely, that a man should "Deal" unconscious, amoral nature "no scorn, no note of malediction" but should "Assist her where thy creaturely dependence gives thee room, / For thou art of her womb" (ll. 26–28). The speaker of the poem, who is addressing "Time," the somehow articulate child of Mother Nature, to find out why His mother always "wounds the lives she loves," is told that the great world weaver is "blind," that "sightless are those orbs of hers" that bring to man "fearful unful-filments." What the poem seems to suggest, below and beyond the fictional dialogue it purveys, is not so much that Milton was wrong because God is even blinder than he was but, rather, that Milton and his romantic progeny were *terribly* wrong because their blindness to nature's own blindness gave us a vision that deprived us of all sight, making us ask restless, foolish questions like the ones the still-untutored questioner of this poem's first stanza poses: Is Nature an "angel fallen from grace"? How do we explain her "fallings from her fair beginnings"? "Why weaves she not her world-webs to according lutes and tabors"? These, after all, are the very questions Hardy believes Milton, Wordsworth, and Shelley asked, respectively, and Hardy's poem answers them by implying that nature was never angelic but, rather, that we were seduced into a fall from the truth about nature by Milton; that the reason Wordsworthian children, as they mature, suffer "fallings from us, vanishings" of their vision is that their own utterly insubstantial fancy is falling and vanishing; and that if the "world weaver's" artwork seems a bit unrefined it is because poets such as Shelley (here is a horribly reductive misreading of "The Witch of Atlas") insisted upon making their own spritely imaginations the *sine qua non* of their definitions of divine creativity. Thus they blinded our orbs to the possibility that to believe in such a creator is to expect too much; thus they precipitated our fall into despair by encouraging us to do what the Satanic Byron of Carlyle's heretical criticism did, namely, to "strain after the unlimited."

In a poem collected with "The Lacking Sense" in *Poems of the Past and the Present* and roughly dated 1883 by the autobiography, Hardy uses the rather baffling, but perfectly Swinburnian technique of personifying nature in order to have her deny that she is an ordered or communicative or moral entity desiring or deserving of the celebration, the cursing, and (in either case) the allegorization and personification which she has so long elicited from mankind. No realm of moons like "Night queens," no harborer of "stars . . . sublime," this Herthian mother of mountains and men deplores the "mountings of mind-sight," the recently elevated "range of" man's "vision," which now allow him to see so far and dream so high that he inevitably finds only "blemish / Throughout my domain," that is, throughout the only reality man will ever know. The unfortunate belief, at once romantic and melioristic to stay within Swinburne's terminology, that "Every best thing . . . to best purpose / Her powers preordain" brings such bitter disappointments and even such social violence that Hardy's speaker hopes, in the final stanza of her poem, to

> grow, then, but mildews and mandrakes,
>   And slimy distortions,
> Let nevermore things good and lovely
>   To me appertain. . . .
>   ["The Mother Mourns," ll. 75–76, 85–88]

Hardy's new, reduced expectations about nature do not prevent him from using that convention of pathetic fallacy which marked his first poems almost as heavily as it filled Swinburne's early work with intense, brooding inner and outer landscapes. The difference lies in the way in which Hardy *uses* the pathetic fallacy. Just as he begins to use romantic love as a straw man to knock down in favor of new definitions of love in his post-1870 poetry, he uses the pathetic fallacy in his later work as a symptom of that romantic faith in the unity of self and nature which his own poetry denies. In "The Milkmaid" and "The Seasons of Her Year" (entitled "The Pathetic Fallacy" in the manuscript), Hardy uses his structure of progressive, point-by-point poetic didacticism to show that there is absolutely no spiritual connection or correspondence between inner life and external nature except that which is fancied by dreamers (or poets) oblivious to the reality of the perfectly mute and morally blank natural world. In the only slightly more bearable third poem of the group, "The King's Experiment," he creates yet another meaningless, unconscious, indifferent, yet somehow garrulous Dame Nature to ridicule a romantic lover who, because of his own temporary happiness, somehow feels at one with the One:

> "Why warbles he that skies are fair
> And coombs alight," she cried, "and fallows gay,
> When I have placed no sunshine in the air
> Or glow on earth today?"
>
> [ll. 5–8]

In poems like "The King's Experiment," Hardy uses what he believed to be a peculiarly romantic tradition (of "seeing everywhere the image of [one's] own mood")[28] to challenge some of the foibles of that romantic vision of nature communicated by the tradition. Alone in a country setting, the speaker of "Nature's Questioning" hears nature sounding a little like Mycerinus, for it is "lipping" such Arnoldian questions as: "Has some Vast Imbecility, / Mighty to build and blend, / But impotent to tend, / Framed us?" "Or come we of an Automaton / Unconscious of our pains?" Or are we scourged by "some high Plan . . . / As yet not understood?" As the poem progresses, of course, we become aware that the "Questioning" is the poet's, not "Nature's," the final stanza reminding us that

> . . . the winds, and rains,
> And Earth's old glooms and pains
> Are still the same, and Life and Death are neighbors nigh.

Just as Hardy surrounded a youthful, romantic identity with a more mature and stoical voice in "The Temporary the All," here he places one vision of nature (that of "Field, flock, and lonely tree" which "All seem to gaze at me . . . / Their faces dulled, constrained, and worn") within another (that of "winds, and rains . . . and Life and Death"). Thus he allows the latter to show up the former for what is is, namely, a projection of the disappointment the speaker feels when, having gone "Omen scouting" in the natural world for "Glad things that men" may "treasure" ("To Outer Nature"), he finds only a chance-ridden realm where "Good" and "gloom" and "Plan" and "pains . . . are neighbors nigh" ("Nature's Questioning," ll. 21–28). By the time the speaker "responds," in the poem's final stanza, to the "questions" which "Nature" asks by mumbling, "No answerer I," we are all too aware of the involution of reality which the romantic effects: it is Nature that has no answers, and it is the poet who is "dulled" and "worn" by his own metaphysical questions.

Far from being a system of images which in some way corresponds to man's individual and collective consciousness, nature for Hardy becomes a dumb, organic system that merely ferments individualized units of life and then, upon their extinction as individual beings, unconsciously and amorally disintegrates and reincorporates them into its own great compost heap. Speaking of "Shelley's Skylark" (1887?), Hardy defines his departure from the "faint penumbra" of the influential predecessor by celebrating not those elevating powers which were symbolized by the bird of Shelley's lyric but, rather, the fact that "Somewhere afield here something lies / In Earth's oblivious eyeless trust," a bird "That moved a poet to prophecies— / A pinch of unseen, unguarded dust" (ll. 1–4). Thus, for Hardy, the unseen bird of Shelley's "ecstatic" vision can only be doubly unseen (hence the pun, "unseen, unguarded"); a quest for it would be utterly impossible (even the quest for the body of the literal bird unseen by Shelley is a quest fit for "fairies"). All that Hardy can hope to "find" in his latter-day hymn is the fact that "the lark that Shelley heard" sang and "lived" just "like another bird" and "perished," a "ball of feather and bone."

As Walter F. Cannon has argued in an essay on nineteenth-century paleontology, "Poetry had to revise its habits. 'Thou wast not born for death, immortal bird,' was true, to Keats's knowledge; it is simply silly to a modern student. Nightingales will be fossils a million years from now."[29] Like Teufelsdröckh's later view of nature as a mysterious, unconscious, and amoral life-eroding, life-creating cycle that quickly covers and metamorphoses human battlefields and monuments,[30] and like Swinburne's similar conception of the natural realm in *Songs before Sunrise* and *Erechtheus*, Hardy's vision of nature after 1870 comes to be that of an indifferent organic system of recycling energies. In "Voices from Things Growing in a Country Churchyard," the flowers all declare whose bodies they incorporate, and in "The Dead Drummer" (1899), later entitled "Drummer Hodge," Hardy anticipates poets like Brooke, Owen, Thomas, and Rosenberg, by saying that "portion" of the field where the young man fell "Will Hodge forever be; / His homely Northern breast and brain / Grow up a Southern tree" (ll. 14–16). (For poets of the later era, of course, the English flesh transformed the tropical "Southern tree" into an English yew.)

In another short Hardy poem, entitled "Transformations," the poet's sole concern is with this theme of the dead who remain forever within the chance-ridden realm of living nature. In the final stanza of "Transformations," the poet simultaneously echoes not only ancient folk ballads but also Swinburne's "Anactoria," FitzGerald's *Rubáiyát*, and T. H. Huxley's assertion in "The Physical Basis of Life" (1868–69) that, in the context of the ever-continuing cycle of natural life, "so far as form is concerned, plants and animals are not separable," since a man who lives by nature's store will soon be fertilizing its continued organic production.[31] Hardy, like Huxley, states that the material essences of the dead become incorporated in the eternal fibrous life of nature. By so doing, he cleverly revises the Easter morning (and thus preempts the Judgment Day) scenario: tomb-site utterances like "He is not here, but is risen" now become preludes to mere arboreal inspection:

So, they are not underground,
But as veins and nerves abound
In the growths of upper air,
And they feel the sun and rain,
And the energy again
That made them what they were!

[ll. 13–18]

A man can never transcend, avoid, or reverse the process that time, chance, and nature determine for him. Hardy knew all too well, with Moschus, that men, "so strong and tall and wise," once they "be dead," lie and "sleep . . . both sound and long a sleep that is without waking" ("Lament for Bion," ll. 100–104). Once the skylark or the soldier has fallen, the substances of that brief life "will for ever be" subject to nature's unpredictable, indifferent cyclic powers. In Shelley's "Adonais," the shapes and fragrances of symbolic flowers are ultimately transformed, after frost, into the fiery radiance of eternal stellar light, but, as the belated and stoical "Rain on a Grave" reminds us, once Hardy's first wife has perished, her only hope for an immortal existence lies in the springtime fact that

> Soon will be growing
>   Green blades from her mound,
> And daisies be showing
>   Like stars on the ground,
> Till she form part of them—
> Ay—the sweet heart of them,
> Loved beyond measure
> With a child's pleasure
> All her life's round.
>
> [1913, ll. 28–35]

It is more accurate to refer to Hardy's mature work as a poetry of strength, endurance, and stoical acceptance than as a poetry of optimism or of celebration, for Hardy's works, although they anticipate the last pages of *Go Down, Moses* (a veritable paean to recycled organic material),[32] by no means attain the triumphant tone of Faulkner's prose. Nevertheless, it is clear that in the Phoenix-like descent and, in descent, rebirth, the poetry has rid itself of, and emerged from, that agonized and defeated tone characteristic of the earliest, anti-romantic laments, poems paralyzed between the fraudulence of past faiths and the horror of life without them. As Hardy stoically writes in "The Impercipient," one of his post-1870 *Wessex Poems*, "O, doth a bird deprived of wings / Go earth-bound wilfully!" (Swinburne had characterized his own maturation as having his "wings clipped,"[33] and in "A Match," his heretical ode to the God of Love, he had sought to "Pluck out" love's "flying feather.")

Hardy has gained a perspective on the past in part by framing its pain in his mature poetry. He surrounds the crises, the troubled progress, of a more youthful life and art with the knowledge possessed in the present, with a progressive and didactic structure that deflates weak dreams into stoical assertions. By doing so, he distances himself from, analyzes, and uses his own past (much as Swinburne did in "Prelude" and in *Erechtheus*) to methodically demonstrate the pathos, the conflicts, and sometimes even the tragedy brought about by all romantic overreaching. By doing so, he also manages to illustrate the value of not expecting too much from life and of seeing other men as delicate, perishable beings whose sufferings, while they cannot be transcended, can be shared.

It is through the theme of shared suffering—a theme common to countless of his poems and ballads—that Hardy, in his mature poetry, comes closest to redefining the belief in the unity of the human spirit which had been so important a component of what Hardy saw as Wordsworth's and Shelley's romantic faith. For Hardy's poems, whether they be the microcosmic depictions of the pains and pleasures of rural life through the medium of the folk ballad, those more macrocosmic surveys of limitless universal chaos and powerless gods, or both (in the case of hybrid poems such as "Channel Firing"), insist that the only unities we can count on, the only meliorisms we may hope for, are those which we forge ourselves when, having accepted the world as a diminished thing and man as a creature with limited resources, we work and sacrifice out of loving-kindness to preserve each other from annihilation.

The tragedy brought about by the speaker of "The Tramp-woman's Tragedy" (1902), for instance, when translated into perhaps over-dignified terms, turns out to be the tragedy of believing that friends and lovers are extensions of one's own being and, therefore, that teasing is harmless, jealousy a contradiction in terms. The catastrophe of "A Sunday Morning Tragedy" (1904), in turn, is the refusal to admit to the untranslatable physicality of mankind, and "The Flirt's Tragedy" (1906) results from a man's inability to accept the smallness, the coarseness, of his identity, the bitterness of love, and time's triumph, in other words, the mere vicissitudes of chance and circumstance.

What Hardy suggests indirectly, by negative example, through ballads like "A Trampwoman's Tragedy" or "A Sunday Morning Tragedy" (both of which were almost certainly influenced by Swinburne's 1889 poem, "The Bride's Tragedy"), he makes known more blatantly, if in somewhat different terms, in poems like "God's Funeral," "A Plaint to Man," ΆΓΝΩΣΤΩι ΘΕΩι, or

"God-Forgotten." Each of these allows a "God" much like the dumb, indifferent "Nature" of Hardy's "The Lacking Sense" or "The Mother Mourns" to confess his own impotence, indifference, even unconsciousness. In the process, the poems illustrate the need for fortitude, responsibility, loving-kindness, even self-sacrifice.

This "God" who speaks in these three poems and, with only minor changes of name and mien, in perhaps a dozen others is perfectly analogous to the God of Swinburne's "Prelude," "Genesis," "Hymn of Man," and "Before a Crucifix" (1871), a sick and dying God whom man, out of his own insecurity, once created in his own image. He is one and the same, moreover, with the shadowy gods who terrify the collective human soul in *Erechtheus*. Hardy's God, like Swinburne's Poseidon, is a man-created abstraction who "causes" (and therefore excuses) human failure and human violence and who must be annihilated by man—individually and collectively—if there is to be a future for human society. He is, furthermore, a power who year by year prevents the birth of the true God, the God of whom Swinburne speaks in "To Walt Whitman in America," to whom he alludes in "Before a Crucifix," and the God who actually speaks to man in "Quia Multum Amavit"—the God of man's freedom from all imaginary divinities.

The God-seeking speaker of Hardy's "God-Forgotten," for instance, meets up with a cosmic "Lord" who chastizes,

"Thou shoulds't have learnt that *Not to Mend*
For me could mean but *Not to Know*. . . .

[ll. 41–42]

The speaker of the poem thus learns, we may assume, the lesson which the poet of ἈΓΝΩΣΤΩι ΘΕΩι has realized just prior to beginning his agnostic confession, namely, that the omniscient and omnipotent goal of his quest was a fancy of his own devising, that

Long have I framed weak phantasies of Thee,
    O Willer masked and dumb!

[ll. 1–2]

Hardy thus implicitly acknowledges that, just as "romantic" men tend to "shape" a spiritual world, usually benevolent but occasionally malign, according to the random pleasures, hopes, or disappointments they feel in the moment, so "religious" men (for Hardy, as for Swinburne, Carlyle, and Arnold, they are much the same) "frame" various "phantasies" of a personal God or "Fate" or

"Doom" according to their own temporary doubts, dreams, or dissatisfactions. Thus, in these poems of agnostic acknowledgement, Hardy manages to "frame" himself in the act of "framing" or "shaping" weak fantasies, that is to say, he manages to step outside of the agonized agnosticism of his own past and thus emerge from it, moving himself as well as his reader beyond disappointment, beyond fantasies, "beyond church."

The "God" which men would have speak to them is, then, according to Hardy, like the romantic "Love," the moral force of "Nature," and the heroic, transcendent identity which the modern self so often seeks but never finds. That is to say, the God whom the reader confronts in Hardy's poetry after 1870 is the God of man's own unbridled imagination and, hence, of man's own wish-fulfilling creation. In the poem "God's Funeral" (1908), Hardy brilliantly uses a funeral train as a metaphor for man's modern, philosophic burial of his own anthropomorphic God. The speaker of the poem looks upon the bier and says:

> The fore-borne shape, to my blurred eyes,
> At first seemed man-like, and anon to change
> To an amorphous cloud of marvellous size. . . .
>
> [ll. 9–11]

The mourning of this "man-like" figure's passing makes the poem a clever reversal of the Biblical notion of creation, for in Hardy's poem, God is one whom man himself created in his own image, in Swinburne's terms, "the shade cast by the soul of man."[34] The speaker at "God's Funeral" continues:

> "O man-projected figure, of late
> Imaged as we, thy knell who shall survive?
> Whence came it we were tempted to create
> One whom we can no longer keep alive?
>
> "Framing him jealous, fierce, at first,
> We gave him justice as the ages rolled,
> Will to bless those by circumstance accurst,
> And longsuffering, and mercies manifold."
>
> [ll. 21–28]

In response to this self-inflicted, latter-day sermon, the poet goes on to ask what, in human life, can suffice as a significant ideal in a universe unswept by any divine, let alone millennial, esemplastic forces:

Still, how to bear such loss I deemed
The insistent question for each animate mind,
And gazing, to my growing sight there seemed
A pale yet positive gleam low down behind. . . .

[ll. 57–60]

This symbolic light, representing that which will make life bearable
in a dumb, indifferent universe, is as pale in definition as the real
light upon the landscape's gloomy horizon. In spite of the symbol's
lack of clarity, however, the image of the "few . . . good" men
who stand "aloof" but "together" in the final two stanzas of the
poem seems hazily to indicate something of the author's belief in
the dire necessity of some combination of liberty yoked with
responsibility, duty, and brotherhood:

Whereof, to lift the general night,
A certain few who stood aloof had said,
"See you upon the horizon that small light—
Swelling somewhat?" Each mourner shook his head.

And they composed a crowd of whom
Some were right good, and many nigh the best. . . .
Thus dazed and puzzled twixt the gleam and gloom
Mechanically I followed with the rest.

[ll. 61–68]

If this light upon the horizon which provokes "the good" and
"the best" "Mechanically" to follow seems too pallid an answer to
the question of what can give meaning to life in such a universe, then
another poem, entitled "A Plaint to Man" (1908), will surely be
found to be adequately explicit. The anthropomorphic God in this
poem asks why man ever made "the unhappy mistake of creating
me" and ends what is otherwise a rather pitiful complaint with
these words:

The truth should be told, and the fact be faced
That had best been faced in earlier years:

The fact of life with dependence placed
On the human heart's resource alone,
In brotherhood bonded close and graced

With loving-kindness fully blown,
And visioned help unsought, unknown.

[ll. 26–32]

Hardy, like Swinburne, thus gives voice to various deities in order to suggest that the building of a free, just, and workable, if never millennial, society demands both the avoidance of "vision" and, simultaneously, the psychic, spiritual annihilation of a transcendent God. (This is a departure from Shelley, for whom Promethean redemption meant the stripping away of illusion, but who, nevertheless, had some conception, however indefinite, of an eternal abode.) Just as the revolutionary battle for social liberty described by *Erechtheus* necessitates that corresponding, convulsive inner revolution that, annihilating man's very conception of eternality, puts the responsibility for the human condition on man and man alone, Hardy, too, in "cosmic" poems like "A Plaint to Man" and "God's Funeral," sees the future of society as dependent upon the revolutionary eradication of man's proclivity to dream of states of transcendent being and perfection.

The fact that we can make comparisons of Hardy's agnostic manifestos with Swinburne's *Erechtheus* or "Hymn of Man," or of "The Mother Mourns" with "Hertha," or of "A Sunday Morning Tragedy" with "The Bride's Tragedy" is, on one hand, incontrovertible evidence that even after Hardy emerges from his early period of crisis, a period in which his devotion to Swinburne's troubled early poetry is immense, his thinking continues to parallel that of the "brother poet" whose "new words" first enthralled him in 1865.

On the other hand, there is a great difference between parallelism and thralldom. "Revulsion" thinks like Swinburne, sounds like Swinburne, feels like Swinburne. The philosophy of late poems like "God's Funeral" or "The Lacking Sense" parallels—sometimes almost perfectly—the philosophy of, say, "Prelude" or "Quia Multum Amavit." To the extent that most nineteenth-century philosophical poems are instructive, didactic arguments developed through a logical (not lyrical), linear (not circular) poetic structure, their philosophical parallelism is underscored by a certain amount of aesthetic similarity. But, beyond that, these mature Hardy poems are distinct and independent, in accord with Swinburne but —in tone, mood, diction, rhythm, and image—all the things that contribute to a poem's linguistic texture—outside the bounds of thralldom.

This is not to suggest, however, that parallelism is never evidence of considerable influence or that, once Hardy emerges from his own agnostic agony, Swinburne's work becomes unimportant. In a rather late poem about dying Gods and repressed human spirits entitled "Aquae Sulis" (1911), Hardy admits, through a striking parallel to Swinburne's "Hymn to Proserpine," that while his own poetic forms may now be independent from his mentor's, Swinburne will always be an intellectual predecessor and, therefore, always more than a "mere" parallel. At the scene of "Roman . . . excavations," the voice of "the Goddess" long buried "beneath the pile / Of the God with the baldachined altar overhead" addresses that later deity who, having superseded the Olympians, has "set up crucifix and candle" where once, in a "stately and shining . . . temple" of the deep past, man worshipped gods but celebrated humanity as well.

Hardy, trying to go Swinburne one better, allows the Olympian herself to bemoan the coming and predict the passing of the "God" of the present, but the language his post-Swinburnian deity uses comes straight out of Swinburne's "Hymn" and his later poem, "Before a Crucifix." The superseded "Goddess" tells Christ that his "crucifix," like her "shrine," shall fall "worm-eaten." (The pale successor admits fully that "We are images both," made to be "twitched" out of sight and mind "by people's desires.") The real pity, the unnamed but surely Proserpinean deity adds, is that man ever freed himself from the humane life of liberty he enjoyed during her own reign and enchained himself to the pale but conquering new god of his making, Christ, the grey Galilean:

> Your priests have trampled the dust of mine without rueing,
> Despising the joys of man whom I so much loved.
>
> [ll. 17–18]

To the extent that Hardy speaks more through the voice of his "Proserpine," it would seem that he, like Swinburne before him, would rather "unearth" an old and relatively unoppressive deity than continue being "trampled" by the "priests" of the present. To the extent that "Aquae Sulis" converses with a poet of the past whose ideas, if resurrected, would trample Christ even as Christ's precursors had been down-trodden, the presiding imagistic motif of "excavation" is metapoetic as well as literal; the poet implicitly seeks to "unearth" early Swinburne to help him in the task of razing the temple of what Swinburne, in his letter to Ruskin, had called the "dead and doubtful gods."

Here, then, is a poem which, if not quite Swinburnian in setting or mood, nevertheless accounts for its origins, admitting that Swinburne's ideas are still attractive and betraying just enough edginess to testify to the older poet's continuing influence. Excavation, after all, implies that Swinburne is dead and buried which, though true in the physical sense, in an aesthetic or historical sense may be wishful thinking on Hardy's part.

However much Hardy becomes a poet in his own right, the careful critic can always sense the presence of a lingering indebtedness; most often through the ideas about God and man and nature, occasionally through the presence of a particularly Swinburnian theme or motif, as in "Aquae Sulis," and once in a poem that mysteriously describes, at least to my mind, Hardy's failed attempts as a mature poet to convince himself of his own originality, his coming to grips with Swinburne's faded, but never quite forgotten, poetic presence. In a poem composed in 1899 and entitled "I Have Lived With Shades," some still animate ghosts conduct the poet through dim rooms in the realm "To-be" and suddenly say "Now turn" and "Look whence we came, / And signify his name / Who gazes thence at thee." "Nor name nor race / Know I," the speaker bluntly retorts, "Of man / So commonplace."

"He moves me not at all;
I note no ray or jot
Of rareness in his lot,
Or star exceptional.
    Into the dim
    Dead throngs around
    He'll sink, nor sound
    Be left of him.

"Yet," said they, "his frail speech,
Hath accents pitched like thine—
Thy mould and his define
A likeness each to each—
    But go! Deep pain
    Alas, would be
    His name to thee,
    And told in vain!"

[ll. 24–48]

It is a poem that, admittedly, may bear up to more than one interpretation, but to my mind, the "Shade" whose "accents" the speaker thinks will "sink" into "silence," whose "mould" would seem to "define" the speaker's own, is almost certainly Swinburne. For the room in which the "frail" ghost stands is a place full of "dwindled dust / And rot and rust / Of things that were" (ll. 14–16), the very place which Swinburne created in his early "Ballad of Life" and "Ballad of Death," two of the poems which so tantalized Hardy on "that far morning of a summer day" in 1866, a place whose only colors are "Pale stains of dust and rust," a world where "rusted sheaves" stand "rain-rotten in rank lands." Hardy moves, in the poem, far enough into the future to kill Swinburne off, to reduce him to a ghost of the past, but he leaves him a ghost who cannot be forgotten or denied—at least not without anxiety and guilt—in a past at once painful and definitive.

The Temporary the All

Continuity and Change in Hardy's Fiction

5

The novels Hardy published during the 1870's, like their mature, lyric counterparts, are carefully structured works that establish the dangers of romantic overreaching and the necessity of leading the humble, controlled, responsible life amidst nature's indifferent landscapes. That is not to say, of course, that these novels converse only with poems. Hardy learned a great deal from novelists, and his novels, early and late, openly admit their debts to writers such as George Eliot, whose *Adam Bede* provided Hardy with characters, scenes, plot devices, and even a "Harvest Supper" fit to be warmed over twice.[1] But the *sensibility* Hardy wrestles with in his fiction, the epistemology he radically contests in the early novels, is one that comes to him by way of poets (or, just as often, by way of a pervasive, popular misreading of poets).

The protagonists of these early works of fiction are made to order for the foreshortened horizons of the post-romantic world. Elfride Swancourt, the center of interest in *A Pair of Blue Eyes* (1873), is as much a new Eve as Swinburne's Chthonia. Like the scenery of that Boscastle region of Tintagel she calls home (a favorite spot for both Swinburne and Hardy), "She was a combination of very interesting particulars," but interesting for the "combination itself rather than" the "individual elements combined." As to her person, "you did not see the form and substance of her features"; "as to her Presence, it was not powerful."[2] Controlled by her "womanly instinct" (1:59), Elfride, the narrator tells us with a wink, is "seldom" inclined to entertain any intimations of immortality, "thoughts that lie too deep for tears" (1:5). She believes only "that a thin widespread happiness, commencing now, and of a piece with the days of your life, is preferable to an anticipated heap far away in the future" (2:55–56). Her needs and wants, rather than being founded upon any dreams, religions, or far-off visions, are "modified by the creeping hours of time" and by the "circumstance[s]" of her "history" (1:2–3). Elfride "could slough off a sadness," Hardy says, "as easily as a lizard renews a diseased limb"; she could "swallow . . . agony" as "a draught" (2:2–3).

The land worked by Gabriel Oak, that cheerful, resourceful, and adaptive new Adam of *Far from the Madding Crowd* (1874), is the land which Carlyle had foreseen when the "beatific vision" of nature would "melt away; and oxen and sheep be grazing in its place."[3] It is a "cold," "indestructible," "featureless" land of "chalk" and "soil" where "dry leaves" have "simmered and boiled" as long as the "ancient and decaying" forests have felt the wind's "keenest blasts."[4] It is, the antiapocalyptic narrator tells us with a touch of amusement, "an ordinary specimen of . . . the globe" which will probably remain "undisturbed" on that "day of confusion" when all the "grander heights" known to man will "topple down" (1:11). To the extent that Gabriel embodies a new artistic departure, it is fitting that his sensibility be perfectly in harmony with this rough but enduring scene. Immediately after introducing us to "the poetry of motion" in mutable nature and in the restless shifting of the heavens, the narrator sees that we recognize, as part of the scene, the "muffled," "not . . . unhindered," somewhat "curtailed," but nonetheless appropriate "notes of Farmer Oak's flute" (1:13–14).

Oak, the artist and shepherd of these blasted but indestructible fields, is perfectly suited to the demands they exact. "A man of misty views" whose "features adhered . . . to the middle line" between "beauty" and "ugliness" ("not a single lineament could be . . . called worthy either of distinction or notoriety"), Gabriel "occupied morally" the "vast middle space of Laodicean neutrality," and a "quiet modesty" resulted from and reinforced his impression "that he had no great claim on the world's room" (1:1–4, 9). If he were given to philosophizing, he might well admit (as Swinburne had eventually confessed to Ruskin) "I don't want . . . more suffering and failure than I can avoid; but I take what comes as well and as quietly as I can; and this seems to me a man's real business and only duty."[5] Oak embodies that "creed of self sufficience" which Swinburne applauded in Arnold's poetry,[6] that "self-control, the *virtus verusque* labor" that Arnold found so wanting in most romantic poems.[7] "He had just reached that time of life," the narrator tells us, at which "intellect and . . . emotions" become "clearly separated," having "passed" through "the time during which the influence of youth indiscriminately mingles them [thought and feeling] in the character of impulse" (1:5). Hardy will later define Troy's "impulsive" and "youthful" character as "Romantic"; therefore, in some sense, Oak is a prototype of those who have escaped the "influence" of those romantic "youth" who "indiscriminately mingle" the "intellect and . . . emotions." A farmer whose countenance reminded the beholder of "a rising star," the "rising . . . moon," or of "rays in a rudimentary sketch of the rising sun" (1:1, 27), he is the incarnation of that actual which *is* the ideal, the temporary power that is all we know and all we need to know of the divine. His gnarled hand is the "hammer" of "Thor"; when sharpening his shears he is pictured as an "Eros . . . sharpening his arrows"; at supper he ate, drank, and talked "merry as the gods in Homer's heaven" (1:179, 219, 260–61).

To convince us that such characters are valuable citizens and valid literary protagonists, of course, Hardy must set them in opposition to another kind of character, that of the ineffectual, dangerous, and self-destructive romantic. Eustacia Vye, that raging Queen of the Night who nearly destroys the world of *The Return of the Native* (1878), comes immediately to mind as an example. Physically, Eustacia is of a piece with Egdon's "subdued" and "solemn" contours.[8] Describing her monochromatic outline on one of the heath's innumerable crests, Hardy says that her "form was so much like an organic part of the entire motionless structure that to see it move would have impressed the mind as a strange phenomenon" (1:24). And yet, in spite of Eustacia's "organic oneness" with the heath, "Egdon was her Hades" (1:149). She longs to transcend the drabness of possibility and, thus, to experience a condition at variance with the inevitable. "[R]omantic recollections" and "fancies" cause her to see "esplanade[s]" and "gallants" standing "like gilded uncials upon the blank tablet of surrounding Egdon" (1:151). Like Milton's Satan and the Satanic Byron of Arnold's heretical, post-romantic criticism, Eustacia spends her life "straining after the unlimited";[9] like the Satanic Coleridge of Pater's "appreciation," she represents the "inexhaustible discontent, languor, and homesickness, that endless regret, the chords of which ring all through our modern literature."[10]

Hardy doesn't leave the reader to guess too long at which shrine this "Romantic" with a "soul" which was "flame-like" and with "moods" which "recalled" the "lotus-eaters" will begin to genuflect (1:147–48). "To be loved to madness—such was her great desire," he tells us. To her, "A blaze of love, and extinction, was better than a lantern glimmer of the same which should last long years"; she longed "for the abstraction called passionate love more than for any particular lover" (1:153–54). The local gallant Wildeve is, for Eustacia, more an "ideali[zed]" image of a lover than a true beloved (he seemed "some wondrous thing she had created out of chaos"). Every time he showed real interest the "glory and the dream" of her romantic affection entirely "departed" (1:134, 158, 227).

The heath, although it may be something of a *tabula rasa* for discontented visionaries—a chaos out of which to create romantic forms—is not a place where glorious dreams are realized. It is, rather, a new, scaled-down landscape for an era of reduced expectations. Standing on its timeless, decaying surface as it makes a "transitional . . . roll," the narrator tells us that "A Saturday afternoon in November was approaching the time of twilight, and the vast tract of unenclosed wild known as Egdon Heath embrowned itself moment by moment." At "this transitional point," Hardy says, "It could best be felt when it could not clearly be seen" (1:3–5). Seasonally, Egdon stood at that point which "followed the green or young fern period, representing the morn" of the year, "and preceded the brown period," the autumnal or "evening . . . season" (2:233). The movement of Egdon out of morn and into evening, out of spring and into autumn, out of the realm of vision and into a realm of tactile presence, represents a "transitional," "twilight" period in history, an emergent time when nature must inherit new qualifiers to replace those adjectives of divinity, glory, and harmony so often and easily awarded her in the past. "Haggard Egdon appealed" to a "recently learnt emotion," Hardy says. To an age in which "spots like Iceland," "a gaunt waste in Thule," and the "sand dunes of Scheveningen" are retreats increasingly preferable to "the Alps," the "Vale of Tempe," and the "vineyards and myrtle gardens of South Europe," Egdon, in its "antique brown dress," its "swarthy monotony," is "at present a place perfectly accordant with man's nature." Both, Hardy says, are "slighted and enduring" (1:6–10).

Clym Yeobright, like Eustacia Vye, is described as being physically continuous with the "haggard" landscape. He, like his environment, possesses "the typical countenance of the future," a face the depiction of which constitutes "a new artistic departure," a demeanor which mirrors "the view of life as a thing to be put up with" (2:73). In spite of his countenance, however, Clym has spent much of his recent life in pursuits as blind, impractical, and quixotic as Eustacia's quest for a "perfect" lover (in his own guise). Upon returning to his native society from the far-off "Paris" of Eustacia's "Romantic" dreams, he has sought to revolutionize it in accordance with the dictates of his own naïve social dreams. With "a conviction that the want of most men was . . . wisdom rather than affluence" (2:84), he is one of those dreaming men who try in vain to "make a globe to suit them" (2:160).

But of all those characters who go down the primrose path wearing rose-colored glasses, it is Farmer Boldwood, and not Clym Yeobright, who is most totally blinded by his own romantic vision. Immediately after receiving the deceptive valentine which he chooses to believe is "prophetic" (1:214), he begins to see a resourceful and resilient farmwoman named Bathsheba as a "perfect one of an imperfect many," a "misty shape," a "vision" (1:195, 166). His "equilibrium" of "enormous antagonistic forces—positives and negatives in fine adjustment"—is so "disturbed" that he enters into that "extremity" of imaginative life (1:201) which Hardy defines through a vague allusion to Shelley (Boldwood is "lighted . . . up" by love "as the moon lights up a great tower") and a wry reference to Keats's superficially Miltonic definition of the imagination: "Adam had awakened from his deep sleep, and behold! there was Eve" (1:203–4, 194). All "sensation," "Devotion," and "tenderness" owing to this "apotheosis" that "took place" only "in his fancy," Boldwood becomes "surcharged with the compound, which was genuine lover's love," says Hardy (1:208, 204). Ever more energized by the electro-chemical (read romantic) passion for a "mystery" of his own making, and unable to translate his lunar epipsyche, Adam's dream, into a new Eve in a Paradise of fact, Boldwood gradually becomes the victim of his unchecked hopes. Once his "perfect one" has shown her preference for a dissolute charmer, Boldwood, like Swinburne's Sappho, "trod . . . the threshold of 'the injured lover's hell'" (1:197).

Sergeant Troy, who competes successfully with Boldwood for Bathsheba's attentions, is, to use Arnold's terms, a Byronic egotist.

He is a young man "brilliant in speech" but "commonplace in action" (1:280). Hardy several times refers to him as a "Romantic" (he even entitles a chapter "Troy's Romanticism," in which he speaks of "the futility of these romantic doings" [2:189]). Troy is a frenetic, impulsive, selfish, deracinated spirit who exists, as much as any man can, outside the constraints of time, living as if there were neither a yesterday nor a tomorrow. Variously described as a "black hound" (2:59), a "flatterer" (1:293), a "juggler of Satan" (2:59), Troy is what Boldwood says he is: a deceiver for whom his deluded romantic victims would "sell soul and body" (2:55). Unlike "Oak, whose defects were patent to the blindest" and whose deeper "virtues" were as bright "metals in a mine" to anyone who could see, Troy possesses Satanic "deformities" that lie too "deep down . . . whilst his embellishments" afford a "revelation" which "blinds" the beholder to true "vision." Bathsheba, consequently, no sooner looks at the "brass and scarlet" of this dazzling creature than he undergoes, in her imagination, a "fairy transformation" from a "soldier" to a "revelation" (1:271, 315–16). In short, Hardy playfully suggests, "she was enclosed in a firmament of light" (1:309).

As Bathsheba's visionary incarceration indicates, the rugged and resilient post-romantic protagonist is perfectly free to fall into romantic error; indeed, the didactic structure of Hardy's early fiction is one which illustrates the danger of lapses of this sort. Bathsheba had first fallen into the habits of romantic deception, sending her overstated valentine to Boldwood simply because "It is romantic to think" about a "man" with "more sense than to waste his time upon me" (1:154–55). As soon as she realizes that Boldwood is "a species of Daniel in her kingdom who persist[s] in kneeling eastward" when she lives to his west (1:161), she begins "fluttering under the onset of a crowd of romantic possibilities" (1:121). Then, after she has won the "worship" of one whose unbelief was better left unhealed, she becomes, herself, the victim of a delusion. Once she sees a "soldier" as a "revelation," once a "commonplace" sergeant has undergone a "fairy transformation" in her fancy, she becomes, like Elfride before her, "Disabled by her moods" (1:247) and begins to blunder through life with a "wild and perturbed" demeanor (1:326). "Oh, I love him to very distraction and misery and agony," she declares to her serving woman, "It is wearing me away!" (1:329).

As Bathsheba stands in relation to Boldwood and Troy, so

Elfride Swancourt stood in relation to her two suitors. Her first, Stephen Smith, might appear, on first impression, to be an unpretentious sort of man perfectly attuned to a world of limited possibilities. A "practical professional man" (1:8), Stephen seems a "quiet," "no nonsense fellow" who could make anyone "feel quite at home" (1:41, 77). Time, however, together with a few authorial allusions to romantic proclivities (Stephen longs to escape "'the weariness, the fever and the fret'" of London life) gradually proves him to be more nearly an unworldly romantic (1:23). While Elfride sings Shelley's "When the lamp is shattered," her "frizzled hair" comes between Stephen and the candlelight. The young man clearly anticipates Farmer Boldwood, for he manages to see, in a "nebulous haze," a "crown like an aureola," a "special medium of manifestation," "a visitation." Once Elfride's reality has been sanctified as in a "dream" through the "effort" of "her true love's fancy" (1:38–39), Stephen's countenance, conversations, and correspondence soon speak "concerning nothing but oneness with her" (2:31). With Stephen, Elfride falls into the romantic habit of "ruling" a "heart with absolute despotism." She piques her entranced worshipper with questions such as "Do I seem like *La Belle Dame sans merci*?" and by quoting Keats's poetry to him (1:122–24).

Elfride's second suitor, Henry Knight, is hardly more "practical" or less immune to "nonsense" than Stephen. Like his young friend, he insists upon loving Elfride "philosophically," as an "idea or ideal." When he first met Elfride, "He had simply thought her weak." Not "till they were parted, and she had become sublimated in his memory, could he be said to have even attentively regarded her." Then, and only then, did he fall "in love with her soul," or, at least, with "disembodi[ed]" "images of her which his mind did not act upon till the cause of them was no longer before him" (2:124–26). In her relationship with Knight, Elfride becomes, as Bathsheba becomes with Troy, the romantic victim. Once Knight relates his "invincible objection to be any but the first comer" to a lover's affections (2:127), Elfride lapses into an existence in which she expends all her energies maintaining an identity approximately that of the ethereal "Phantom of Delight" in Knight's imagination. The growing "allegiance she bore him absorbed her whole soul and existence" (3:65). Both pained and "proud" to be "bond-servant" to a lover practiced in "Poetic study" and "poetic pains," Elfride "presume[s] upon . . . devotion" (3:86–88), "read[s] Words-worth," and thus becomes, almost by definition, "one of those who sigh for the unattainable" (2:157–58).

It is, however, in *Far from the Madding Crowd* and through Gabriel Oak's fall into self-consciousness and ineffectuality that Hardy most clearly demonstrates the danger of suddenly back-sliding into that "influence of youth" which tempts the dilution of reason in exalted mood or feelings. Oak's affection for the rugged, efficient, and independent mistress of Weatherbury Farm, Bath-sheba Everdene, depends, after all, upon the "estimate" (or mis-estimate) of a man whose "soul," for some reason, increasingly "required a divinity." "Having for some time known the want of a satisfactory form to fill an increasing void within him, his position moreover affording the widest scope for his fancy," Oak begins to "colour and mould according to the wants within," to "idealize" his "object," and to be longing for "the secret fusion of himself in Bathsheba to be burning with a finer flame" (1:23, 54). This Shelleyan yearning to become, through love, "two meteors of expanding flame" which "touch, mingle, are transfigured" into "the same" ("Epipsychidion," ll. 576–77) soon makes "appreciable in-roads upon the emotional constitution" of the formerly stoical, self-reliant man, for to "require" a "divinity," to "want" and even to expect a perfect "fusion" of the self and the godly, is to presume too much, is to seek heights of experience which, unfound, inevitably make the inevitable seem inadequate (1:38).

Agnostic man must, as Milton's Mammon suggested, learn to see his place not as hell but as an acceptable home. The romantic temptation is to look too high, to suppress or deny the only sensibility attuned to reality. Oak, having commenced his quest for a divinity, makes the pathetic resolve "never" to "let Bathsheba see him playing [his] flute" (1:110). The temptation to underplay the post-romantic song of experience, moreover, is a temptation which Hardy admits that he occasionally finds as alluring as does Oak. Gabriel's eyes are following not a real woman but "a nebula" when he secretly watches his beloved traverse the Norcombe landscape. Hardy's vision once comes treacherously close to his protagonist's distorted fancy; his narrative focuses the reader's eyes on "the bed-room window" of Bathsheba's farmhouse and then suddenly slips just enough out of focus to suggest that the heroine's "dimly seen" "head and shoulders" were actually "robed in mystic white" (1:23, 114).

Most of the time, however, the narrator is well above reproach, telling us exactly when and exactly where his characters make their romantic mistakes. When Oak begins to "idealize" his "object" to the extent that he yearns for possession not of attainable woman but, rather, an unattainable bliss, Hardy epigrammatically warns us that Oak sees Bathsheba in much the same way "as Milton's Satan first saw Paradise" (1:21). Whenever Stephen envisions Elfride as some kind of divine "visitation" or "manifestation," Hardy steps in with his own words of wisdom or the voice of a yet unfallen Elfride and a formidably Swinburnian landscape to put Stephen's view of things in perspective. "Our most intimate *alter ego*," the narrator reminds us in the sobering language of "The Temporary the All," "is really somebody we got to know by mere physical juxtaposition" (1:297). Standing on a "huge blue black rock" encircled by "white screaming gulls" and flanked by "the toothed and zigzag line of storm-torn heights," Elfride offers a somewhat similar warning. "Stephen," she says, "I am content to build happiness on any accidental basis that may lie near at hand; you are for making a world to suit your happiness" (1:126–27, 131–32).

Sometimes Hardy deprecates the romantic penchant for deception or self-delusion with a sardonic witticism that borders on caustic satire. After Eustacia abandons Wildeve for Clym—"because she had . . . determined to love him," this "entrancing" lover supplied by her "imagination"—Hardy cynically muses that "the perfervid woman" was "in love with a vision," and if "The fantastic nature of her passion . . . lowered her as an intellect [it] raised her as a soul" (1:259, 264, 2:16). If we are tempted to feel sorry for the all-too-available Wildeve, abandoned by a woman in pursuit of the romantic and remote, Hardy effectively prevents us from doing so by lightly satirizing a man whose "nature," no less than his lover's, is "To be yearning for the difficult, to be weary of that offered; to care for the remote, to dislike the near." Although his "fevered feelings had not been elaborated to real poetical compass," he was a perfect "man of sentiment," he "might have been called the Rousseau of Egdon" (2:182). As for Clym, that rival who is not without "poetical" and "Rousseauist" tendencies of his own, Hardy says, with a wry smile, that "Yeobright preaching to the Egdon ermites that they might rise to a serene comprehensiveness without going through the process of enriching themselves was not unlike arguing to the ancient Chaldeans that in ascending from earth to the pure empyrean it was not necessary to pass first into the intervening heaven of ether" (2:86).

In addition to using authorial commentary, characters' conversations, and landscapes, Hardy sets up symbolic *tableaux*, develops metaphorical systems, and makes pointed allusions in order to criticize a sensibility he would characterize as romantic. He employs a dramatic scene in *Far from the Madding Crowd*, for instance, to show that the only romantic electricity which really flows between Bathsheba and her soldier is a one-way discharge of destructive energies. Bathsheba sees "the point" of Troy's sword "glisten towards her bosom and seemingly enter it." "All was quick as electricity" (1:311, 308). Even if such obvious *tableaux* weren't present, we would be conscious that this attraction is as destructive to Bathsheba as her earlier romantic infatuation was to Boldwood. As he does to Elfride, Boldwood, and the various trees felled by the romantic overreachings of "The Ivy Wife," Hardy attaches metaphors of bondage to this victim of "thought" weakened by "feeling." Bathsheba, he says, "was conquered. . . . She chafed to and fro in rebelliousness, like a caged leopard. . . . She hated herself" (2:124–25). We know that Boldwood is similarly entrapped by a romantic illusion when Hardy refers us to a literary predecessor (subsequent editions say "Keats"), cautioning us that "What the poet calls a too happy happiness" leads to the "abstraction by love of all dignity from a man" (1:265). "The rarest offerings of the purest loves," Hardy says, "are but a self-indulgence" (1:217). Arnold, of course, had spoken of Keats's "too happy happiness," his love for Fanny Brawne, as "relaxed self-abandonment," an "indulgence" that soon led to "the abandonment of all . . . dignity."[11]

About the best evidence, in Hardy's early novels as in his mature poetry, that a person has abandoned dignity and self-control is his tendency to blame malicious gods once it becomes clear that mere reality cannot measure up to his "perfervid," "self-indulgent" expectations. Once Bathsheba's fancy for a "flatterer" leads to "misery and agony," she declares to her serving woman, "I shall never forgive my Maker for making me a woman" (1:329–31). The narrator, however, is not so sure the fault is God's, reminding the reader in epigram after epigram of the predictability of Bathsheba's pain. She "loved Troy," after all, "in the way that only self-reliant women love when they throw away their self-reliance" (1:314).

"Her love," he goes on to tell us, was "as a child's," that is, she made "no attempt to control feeling" (1:315). For a short while after their marriage, Eustacia and Clym live "in a sort of luminous mist, which hid from them surroundings of any inharmonious colour" (2:234). However, Eustacia's unquenchable desire "to be one" in an "absolute solitude" of "reciprocal thoughts" (the kind of "thirst" which, Hardy often reminds us, "a little more self-control" would have "killed off" [2:234, 1:264]) inevitably leads her to bitter disappointment in marriage and, beyond that, to that agonized agnosticism that fears "the satire of Heaven" controls her every move (2:275), the paranoid belief that a malign "Destiny" stands opposed to her thwarted romantic will (1:153). The irony is, of course, that this "rebellious" woman with "abstract . . . desires" and "visions" of "palaces" and "towers" (1:149–53), who now sees "demons in the air, and malice in every bush and bough," is in fact becoming the romantic demon destructive in her overreaching (3:221). However "congenial to philosophy" those individuals may be who have "not . . . acquired a homely zest for doing what [they] can," Hardy warns, they are also "dangerous to the commonwealth" (1:157–58).

Prefiguring Angel Clare, Henry Knight quickly and cruelly abandons his lover once his superficial idealism confronts the reality of her simple humanity. Then, with the help of an ironic narrator happy to plunder romantic poems in order to suggest wryly the destructive absurdity of romantic expectation, he projects his self-perpetuated disappointments upon nature. "There had passed away a glory" from the earth, Knight thinks, "and the dream was not as it had been of yore" (3:122). His feeling that the "very land and sky . . . suffer" his own personal loss with him is, of course, only the logical extension of a romantic faith in correspondences between self and world which he has held all along (3:155). Earlier, while hanging precariously from a crumbling cliff above a storm-tossed ocean, he felt "himself in the presence of a *personalized* loneliness" (2:179).

And yet each time, in the novel, Knight projects imaginative visions of a meaningful nature upon its blank and chaotic forms, Hardy quickly surrounds the "fanciful" speculations of this "writer" with "poetical tendencies" that cause him to "only . . . half know" the "thing" he "writes about" (we may safely assume that Knight "half creates and half perceives") with deflating, post-romantic knowledge (1:295–96). " 'This is a summer afternoon,' he said, 'and there can never have been such a heavy and cold rain on a summer day. . . . ' He was again mistaken. The rain was quite ordinary in quantity; the air in temperature." Knight "turned to contemplate the Dark Valley and the unknown future beyond. Into the shadowy depths of these speculations we will not follow him" (2:189, 192). In the words of "God's Funeral," Hardy's early novels "frame" their idealists (in this case the idealist is a writer thinking thoughts not unlike those which Hardy entertained in his Swinburnian youth) in the act of "framing" supernatural presences that simply do not exist. By so doing, they move readers, and eventually some characters, out of the confines of belief and suspicion, into an anxious life outside the shadow world of dream, and eventually beyond the dialectic of faith and paranoia into revisionary understanding.

In the final chapters of *Far from the Madding Crowd*, Bathsheba emerges from an unrealizable passion, that is, from that "discord between mood and matter" (2:66) that spawned Swinburne's early poetry and Boldwood's suicidal insanity, into a solid affection for a now sadder but wiser Gabriel Oak. The reader, like Hardy and his heroine, embraces not only that scaled-down definition of the heroic self for which Oak, once again, stands as symbol but also a revisionary definition of love. On Christmas day just one year and a day after the fateful party, the return of Sergeant Troy, and Boldwood's consequent lapse into homicidal madness, Hardy links the lovers' arms and declares that "Theirs was that substantial affection which arises . . . when two who are thrown together begin first by knowing the rougher sides of each other's character." Theirs was a "romance growing up in the interstices of a mass of hard prosaic reality," he says, a "good-fellowship" or *"camaraderie"* developing "through similarity of pursuits," a "love . . . beside which the passion usually called by the name is evanescent as steam" (2:332).

If *Far from the Madding Crowd* dramatizes the emergence from a crazy old myth about passionate heroes and heroines in romantic love—a love that Swinburne had said "goes out like steam"[12] and that Hardy called "the passion evanescent as steam"—*The Return of the Native* describes a "transitional . . . roll" into another new, if limited, vision of things. Clym, for he is the most important character to survive the events of the novel, may be seen as the *exemplum* of that gradual change in sensibility the fiction sees as necessary for survival. As Clym consumes himself in fantasies of the mind and of the printed page, Hardy sees to it that his self-determining folly meets an appropriate "Circumstance": his re-forming fires burn up his eyes, making impossible both his physical and his social "vision." It is an aesthetic, not a deific fate, that returns Clym—visionless—to the earthy sights, sounds, smells, and textures of a proto-Lawrentian world brimming with life in all its imperfect glory, an Egdon where "Tribes of emerald-green grass-hoppers leaped over his feet, falling awkwardly . . . as chance might rule," where "snakes glided in their most brilliant blue and yellow guise, it being the season immediately following the shed-ding of their old skins," where "young rabbits came out . . . to sun themselves," the "hot beams . . . firing" their ears "to a blood-red transparency" (2:262–63).

Clym, like Gabriel Oak, eases his romantic disappointments by turning back to a life of unself-conscious toil upon the brown face of an earth seething with life. When the still-raging Eustacia decries his new-found stoicism, Clym can retort with a terse, almost epigrammatic admonition that, at this late stage of the narrative, is tonally indistinguishable from Hardy's typically stoical, post-romantic voice. "Now, don't you suppose, my inexperienced girl," he says, "that I cannot rebel, in high Promethean fashion, against the gods and fate as well as you. I have felt more steam and smoke of that sort than you have ever heard of. But the more I see of life the more do I perceive that there is nothing particularly great in its greatest walks, and therefore nothing particularly small in mine of furze-cutting" (2:269).

With the narrator's point of view, Clym Yeobright has been carefully brought into focus. Like Oak, he has passed through a period of yoked thought and feeling and into an era of persever-ance, work, and responsibility. Unlike Oak, however, Clym is less than an attractive figure. Hardy may have written to Gerard Manly Hopkins to tell him that Clym was the novel's most "important" character; he may even have believed that Clym was the "nicest" of his "heroes";[13] but there is an undercurrent in the last book of the novel which would seem to murmur that Hardy prefers to see Eustacia die rather than allow her to become another bland and self-sacrificing Clym or, worse, that meek, mild, meddlesome extension of humble and resourceful Gabriel Oak, namely, Diggory Venn. Thus *The Return of the Native* would seem to veer away from the ordered world of a novel like *Far from the Madding Crowd*. Rather than being a declaration of the muted glory of a new day, it is a work that almost lapses into nihilism. The characters who survive circumstance seem hardly worth keeping alive. The one incurably romantic character who refuses to learn that lesson implicit in the structure of the plot and the moral intonation of the narrator is much, much more than a *persona* to be perforated by narrative revelations.

The Return of the Native is not the first Hardy novel to end with a death. It is, however, Hardy's first tragedy.

If *Far from the Madding Crowd* can be said to be the first of Hardy's novels to demonstrate (and, to some degree, to predict) the dangers of the romantic relapse, then *The Mayor of Casterbridge* (1886) can be said to hasten the blazing fall backwards which Hardy precipitates with the creation of Eustacia Vye in *The Return of the Native*. Michael Henchard, the tragical and unswervingly romantic hero of this, the author's next great novel, bears far more resemblance to Hardy's pouting, petulant Queen of the Night than to that tempted but for the most part temperate paragon of duty and humility, Gabriel Oak.

In spite of the fact that he has sworn off drinking and taken the public oath of office, Henchard's character has never been rid of that self-centeredness and irresponsibility which motivated the one heinous action in his past. Like the Burns of Carlyle's not entirely uncritical appreciation, he is primarily a "self-seeker and self-worshipper"; like the Blake of Swinburne's creation, his are "the loud and angry habits" of "seeing everywhere the image of his own mood."[14] This "fitful" and "oppressive" man, once so convinced that his wife was his, body and soul, that he sold her at a country fair, is still intent upon complete possession of his friends, children, lovers. He can tolerate neither Donald Farfrae's independence of mind ("headstrong," he fires him in a "jealous temper" when the younger man makes allowance for meteorological chance with a treetop canvas) nor Elizabeth-Jane's genetic independence (he abandons her upon learning that he is not her biological parent).[15] The occasional object of Henchard's romantic desire, in turn, seems more an image, fancy, or idea entirely of his own making than a flesh-and-blood woman named Lucetta Le Sueur. When Lucetta is available to Henchard, his desire is "chilled"; when she is "qualified" with "inaccessibility," then she once again becomes, like the "disembodied . . . Elfride" of Henry Knight's "poetic imagination," the *sine qua non* of his own romantic will (2:19).

Boredom with reality and simultaneous longing for the inaccessible forms of the romantic imagination, of course, soon make Henchard so hypersensitive that, like Knight, Eustacia, the poet of "Hap," and the Swinburne of 1865–66, he is obsessed with the fear that his own disappointments may be bringing calculated joy to some malign presence. And yet, each time he wonders "if it can be that somebody has been . . . stirring an unholy brew to confound" him (2:49), whether "the scheme of some sinister intelligence is bent on punishing" him (1:240), the mature voice of Hardy's narrative is quick to add that the fantasies arising out of such "hours of superstition" (2:50) are not to be lent too much credibility. "Character is Fate, said Novalis, and Farfrae's character was just the reverse of Henchard's, who might not inaptly be described as Faust has been described—as a vehement gloomy being, who had quitted the ways of vulgar men without light to guide him on a better way" (1:218).

In Hardy's dialectical world of human personalities, Donald Farfrae stands in relation to "Faustian" Henchard just as Gabriel Oak does to "Romantic" Francis Troy, just as Diggory Venn does to "Rousseauist" Wildeve, just as Giles Winterborne will stand to the "Transcendentalist," Dr. Fitzpiers, in *The Woodlanders*. Hailed by the narrator as a "distinct" "new arrival" (1:68), even as a "poet of a new school" (1:98), Farfrae is a master at using his practical intelligence to make all he can out of those temporary opportunities afforded by circumstance. His restoration of the mouldy grain harvest recalls Oak's revival of Bathsheba's bloated and dying sheep; his instinctive feel for nature's changing moods allows him to prepare for the same rainstorm that ruins Henchard's expensive fair. (In this case, the contrast between Oak on one hand and Troy and Boldwood on the other during the night of the great rain must have been on Hardy's mind.) When his good sense produces circumstances even more unexpected than the storm, namely, Henchard's anger and his own consequent unemployment, Farfrae again adapts without demur, "quietly assent[ing]" to the stunning news. "[W]hen people deplored the fact, and asked why it was, he simply replied that Mr. Henchard no longer required his help" (1:206).

Like Elfride, who "could slough off sadness . . . as easily as a lizard renews a diseased limb," Farfrae possesses a certain cold-bloodedness which allows him to endure while more passionate men and women perish. His moods—"romantic" and "commercial" —are usually "intertwisted" like "colours in a variegated cord." As Lucetta explains it, Donald's having "both temperatures going on in [him] at the same time," "warm" and "cold," allows him to succeed while Henchard dreams, fails, and cries out in defiance (1:303–4). There may be something bothersome about a character unconsumed by inner fires, but it is not easy to fault Farfrae's morality. After learning that Henchard has lost everything in a Faustian scheme to buy atmospheric secrets and, through the knowledge of Nature's mysterious power, ruin Farfrae's independent grain business, the younger man offers to buy his former employer a profitable seed shop. After Henchard has refused the offer, publicly cursed him, even tried to kill him, Farfrae still retains him as a hired man.

The structure of *The Mayor of Casterbridge* points to the union of Farfrae and Elizabeth-Jane Henchard as surely as *Far from the Madding Crowd* predicted the final return of Bathsheba to Oak. There was a "reasonableness" about "almost everything that Elizabeth-Jane did," the narrator has told us. Never did she triumph but that "triumph was tempered by circumspection; she had" the respect of a "field-mouse" for "the coulter of destiny" (1:163–64). She adapts calmly and quietly to the (incorrect) information that Henchard, not Newson, is her father, and after learning that Donald Farfrae's first romantic interests lie with Lucetta La Sueur and not herself, she "live[s] on, . . . quenching with patient fortitude her incipient interest," bearing up to "the frosty ache" as "she had borne up under worse things" (1:253, 2:18). When Farfrae finally turns his attentions to this perfectly kindred spirit, their consequent union solidifies that "delicate poise between love and friendship" which has always characterized their relations, the only bond "unalloyed with pain." The "scope" of Elizabeth-Jane's "married life" is defined by her mission of "discovering to the narrow-lived ones around her the secret (as she had . . . learnt it) of making limited opportunities endurable." She teaches, Hardy says, "the cunning enlargement" of "those minute forms of satisfaction that offer themselves to everybody" (2:19, 311).

Elizabeth-Jane is a character who can, when necessary, live with the fact that "what she had desired had not been granted her, and

. . . what had been granted her she had not desired" (2:27). That makes her more like Swinburne's Chthonia than King Erechtheus, who had bitterly complained of the Gods that "what they will is more than our desire / And their desire is more than what we will" (4:343). But, strangely enough, it does not make her a heroine, any more than her habit of always "making limited opportunities endurable" gives her the dimensions of a Gabriel Oak. Within the contexts of this later novel, to find recompense for life's pains in "minute forms of satisfaction" seems to speak more of the banality of virtue than true stoicism. The "cool . . . temperature" which characterizes Elizabeth-Jane, her husband, and their chameleon abilities to accept and adapt to everything makes them seem, if not despicable, at least unadmirable, if not immoral, at least characters whose morality is unworthy of attention. Farfrae's superficial love of his homeland and his lack of purpose or plan for his life, the very qualities which allow him to stay in, adapt to, and even control Casterbridge, indicate a certain blankness of will or imagination. Henchard, on the other hand, boasts a passionate willfulness, an imperfect but complex, emotion-charged morality that perfectly simple, perfectly practical characters can never attain. He knows the tragedy of Weydon-Priors was "of his own making" and that "he ought to bear" its responsibility (1:29). The day after he fired Farfrae "his heart sank within him at what he had said and done" (1:206). Well after he has learned of Lucetta's love for Farfrae, he risks his life to save her from danger (2:80), and although he possesses the power to destroy their relationship, he can never quite bring himself to tell the younger man of Lucetta's past. That Hardy's tragic hero can be violent is undeniable, but when Farfrae, beaten in hayloft combat, dares Henchard to take his life, the irascible former mayor declares, "God is my witness that no man ever loved another as I did thee." Then "he withdrew to the back part of the loft, and flung himself into a corner upon some sacks, in the abandonment of remorse" (2:207–8).

There are points at which the novel suggests, without quite saying, that no matter how well Henchard had controlled his destructive impulses, his fate would have been the same. At the beginning, the narrator describes the route between Weydon-Priors and Casterbridge as a "track" (1:35). Anticipating the symbolic use of physical places (Stonehenge, the Brown House) to foreshadow inescapable fates in *Tess* and in *Jude*, Hardy uses images like tracks or, better, the Roman amphitheater, to suggest the tragic pattern of historical process, the inevitability of loss, suffering, even annihilation. The arena, where history has spanned "sanguinary . . . games," hangings, strangulations, executions by fire, and fights to the death, seems to symbolize that fate which is beyond any one individual's control. In an essay on the Dorsetshire (read Casterbridge) amphitheater, Hardy quotes Swinburne's "Faustine" to communicate the aura of inevitability which hangs over that place "Where death must win."[16] Can we, then, agree with Michael Millgate's somewhat bold assertion that, indeed, "Character *is* Fate" in *The Mayor of Casterbridge*[17] and, therefore, any event in the plot which befalls Henchard, such as the return of the haggish furmity woman, is Hardy's way of symbolizing the fact that Henchard's character has not really changed since the day upon which he bartered his wife in the furmity woman's presence? But can it really be true that Henchard, in his ascent from laborer to mayor, has learned nothing? Or don't we also have to see in the nightmarish returns of the furmity woman and sailor Newson a dark, almost surrealistic drama of the absurd,[18] a dramatic rendition of a cosmos which may even contain a hint of that supernatural malignity which Henchard, like Eustacia, so often felt? Can we accept *The Mayor of Casterbridge* as a didactic novel that, like *Far from the Madding Crowd*, describes a world in which men survive in accordance with their ability to lead practical, useful lives? Can such an interpretation be reconciled with the fact that the novel is not only the demonstration of Farfrae's well-deserved successes but also the moving story of Michael Henchard's tragedy? Who *really* is *The Mayor* referred to by the title of this uneasy work? Can we be sure that Hardy was sure it is Henchard? (The question is not so simple: Hardy always maintained that Clym, not Eustacia, was the heroic center of *The Return of the Native*.) How can a character be both a tragic hero and, at the same time, a straw man whose failures help to explain a better man's successes? How can a post-Christian work of art both rhetorically declare that a man's character determines his fate and, through its images and its plot structure, suggest that there is a relentlessness about the track of time which almost identifies the presence of a malign Providence? As J. I. M. Stewart suggests, "All this generating of great misfortunes out of petty chances ingeniously brought to bear *suggests* . . . that Henchard at his most cast down (like Jude Fawley and Sue Bridehead after him) is right, and that we inhabit a kind of goblin universe."[19]

The plot structure (through its elevation of Farfrae's fortunes and its annihilation of Henchard) and the authorial philosophy ("Character is Fate") of *The Mayor of Casterbridge* speak, each in its own way, of such tried and true themes as self-determination, self-control, and responsibility. The grotesque vicissitudes of chance, however, together with the largely sympathetic portrait of a large-souled, if fiery-spirited, romantic dreamer named Michael Henchard suggest that at least half of Thomas Hardy celebrates his Faustian's passionate energy in the face of a chance too malign to be accidental, a fate too necessitarian to bow to any fine adjustments of character. The very same dialectic of rhetoric and character, didacticism and defiance, complicates *The Woodlanders* (1887), the first of Hardy's novels to shatter the pattern of the early fiction, the first undeniable anticipant of Hardy's new fiction of the 1890's.

The narrator makes it clear from the beginning that Grace Melbury is as right for hard-working Giles Winterborne as the speaker of "The Temporary the All" was for his mundane lover, as Diggory was for Thomasin, Bathsheba for Oak, Elfride for Stephen. Grace's father, however, convinces his daughter (recently returned from a fancy boarding school) that common folk like Giles shouldn't be "dragging down to that old level" a girl whose father has "taken so much trouble to lift up."[20] He succeeds in inducing in his dream-prone daughter a Eustacia-like passion for Dr. Fitzpiers, a resident recluse who is, on one hand, a "Transcendentalist," a "Faustian" who is said to be "in league with the devil" (1:11), and, on the other, wealthy enough to offer Grace what Mr. Melbury likes to refer to as "a blithe romantical life."[21]

Fitzpiers, besides being "romantical," "Faustian," and a "Transcendentalist," is "primarily . . . an idealist" who "believed that behind the imperfect lay the perfect, that rare things were to be discovered amid a bulk of commonplace" (2:36–37). For one who is convinced, like so many of Hardy's "idealists," that "There's only Me and Not Me in the whole world" (1:119), for one who, like the Byron of Arnold's "Preface," is so unable to be "impersonal and disinterested" that while "straining after the unlimited" he "hardly" sees "any subject but . . . himself,"[22] Fitzpiers falls in love with Grace (or with his image of Grace as seen in a mirror) in a fairly predictable way. He allows his "Shelleyan" imagination to "think

. . . of an ideal mistress," until "at length the rustle of a woman's dress, the sound of her voice . . . enkindle his soul with a flame that blinds his eyes" (2:13–14). His romantic vision, Hardy would seem to suggest, is mirror love and thus no less blind to what Pater would call "the here and now" and Carlyle "this solid earth" than was Clym Yeobright's social vision.[23] Fitzpiers, like Ruskin's Shelley, has confused "blue eyes" with "the heavens" and "the heavens" with his "own poor little Psychidion."[24]

When not mixing "chemical experiments . . . and metaphysical conceptions," Fitzpiers spends his time explaining to even-tempered Giles Winterborne that his love for Grace keeps him "charged with emotive fluid like a Leyden-jar with electric, for want of some conductor at hand to disperse it." (Melville's Ahab, though not quite a romantic lover, "would fain have shocked into" another human being "the same fiery emotion accumulated within the Leyden jar of his own magnetic life" [*Moby Dick*, ch. 36].) "Human love is a subjective thing," the doctor tells Giles. It is "the essence of man," a fancy, an image, or an "idea which we project against any suitable object in the line of our vision. . . . So that if any other young lady had appeared instead of the one who did appear, I should have felt the same interest in her and have quoted precisely the same lines from Shelley about her, as about this one I saw" (1:296). (Fitzpiers had quoted *Laon and Cythna* [2:23]; what he *says* about love paraphrases one of Shelley's letters to Thomas Hogg, a letter first made public in 1858 in Hogg's *Life of Shelley*.)[25]

Fitzpiers tells Grace that in her "Nature has . . . recovered her lost union with the Idea," that the "transcendental philosopher" is proven right by her very being, since the beholder is "scarcely able to distinguish between reality and fancy" (2:30–31). But once he marries her and realizes that "chance" has actually allowed his "fancy" to become a real "circumstance" of his life, his "Rapture," in the words of *A Pair of Blue Eyes*, is very quickly "cooled by contact with its cause" (1:283). Overcome by *ennui*, he discards his young wife as yet another face of a tedious reality which, in the words of "The Temporary the All," is "unformed to be all eclipsing," and seeks the perfect antidote to his romantic agony, an adulterous relationship with a charming Frenchwoman whose love, for years, has seemingly been denied by Fate. Grace, like Bathsheba and Eustacia before her, finds boredom and despair where once she had envisioned romance and adventure; Mr. Melbury, instead of seeing his family elevated to new heights of social identity, consoles a heartbroken daughter; Fitzpiers and Felice, finally, are prevented from realizing their dream of union by a crazed South Carolinian who, like Boldwood, would commit murder before allowing his ideal to fall into the hands of a usurper.

In dialectical opposition to these fated overreachers, the novel gives us a character who in summer supervises an orchard and in fall, winter, and spring works diligently for the Melbury family's lumber company. After losing Grace, Giles makes limited opportunities endurable by welcoming her into his life as a friend. Upon losing his modest fortune, he moves into a tiny shack in the woods and takes up a solitary life reminiscent of Clym Yeobright's career as a furze-cutter as well as the gypsy-like existence of the reddleman, Diggory Venn. Finally, when Grace comes in search of Giles one stormy night, despondent over her interminable marriage to Fitzpiers, he relinquishes his cabin, sleeps out in the cold, driving rain, and consequently gives up his life to protect the health (and social reputation) of his beloved.

This is a surprising change in Hardy's fiction, in which the unworldly romantic dreamer has not usually survived while the humble, hard-working character who stands in dialectical opposition succumbs to the inevitable. The mechanics of time had not been kind to Michael Henchard, but they had posed little problem for his more practical counterpart, Donald Farfrae. They had dealt fierce blows to Boldwood, Troy, and Eustacia, but they had never played tyrant to Oak or Venn. It would seem, from the plot structure of *The Woodlanders*, that Hardy's world is losing its sense of priorities. The structure of "The Temporary the All," which had defined man's limited and proper relationship to dumb, indifferent, cosmic forces, now seems to be giving way to a new structure, one that threatens to annihilate those individuals who have accepted the limited terms of that relationship. Suddenly that character who embodies the equation of actual and ideal, mundane and divine (Winterborne is pictured, alternately, as a "fruit god" and a "wood god"), that character who, perhaps as much as any other Hardy character, is autobiographically conceived (Emma Gifford's father spoke of that "low-born churl who had presumed to marry into my family"),[26] dies a pathetic death. And what about his romantic counterpart, that character who, most of the time, is treated ironically, even sarcastically, by the narrator? Were it not for the wisdom of editors, he might well have been advertised as *Fitzpiers at Hintock*, the novel's titular hero.[27] Hardy's apparent confusion over his protagonist, together with his implicit self destruction, attests not only to a profound tension in the world of the novel but, more importantly, in the changing sensibility of its creator.

The imp of the perverse which cuts down Winterborne continues its reign of misrule by undermining the author's long-standing definition of nature as an unconscious, amoral cycle. To be sure, *The Woodlanders* has wry fun with the dilemma of Marty South's father, an old man who, certain that his own being is in some mysterious way connected with the forces of nature, promptly dies when a tree outside his window is cut down. The narrative even goes so far as to point out that there is a direct link between John South's pathetic belief and the unexpected misfortune of Giles, since it is upon South's death that Giles's property reverts to Felice Charmond. And yet, in the descriptive passages of the novel, Hardy demonstrates that, like Henchard and John South, he too entertains the discomforting suspicion that nature is more meaning-ful than blank, more antipathetic than apathetic, or, in the terminology of Swinburne's early poems, more poisonous than indifferent. In the first three paragraphs, we learn that "Nature," without "human companionship," is the "incubus of the forlorn" in a man's heart (1:3). In spring, Hardy says, it is hard to avoid hearing the saps "beginning to heave," unitedly, "with the force of hydraulic lifts inside" (3:3). Anticipating the second chapter of *Tess*, Hardy mentions that the boughs of the trees in the summer woodlands "cast green shades, which hurt the complexion of the girls who walked there."[28] Later, on old and dying trees, "huge lobes of fungi grew like lungs." The "leaf" of the autumn wood-land was "deformed, the curve was crippled, the taper was inter-rupted; the lichen ate the vigor of the stalk, and the ivy slowly strangled to death the promising sapling" (1:127–28). Still later in the year, nature manifests itself in landscapes that adumbrate the grinding, grey, nightmare world of *Jude*. A "sunless winter day," Hardy says, "emerged" from night "like a dead-born child," while "Owls that had been catching mice . . . rabbits that had been eating winter-greens in the gardens, and stoats that had been sucking the blood of rabbits . . . discreetly withdrew from publicity" (1:51).

When Grace and her father walk into the forest to look for the errant Dr. Fitzpiers, Hardy guides them through hellish landscapes not unlike those of Swinburne's "Anactoria" and "Laus Veneris": they "halted beneath a half-dead oak, hollow, and disfigured with white tumors, its roots spreading out like claws. . . . A chilly wind circled round them," the "vale was wrapped in a dim atmosphere of unnaturalness, and the east was like a livid curtain edged with pink" (2:245). In earlier novels, of course, Hardy's narrative was always quick to point out that such are only the wild imaginings of the disturbed visionary consciousness, but no such disclaimers are made here. When the "smooth surfaces of glossy plants" are described as "weak, lidless eyes" or the branches of trees as "cloven tongues," lest the reader attribute such a vision to the wild fancy of an emotionally strained child-bride, the narrator hastens to add that since "Grace's fear . . . was not imaginative," she was seldom prone to heed "such impressions" (3:139–40). It is Hardy's *own* narrative voice which calls nature an "intense consciousness . . . oppressively contrasting with" man's "active emotions"; we are aware of Hardy's *own* darkening vision when he compares the "sudden lapse from the ornate to the primitive," the growing gloom of nature in winter (and in this novel), to the "retrogressive step from the art of an advanced school" (2:126, 1:125).

Perhaps, with Grace Melbury, we should simply fail to heed such impressions. And yet the attribution of repulsive, anthropomorphic characteristics to nature by the author's narrative voice in *The Woodlanders* is as significant to a study of transitions within the author's changing world as is the trivialization of characters such as Giles Winterborne or Donald Farfrae, men who could have served as the cool and practical post-romantic heroes of many an earlier novel. For these are transitions that, year by year, are moving the Dorsetshire artist out from under the Greenwood tree (where a man's character was his only fate) into the perversely providential labyrinth of *Tess of the D'Urbervilles*, *Jude the Obscure*, and *The Dynasts*.

The belief that natural forces could be part of a malign order had been classified by Hardy's early fiction as a foolish romantic mistake—an error commonly committed by irresponsible dreamers unable to live by the random handouts of mother chance. By the time Hardy begins *Tess*, it is clear that what seemed romantic paranoia in earlier works has become an increasingly haunting fact.

His narrator, no longer able to dismiss the romantic's vision of nature as the guardian and guide of all our moral being with a father's amused chuckle at a child's heady hopes, now lashes out at those who peddled such painful follies. "Some people would like to know," he sneers near the beginning of *Tess*, "whence the poet whose philosophy is in these days deemed as profound . . . gets his authority for speaking of 'Nature's holy plan'."[29]

Alec D'Urberville, "the blood-red ray in the spectrum" of Tess's "young life" (1:75), is nature in its rankest, rawest, least romantic human form. With his red, "swarthy complexion" and "full lips badly moulded, though red and smooth," there is a "barbarism in his contours." The narrator, moreover, demonstrates that Tess's natural reaction to the strong, "red . . . force" of this supposed "blood relative" is immediate, however prudently she attempts to disguise it. When Alec "stood up and held" a huge strawberry "by the stem to her mouth," the narrator says, Tess "parted her lips and took it in." Then, after he "filled her little basket" with his "large" and "specially fine" fruit, "the two passed round to the rose-trees, whence he gathered blossoms and gave her to put in her bosom. She obeyed . . . like one in a dream." Though "Tess Durbeyfield did not divine" as much as she looked down upon the bright red "roses in her bosom," the "tragic mischief in her drama" had already begun (1:70–75).

The nature that courses through the veins of human as well as non-human forms in *Tess of the D'Urbervilles* is far more sinister, deterministic, and tyrannical than either the temperamental but productive nature of *Far from the Madding Crowd* or the muted, faceless nature of *The Return of the Native*. Hardy conveys this fact best through suggestive *tableaux*, *tableaux* like the death of the Durbeyfield horse, the "blood-red" fruit-eating, rose-plucking scenes of Chapter 5, or the scene describing Tess's nighttime visit to a country barn dance where, "through . . . floating fusty *débris* of peat and hay, mixed with the perspirations . . . of the dancers, and forming together a sort of vegeto-human pollen," the dancers "coughed as they danced, and laughed as they coughed," looking all the world like "a multiplicity of Syrinxes; Lotis attempting to elude Priapus, and always failing."[30] Pagan energies are far from new to Hardy's world (Gabriel Oak had been described in *Far from the Madding Crowd* as an "Eros" in the act of "sharpening his arrows"). Even sexual force as a natural urge to be enjoyed is familiar in the Hardy canon. But "pagan" sexual energy as a tyrant which rapes human hopes, plans, and dreams—this is something quite new. In what other novel, with the possible exception of *The Woodlanders*, does Hardy even suggest "that the serpent hisses where the sweet birds sing" (1:146)? Having described the carriage ride that glides Alec and Tess into the "blackness," the "obscurity" of the forest "primeval," the almost nightmarish loss of direction, and the ensuing turn of events which, like "an unholy brew," lulls Tess into a deep sleep and awakens D'Urberville's passion, the narrator tells us that "Darkness and silence ruled everwhere around. Above them rose the primeval yews and oaks of The Chase, in which were poised gentle roosting birds in their last nap. . . . Why it was," he asks, "that upon this beautiful feminine tissue, sensitive as gossamer, and practically blank as snow as yet, there should have been traced such a coarse pattern as it was doomed to receive . . . many thousand years of analytical philosophy have failed to explain to our sense of order. One may, indeed, admit the possibility of a retribution lurking in the catastrophe" (1:140–41).

After the birth and death of Tess's "Sorrow," that "bastard gift of shameless Nature who respects not the civil law" (1:188), Hardy makes every effort to celebrate that "recuperative power" of "organic nature" (1:195). It allows Tess, after all, to move to Tabothay's dairy in Var Vale, a place where "her hopes mingled with the sunshine in an ideal photosphere" of "transmutation" (1:205–6), a fecund spot where "large-veined udders hung ponderous as sandbags" (1:211), where "Rays from the sunrise drew forth buds and . . . lifted up saps in noiseless streams, opened petals, and sucked out scents in invisible jets" (1:257). Here, at Tabothay's dairy, Tess meets and falls in love with Angel Clare. Here, miles away from the scenes of her past, it almost seems that Tess will, indeed, find happiness in nature, for "Amid the oozing fatness and warm ferments of the Var Vale, at a season when the rush of juices could almost be heard below the hiss of fertilization, it was impossible that the most fanciful love should not grow passionate" (2:34).

And yet can a word such as "hiss," a phrase like the "suck" of "saps in noiseless streams," possibly be accidental, given Hardy's earlier descriptions of Prince, dying while his blood "fell with a hiss into the road" (1:57), or of Tess, coming to the realization that "the serpent hisses where the sweet bird sings"? Var Vale is, undeniably, a place of good omens. As Tess sees morning after happy morning break, it *does* almost seem that earth's "diurnal roll" is changing "the pivot of the universe" to the point where she is to have "a new horizon thenceforward." She sees the "delicate equilibrium" (2:36–41) of her new love as occurring in a "preternatural time" reflected by the "neutral shade," the "grey half-tones of daybreak," the "twilight of the morning" when she and Angel meet to exchange vows (1:260–61). But if we really suppose this equilibrious natural world to be the setting for a new, happier "Adam and Eve," a second "Artemis" and "Demeter" (1:260–61), then we have allowed ourselves to forget everything we have seen both of the surface and of the underlying reality of nature. For Tess and for Hardy, this is a time between times, a time for change, but the change foreshadowed is a tragic turn of events for the heroine and a darkening epistemology for the author. Even Tess knows, Hardy tells us, that "spectres" of the future are "waiting just outside the circumscribing light" (2:132–33), for it is inevitable that in this springtime of earth's fecundity, in this time of love, should lie the hidden serpent of nature's awesome, destructive power. The luscious, "red interior" of Tess's mouth, Hardy warns us, was like "a snake's." She would "stretch" an arm "high above her coiled-up cable of hair"; her "eyelids hung heavy over their pupils" (2:79).

The movement of Swinburne's *Erechtheus* and of Hardy's middle fiction is slowly but surely being reversed in *Tess of the D'Urbervilles*. Inner and outer nature, once seen as a benign and meaningless cycle of opportunity for man, now looks, once again, all the world like Swinburne's early vision of a deadly "coil of things," a temporal and natural process that, like a serpent, gnaws at the root of all human dreams ("Anactoria," ll. 236–40), a wild and sticky and bloody world which "trammel[s] . . . and catches and cleaves." "The outskirt of the garden in which Tess" keeps her fatal *rendezvous* with Angel "had been left uncultivated for some years, and was now damp and rank with juicy grass which sent up mists of pollen at a touch." Tess "went stealthily as a cat through this profusion of growth, gathering cuckoo-spittle on her skirts, cracking snails that were underfoot, staining her hands with thistle-milk and slug-slime, and rubbing off upon her naked arms sticky blights which, though snow-white on the apple-tree trunks, made blood-red stains on her skin" (1:245–46).

Through her relationship with Angel, Tess hopes that she may "snatch ripe pleasure before the iron teeth of pain could have time to shut upon her" (2:97); her foolishness lies in thinking that nature's deadly trap would allow her to make off with such a prize. On her wedding day, when Tess learns that her confessional letter has not been read, the narrator tells us that the stillness of the afternoon was "interrupted by the crowing of a cock" (2:174), an evil omen from the natural world. When the newlyweds arrive at the first night's lodgings, an old D'Urberville mansion, they find portraits of women believed to be Tess's ancestors, "women of middle age, of a date some two hundred years ago," with "long pointed features, narrow eye and . . . bill hook nose." "The unpleasantness of the matter," the narrator tells us, was that in their middle-aged "ferocity" could be seen a kind of genetic map, a pattern in which Tess's future development can be all too clearly read. Her own "fine features," Hardy tells us, "were unquestionably traceable in these exaggerated forms" (2:177–78). When Tess hints to Angel of her past, when Angel assures her that it could not possibly be as objectionable as his own, Tess looks first at the fire, where she sees "a Last Day luridness in this red-coaled glow," and then looks at the Clare family necklace, "at which each diamond on her neck gave a sinister wink like a toad's" (2:194–95).

Old women like Fates, a crowing cock, the hellish glow of fresh carbon, together with the chilling "wink" of a billion knowing years of pressed carbon all prove prophetic. At Tabothay's Tess had attempted "to escape the past . . . to annihilate it" (1:195); through her engagement "She dismissed the past—trod upon it and put it out" (2:128). Within an hour after her wedding, however, she and Clare are married in name only, and "she knew . . . that Time was chanting his satiric [Swinburnian] psalm at her then—"

> Behold, when thy face is made bare, he that
>   loved thee shall hate;
> Thy face shall be no more fair at the fall
>   of thy fate.
> For thy life shall fall as a leaf and be
>   shed as the rain;
> And the veil of thine head shall be grief,
>   and the crown shall be pain.

[2:208]

"Nature, in her fantastic trickery," her "vulpine slyness" (2:220, 233), Hardy says, had turned Tess's happiness into unutterable despair. "The night," while seeming "unconcerned and indifferent," he tells us, "had already swallowed up . . . happiness, and was now digesting it listlessly; and was ready to swallow up the happiness of a thousand other people" (2:216).

As relentless and as mechanistic as the great, "Plutonic" harvesting engine which stands as its symbol (3:128), nature propels Tess pell mell into Flintcomb Ash, a "starve-acre" place where stones "outcrop" in "bulbous, cusped, and phallic shapes" and "strange birds" glide by which have "been half blinded by the whirl of colossal storms and terraqueous distortions" (3:43–44, 50). But Flintcomb Ash, horrible as it is, is only a sufferable way station; in short time Tess is driven towards violence and, finally, towards her own execution. The season of the year is winter, and the nights are blackened by "equinoctial darkness," save where they are pierced by "the steely stars" (3:168). Here, under lowering, frigid skies, Tess once again finds herself on the track of Alec D'Urberville, his "passion," his "ferocious" "rude energy" as strong and as insistent as ever (3:86–87). Here, reduced to that "cadaverous and saucer-eyed" shade of her former self so precisely pictured by the ancestral portraits (3:145), Tess seeks to act out her final, heroic act of defiance against nature's plan for her life. She kills Alec, as "in a dream" (3:237), and rejoins her now repentant "Shelleyan" Angel in a brief life outside of reality (2:128), where there can be "an unpractical vagueness in their movements" and where, though "all is trouble outside," inside there is "content . . . affection, union" and momentary peace (3:262). Their inevitable separation comes, of course, at Stonehenge, "a forest of monoliths" which serves as Hardy's bitterest perversion of a romantic motif. For Stonehenge is an Aeolean harp that sings only of the monotony of human endeavor and reward; "the wind, playing upon the edifice, produced a booming tune, like the note of some gigantic one-stringed harp" (3:266). And yet, though Tess's and Angel's romantic dream life lasts only a few days, there is something in this momentary reunion of frail, imperfect lovers beside which the cruel machinations of nature seem "as evanescent as steam."

In Hardy's earlier fiction, men and women had learned to make the best of circumstances by living close to nature and by adapting their love affairs (*Far from the Madding Crowd*), even their system of social organization (*The Mayor of Casterbridge*), to the peculiar problems of survival posed by their own, local landscapes. Once nature comes to be seen as a grotesque and omnipotent mechanism whose unholy plan is pitted against human prosperity and even survival, however, the whole basis of Hardy's earlier celebrations of social cooperation, social brotherhood, is called into question.

Where time had once permitted momentary harmonies among men and women bound by common interests and loving-kindness, it now "chants its satiric psalm" to the unwilling ears of isolated, alienated dreamers, men and women who, like Tess and Angel, turn to their most precious, most unrealistic dreams in order to find the bliss of momentary peace. Children such as Jude Fawley inhabit a cold and barren country where girls give "themselves to lovers who would not turn their heads to look at them," where a boy's attempts to be kind to animals, "the only friends he could claim," are rewarded by a fierce beating, and an even crueler release from employment.[31] "Nature's logic," Hardy tells us in *Jude the Obscure* (1895), "was too horrid" for Jude "to care for. That mercy toward one set of creatures was cruelty toward another sickened his sense of harmony. As you got older . . . you were seized with a sort of shuddering, he perceived. All around you there seemed to be something glaring, garish, rattling, and the noises and glares hit upon the little cell called your life, and shook it, and scorched it. . . . He did not want to be a man" (p. 15).

The child's refusal to participate in nature's cruel logic—the very logic which spawns that insane social tendency to punish the merciful—leads him, ultimately, to create worlds structured by his own subjective logic. Jude's "dreams were as gigantic as his surroundings were small," the narrator tells us as the child fantasizes about a "Heavenly City," an at once romantic and religious vision of distant Christminster which gradually "acquired a tangibility, a permanence, a hold on his life." Jude rebounds from the rebuffs of his own, impoverished, violent society by imagining an ideal society where poor and rich work side by side toward distant but attainable goals of Truth and Light. He was, in the narrator's words, "getting . . . romantically attached" to "dreams" comparable to "those of the Apocalyptic writer" (pp. 20–22).

Through contrapuntal images, characters, and dramatic scenes, Hardy confesses to the pathetic nature of Jude's social vision. Immediately after Jude describes his "new Jerusalem," a couple of coal tranters remind us that in the real Christminster "there's wenches in the streets" where many a "hobble-de-hoy chap" has supposedly turned himself "into a solemn preaching man" (p. 23). When Jude begins to idolize a doctor who has studied at Christminster, it is a short time indeed before Hardy shows us that the man is a quack, more interested in peddling worthless patent medicines than in helping a young man who thirsts for the precious elixir of knowledge (p. 29). Of course, the most famous example of this methodically structured process of deflation comes when Hardy interrupts Jude's "deep concentration," his "magic lantern" reverie on the ancients and upon his own future in "heavenly" Christminster, with a "cold . . . piece of flesh, the characteristic part of a barrow pig," which, thrown by a wench out for "a bit of fun," "smacked him sharply in the ear" (p. 41). Like Tess, whose momentary dream of perfect bliss in love is undermined by her own genetic makeup and by that larger, universal "coil" of natural urges, Jude is prevented from pursuing his quest for an enlightened society by the "unvoiced call of woman to man" (pp. 44–45). "It had been no vestal who chose to throw *that* missile for opening her attack on him," Jude slyly hypothesizes, and Hardy breaks in to remind us that, though he "had anticipated much pleasure in this afternoon's reading," "a new thing, a great hitch, had happened" to "the gliding noiseless current of his life, and he felt as a snake must feel who has sloughed off his winter skin" (pp. 46, 48).

Where once, in Hardy's fiction, the romantic's yearning for complete mergence with a beloved had earned the traditional, Petrarchan metaphors of imprisonment, invasion, missiles, and attack, that democratic antidote to the tortures of high romance, mere sexual enjoyment, is now penalized by the same loaded terms. Where once the snake's instinctive ability to shed its skin stood as symbol for the natural man's instinctive ability to slough off the ravages of time and change, that very image now serves as a symbol of those fiendish natural urges which invade and infest the paradisiacal gardens of man's most idealistic social dreams. Jude gives up his dream of life in a heavenly city for the "fresh wild pleasure" of Arabella's body, but that seemingly tangible pleasure quickly evaporates into a haze of deceptions as soon as physical union has been eternalized by the trammel of society's marriage laws. Soon despondent over the deceptions and degradations of his unsuccessful marriage, Jude, for the second time in his life, withdraws into his amniotic, idealized vision of distant Christminster. The far-off "sight of it," Hardy says, "lit in his soul a spark of the old fire. Surely his plan should be to move onward . . . —to do good cheerfully," in the words of "Spinoza." So, boasting a new plentitude of romantic faith, Jude begins to test the reality of a dream by trudging off in the direction of the "Heavenly City," where soon, across the miles of hills and valleys, there "actually arose the faint halo, a small dim nebulousness, hardly recognizable save by the eye of faith" (p. 87).

The enchantment of Jude's halo-ringed vision of Christminster society is not entirely dissipated upon his nighttime arrival in the city. Wandering about the walls of what seems a fairy-built university, Jude has a vision in which poets (including Swinburne), philosophers, theologians, and statesmen of past and present are in his presence. He "found himself speaking out loud, holding conversations with them . . . like an actor in a melodrama" (pp. 96–98). Morning, however, with its cold, clear, prosaic rays, soon enlightens both Jude and the reader to the reality of Christminster. "[T]he colleges," Hardy says, "had treacherously changed the sympathetic countenances: some were stern; some had . . . the look of family vaults," and "something barbaric loomed" in the aspect "of all" of them. "What at night had been perfect and ideal was by day the more or less defective real" (p. 99). When Jude rebounds from this visual disappointment by pursuing his original plan of joining in the *genius loci*, he soons learns that "their associations and privileges were not for him." As T. Tetuphenay, Master of Biblioll College, tells Jude, "I . . . think you will have . . . success in life by remaining in your own sphere and sticking to your trade." Within no great length of time, Jude's vision of "Heavenly" Christminster is perforated by the most painful kind of knowledge, that which comes when "an imaginative world," the lifelong hope of a "dreaming youth," is "burst . . . like an iridescent soap-bubble" (pp. 138–43).

When Jude abandons his dream of university society, he opts for a temporary life of revelry in town society, where "the two sexes had met for loving, hating, coupling, parting; had waited, had suffered, for each other; had triumphed over each other; cursed each other in jealousy, blessed each other in forgiveness" (p. 144). The earthy life of the Crossways might well have satisfied the humble heroes of Hardy's early fiction; it soon leads to malaise, scorn, and even self-contempt in the minds of the aspiring romantics who populate his later, darker works. No sooner do the "frolicsome," Arabella-esque girls of the town make "advances" than "the spirit of Sue" Bridehead "seemed to hover around him" (p. 144). He found himself drawn by the "magnetism," the "untranslatable . . . mystery," of his beautiful Christminster cousin. She was the "ideal character" of his own "fantastic daydreams," Hardy says, the girl who "haunted" "the impressionable and lonely" Jude even though he had seen her only in one of his aunt's photographs (pp. 92, 106, 110–11). When Jude finally seeks Sue out and makes her acquaintance, he is drawn by some strange force of attraction toward this "hellenist," a "liquid-eyed, light-footed young woman" who collects statues of "Venus, . . . Diana, . . . Apollo, Bacchus, and Mars," (pp. 111–12) and who liberally mixes into her own conversation verses from Shelley (e.g., p. 307) and the passionate lines of Swinburne's *Poems and Ballads* (e.g., p. 115). To Jude, she becomes "almost an ideality" (p. 118), later "almost a divinity" (p. 179); together, the two of them are "enshered by the same harmonies" (p. 110).

Sue Bridehead is the Angel of *Jude*; indeed, all of Hardy's insistent efforts to characterize Angel Clare as a "Romantic" could be said to characterize Sue's romanticism as well. Angel, we are told, "though not cold-natured," was "rather bright than hot," a "Shelleyan" spirit who "could love desperately, but with a love more especially inclined to the imaginative and ethereal" (2:127). He often seemed to Tess "an intelligence rather than a man," an "abundance of illuminations" residing at some "unmeasurable . . . altitude" (1:251). He was, consequently, a spirit who "settled practical questions" "by a sentiment which had nothing to do with them" (2:152), unable and, in any case, unwilling to compromise ideals with mundane necessities. His was "the will to subdue the grosser to the subtler emotion, the substance to the conception, the flesh to the spirit." As they were for the poet of "Ode to the West Wind," "Propensities, tendencies, habits, were as dead leaves upon the tyrannous wind of his imaginative ascendency" (2:236). (Hardy makes this statement at the very moment of Angel's departure from Tess; thus, once again, romantic idealism would seem to be implicitly compared with residual Christian sentiment, a comparison equally implicit in the author's depiction of Sue Bridehead's "Shelleyan" purity [p. 290].) It is Angel, but it might well be Sue, who lives the "romantic" conviction that "the best is not to remember that your past doings have been like thousands' and thousands', and that your coming life and doings'll be like thousands' and thousands'" (1:253).

For a short while, Jude and Sue, like Tess and Angel before them, seem to be able to live in a quiet, private dreamland apart from that brutal reality where "all is trouble" (*Tess*, 3:262). During a holiday trip into the country, Sue describes their day together as being "Outside all laws except gravitation and germination," a day which almost recaptures that evasive "life of . . . infancy and its freedom" (p. 170). And when the two return from their country expedition—wet, tired, and too late for Sue to be admitted to her room in the boarding school nearby—she "sleeps" like "a divinity" in Jude's room, with nary a suggestion that their love should abandon its ethereal, platonic basis. "I have never yielded myself to any lover," she tells her somewhat incredulous roommate the next day. "People say I must be cold-natured,—sexless—on account of it. But I won't have it! Some of the most passionately erotic poets have been the most self-contained in their daily lives" (pp. 179, 184).

Just as Jude's two visions of Christminster society were exploded, first by natural law and, later, by that legalistic codification of nature's cruelty in social law and custom, so his most recent dream, this "poetic" one of a transcendent love "outside all laws," is similarly demolished by those very same statutes. For one thing, Jude's own, natural flesh rebels at that relationship with Sue which his mind and spirit treasure so dearly. After months and months of purely spiritual communion with his phantasmal Sue, Jude meets his Wife of Bath, his estranged Arabella, in a Christminster tavern. There, after a few hours of ritualistic verbal billing, he is once again diverted from his most idealistic intentions by that "characteristic part" of everyman's makeup. Social law, like natural law, moreover, is equally insistent upon the infeasibility of Jude's unearthly relationship with Sue. By legally sanctioning his natural response to Arabella's suggestive overture, society insists upon dignifying a long defunct union and, by so doing, drives Sue Bridehead into an equally imperfect union with a schoolmaster.

Master Phillotson, of course, eventually releases Sue from the bondage of an unfortunate marriage so that she can return to her beloved cousin. Together, as Phillotson explains it, Jude and Sue, this "Laon and Cythna," "share each other's emotions, and fancies, and dreams" in a "Platonic" or, more precisely, in a "Shelleyan" relationship which transcends all "ignoble, merely animal" feelings (pp. 289–90). Indeed, Sue does return to Jude as if she were "a Being . . . / Met on . . . visioned wanderings . . . /A seraph of heaven too gentle to be human" (p. 307) and, for a short time, this "phantasmal, bodiless creature" actually succeeds in giving him a great measure of happiness (p. 325). Even in these happiest moments, however, Hardy never allows the reader to forget what he reminded a friend in a letter: that this is a story about "the ideal life a man wished to lead, and the squalid real life he was fated to lead."[32] To remind us that doom hangs heavily over this unworldly relationship, Hardy sees that we are told the story of the Brown House, the place where, on a knoll only a few miles from their home, Jude's and Sue's ancestor was hanged for trying to steal the corpse of his child from the house of his estranged wife (p. 354).

The Fawley ancestry proves just as tyrannical as that of the ancient, D'Urberville women, for the following year brings the arrival of that little grotesque, Father Time, as well as the murder of Jude's and Sue's (divinely conceived) children at the hands of this tiny, human, Old Testament prophecy of those ancient, those returning, "Years of night" (p. 346). The new season also brings an incurable sickness to Jude, the loss of yet another child, poverty and hunger to the family, and, to Sue, a religious fanaticism which borders upon madness. Through Sue's raging and Jude's demise, Hardy's last great novel conjures up just enough *déja vu* to remind us a little of the early fiction. "Childish" romantics, that is, are still the victims of hopelessness and of tragic defeat, while characters like Arabella, Phillotson, Dr. Villiers, and all the men and women of the Crossways manage to continue making the best of limited opportunities.

But here all real similarities end. For in suggesting new, darker definitions of time, nature, love, and society, Hardy has necessarily elevated the cruel fates of his hopeless, romantic dreamers to heights of pathos which had been unattainable in those early novels that celebrated natural process, temporal opportunities, earthy sexuality, and simple loving-kindness, to heights of tragic heroism which seemed confusing, even contradictory, in the epistemologically ambiguous works of the eighties, *The Mayor of Casterbridge* and *The Woodlanders*. The rhetorical and structural underpinning (or perhaps even source) of this moral elevation of dreamers in *Tess* and in *Jude* is a shortening of distance between the authorial point of view and the consciousness of the romantic protagonist. In *The Well-Beloved*, Hardy's final novel, narrator and protagonist become virtually indistinguishable. These last works of fiction, although they torture, sometimes obliterate, their Shelleyan angels, also demand that we participate sympathetically in the romantic downfall. (We hardly cared about Boldwood; Troy got what he deserved.) In a curious way, Hardy's late novels restore the true romantic vision—which was darker and more fatalistic than post-romantic critics admitted—even as they pretend, or perhaps intend, to undercut it once more.

All of these changes, moreover, contribute to what Misao Miyoshi calls "Hardy's revival of Gothicism in the last decade" of the century.[33] Whether or not Hardy really revived "Gothicism" is subject to debate; that he began to create a goblin universe where the paranoid's fears are as often justified as the escapist's dreams are necessary is beyond question. Perhaps Sue is wrong when she hysterically declares that she and her lover are victims of the wrath of God. Still, there can be no doubt that Jude and Sue, like Tess and Giles Winterborne before them, are the helpless victims of natural and social laws totally beyond their control, the heroic victims of what Hardy will begin to refer to in his late poetry as the Immanent Will—an entity which is not God but, rather, that awesome sum of natural (including human) actions, interactions, and reactions. Hardy, by revising both the notions of Providence and self-determination, declares subjective, human wishes to be at once pathetic and heroic, romantic vanities.

The late novels, then, may still be called tragedies of sensibility, so long as we understand that the phrase has taken on a different meaning. In the early novels it was the sensibility that brought about the tragedy; in the last novels the tragedy is that man lives in a world in which the romantic sensibility is but an escapist's dream.

Nothing is All

Swinburne, Hardy, Lawrence, and Romantic Forms

6

Virginia Woolf has said of Hardy's later fiction, "It is as if Hardy himself were not quite aware of what he did, as if his consciousness held more than he could produce, and he left it for his readers to make out his full meaning."[1] One of the things which that fulsomeness of consciousness did produce is a fiction torn by an unresolvable conflict, a conflict between an ironic plot structure that, by the 1890's, had become nothing less than an authorial trademark and a mood or tone in the fiction which would seem to undermine the plot's methodical attempts to demonstrate the foolishness of the quest for transcendence—ecclesiastical, social, intellectual, or spiritual. This mood or tone, which at its best approaches the lyrical pathos of tragedy and at its worst degenerates into a wistful sentimentality, compels the reader to sympathize with those characters who never learn to make limited opportunities endurable, who insist, in spite of the outward circumstances generated by plot, upon dreaming their way into oblivion.

An anguished, almost schizophrenic fiction which, in Woolf's words, may not be quite aware of what it does, is not the only distinguishing feature of Hardy's career during the 1890's. During that very decade he had abandoned the novel forever and turned to poetry once again.[2] He declared that while "there is no new poetry . . . the new poet—if he carry the flame . . . —comes with a new note." Implicitly comparing himself to the composer, Verdi, Hardy echoes Swinburne by pointing out that "from the ashes of his early popularity . . . there arose a sudden sort of phoenix," a "new note" for a new aesthetic and spiritual era.[3]

As I have suggested earlier, many if not most of Hardy's poems written after the 1865–67 group argue for realistic and responsible adaptation to an indifferent world without God (*bonum* or *malum*) and without transcendental possibilities of the social, romantic, temporal, or poetic varieties. However, Hardy composed some late lyrics that adopt a view of things which is at once more superstitious and more sentimental. They are not many and, with the exception of the haunted *Poems of 1912–1913*, they are scattered helter-skelter throughout the various collections published between 1914 and 1928. Nevertheless they exist; there are several poems which lament man's helplessness in the face of a deterministic plan, others which offer a dreamlike escape from a grinding, grey world whose reality is never for a moment questioned, and there are still others which suggest, eloquently and movingly, that if the sanity of the agnostic poet is to be preserved, the former must be balanced by the latter, the poetry of loss must be qualified by the poetry of hope, fancy, dream, escape.

In "The Clock of the Years" (1916), Hardy twists an eighteenth-century notion of universal order by describing the great, cosmic timepiece as a rigid, guillotine-like machine "ordained" to annihilate human hope, action, even life. A grim lyric entitled "Heredity," the idea for which was conceived in 1889 but was not "carried out" in poetry until much later,[4] suggests, as a young, angry Swinburne had suggested back in 1865, that the "trace" of a man's identity (that is, the "reins" that hold him back by prescribing the "track" he is destined to sweep on the clock of the years) is precisely determined by natural patterns over which he has no control. "The family face," Hardy says in lines recalling *Tess*, is the only "eternal thing in man." It lives on as dreams implode and as "Flesh perishes, . . . / Projecting trait and trace / Through time to times anon." And in "The Unborn," dated 1905, Hardy adds his own macabre touch to Shelley's "The Triumph of Life" by describing a deep, uterine "Cave of the Unborn," where "eyes" are "lit with . . . trust," and "Hope" foresees a life of "pure delight." But "as I silently retired," the poet exclaims,

> I turned and watched them still,
> And they came helter-skelter out,

> Driven forward like a rabble rout
> Into the world they had so desired,
>   By the all-immanent Will.

Even while mankind fashions a great ship, a titanic "creature of cleaving wing," this same force that drives the "unborn," the same mindless power that energizes the "grotesque, slimed, dumb, indifferent" "sea-worm," this "Immanent Will that stirs and urges everything / Prepared a sinister mate . . . / A Shape of Ice, for the time far and dissociate":

> Alien they seemed to be:
> No mortal eye could see
> The intimate welding of their later history. . . .
>   [1912]

Not all of Hardy's later poems choose to emphasize this clockwork, tracklike, welded destiny that scorns all man's foolish and idle fancies, including his dreams of self-determination. Many of the later lyrics choose to aspire to moments of vision, far phantasies, rather than offer human shows, satires of circumstance. These poems, although they admit to the improbable, unrealistic, even absurd nature of their quests, seek to keep the dreaming life of the fancy alive precisely because of the unbearable vicissitudes of an all too mechanical existence. In "The Shadow on the Stone" (1913), for instance, the speaker watches the "rhythmic swing" of shadows cast upon a "Druid stone" by a "tree hard by." He wonders why the ghost of a woman, whose intangible presence he feels behind him, would dare reenter "this old track," but he purposely fails to turn around and confront this vision enmeshed with the hard timepiece of the landscape "lest" his "dream should fade." Here there is no authorial intrusion, no puncturing reminder of the foolishness of believing in illusions. Indeed, in this poem, as in others like "A Church Romance" (1906), or in lyrics such as "When I Set Out for Lyonnesse" or "She Opened the Door," the latter a reverie composed shortly after the death in 1912 of the poet's once vivacious wife, there is absolutely no justification for separating the poet from the sentimental speaker:

> She opened the door of Romance to me,
>   The door from a cell
>   I had known too well,
> Too long, till then, and was fain to flee.

> She opened the door of a Love to me,
>> That passed the wry
>> World-welters by
> As far as the arching blue the lea.

The near-deity celebrated by these poems—the "Romance" that liberates the self from the imprisoning "cell" of mere experience, the "Love" that transcends the nettles, the "welters" of the "world" "As far as the arching blue the lea"—is something at once less and more than that love which could be defined as shared work, *camaraderie*, sexual feeling. It is almost as if Hardy had responded to his increasingly despairing vision of nature, time, and social possibility by nourishing a faith in what "Faustian Fitzpiers" had described as a "transcendental," a "romantic," an "entirely subjective ideal" of love.

Certainly, the development of Hardy's Swinburne-reviving idea of "The Well-Beloved" (Swinburne had written, in his 1866 "Notes on Poems and Reviews," of "the transmigration of a single soul . . . through many ages and forms," of "the sudden sight of a living face which recalled the well-known likeness of another dead")[5]; certainly, Hardy's lyrical and novelistic resurrection of this idea is evidence of a transition which almost reverses the well-established process of reducing romantic phantoms of delight into earthy lovers of the here and now. (Another evidence of transition is the fact that Henry Knight's love for the "disembodied soul" of his "beloved" had been treated ironically, even scornfully, by the plot and authorial rhetoric of *A Pair of Blue Eyes* [2:124–26].) The speaker of the 1896 poem, voyaging to meet his intended, idealistically declares,

> "—O faultless is her dainty form,
>> And luminous her mind;
> She is the God-created norm
>> Of perfect womankind!"

A Phantasm of Love then appears and declares that She is a pure and spotless "dream"—a spirit-vision which permanently occupies the lover's mind. In Shelley's "Epipsychidion" the "glorious shape" of which the poet had dreamed and the "mortal form" of a woman had merged in Emily, and in Wordsworth's "She Was a Phantom of Delight," the vision of a phantom and the perception of a living person were conclusively merged in the celebration of a strong and enduring woman—"And yet a spirit still. . . . " But Hardy's poem, although it marks something of a return to a romantic mode, is not quite so romantic as Shelley's or Wordsworth's. The real woman never actually becomes the dream, and the dream never really spiritualizes the intended:

> The sprite resumed: "Thou hast transferred
>   To her dull form awhile
> My beauty, fame, and deed, and word,
>   My gestures and my smile. . . .
> Thou lovest what thou dreamest her;
>   I am thy very dream!"

Nevertheless, the dream does exist for the suitor, even if its delights are unrealizable, save in the reveries of his active fancy. And, if the anxious voices of Hardy's later love lyrics continue to complain about the barrenness of reality (the speaker of "The Well-Beloved" reveals that when he finally "arrived and met" his "bride, / Her look was pinched and thin"), they can also, it would seem, find a reason for existence in a beautiful, changeless realm of imaginative experience which, as long as life lasts, exists apart from the pitiless natural loom of the flesh and its inevitable process of unraveling.

Some of these later lyrics offer an imaginative escape into timelessness, into a world of phantasms which lies, temporarily at least, outside of nature's process, into a perception of things which avoids, momentarily anyway, that stoical and ironical vision that time's relentlessness would seem to require. "Under the Waterfall" (1912) is an attempt by Hardy to use natural experience almost as Wordsworth, or perhaps more nearly as Keats, might have used it—to transmit the imagination back into the lost, the forever static past and thus, in some sense, to transcend both time and the reality of the present. The woman who speaks recalls the day when she, with her lover, rinsed a drinking glass under a waterfall, "Where it slipped, and sank . . . past recall." Now, "Whenever I plunge my arm, like this, / In a basin of water," the speaker claims, "I never miss / The sweet sharp sense of a fugitive day":

> "The basin seems the pool, and its edge
> The hard smooth face of the brook-side ledge,
> And the leafy pattern of china-ware
> The hanging plants that were bathing there."

The poem's ending is absolutely elegiac in tone, and elegy, it must be remembered, is one poetic form the younger Hardy, writing poems equating the temporary with the All, seldom indulged. "Under the Waterfall" ends by envisioning, by sanctifying, by giving poetic voice to the deep drowned "chalice" in the pool:

"By night, by day, when it shines or lours,
There lies intact that chalice of ours,
And its presence adds to the rhyme of love
Persistently sung by the fall above.
No lip has touched it since his and mine
In turns therefrom sipped lovers' wine."

The lovers these dreams, memories, fancies or faiths keep alive are often idealized images of the well-beloved. This is forcefully demonstrated by the fact that, during the two years following the death of Hardy's emotionally estranged and probably insane wife, the poet could write a series of lyrics that all but resurrect her. The *Poems of 1912–1913* are extremely personal reveries which dream, sometimes feverishly, sometimes peacefully, of physical and spiritual reunion. "Rain on a Grave," for instance, recalls the longing of a Byronic Heathcliff for physical reunion with the flesh of Cathy Earnshaw, as well as those powerful lines in "The Triumph of Time" in which Swinburne despairs, "I wish we were dead together to-day, / Lost sight of, hidden away out of sight, / Clasped and clothed in the cloven clay":

Would that I lay here
  And she were housed here!
Or better, together
Were folded away there
Exposed to one weather. . . .

Another of these late, autobiographical love lyrics, entitled "After a Journey" (1913), describes the moment in which Hardy, like Heathcliff, finally sees and speaks to the spirit of his beloved in vision. "I see what you are doing," the speaker cries in painful pleasure; "you are leading me on / To the spots we knew when we haunted here together,"

The waterfall, above which the mist-bow shone
  At the then fair hour in the then fair weather. . . .

Trust me, I mind not, though Life lours,
  The bringing of me here; nay, bring me here again!

Ghosts, visions, phantasms, fancies—all such apparitions were once the exclusive possessions of pathetic, childish dreamers unable to cope with the world. Perhaps these adjectives still fit, but now they characterize the poet, not his straw men, now they are the mark of the sensitive spirit, not the disruptive fool. Hence, apparitions or ghosts have become literary emblems of lost, unattained, or untenable dreams or ideals. In "The Garden Seat," composed between 1917 and 1922, the numerous phantasms who return to that old romantic haunt at night "when reddest flowers are black" seem tender elegies to an old ideal of love:

> With them the seat does not break down,
> Nor winter freeze them, nor floods drown,
> For they are as light as upper air,
> They are as light as upper air!

And in "The Oxen," a quietly sentimental poem written in 1915 and included in *Moments of Vision* (1917), Hardy uses the fantastical belief that on Christmas Eve the oxen kneel in their stalls as an emblem of *all* faith, all hopes, all dreams, all those supernatural ideals that are as necessary as they are absurd. "The Oxen" is a poem in which the will to dream and to believe is as strong as the knowledge that all such beliefs are naïve. As a child, the speaker recalls, "We pictured the meek mild creatures where / They dwelt in their strawy pen, / Nor did it occur to one of us there / To doubt they were kneeling then":

> So fair a fancy few would weave
>   In these years! Yet, I feel,
> If someone said on Christmas Eve,
>   "Come; see the oxen kneel,
>
> "In the lonely barton by yonder coomb
>   Our childhood used to know,"
> I should go with him in the gloom,
>   Hoping it might be so.

It is difficult, if not impossible, to account for Hardy's "return," a somewhat inaccurate word used here to refer to the poet's renewed efforts to proclaim both the insufferability of the here and now and the utter necessity of the will to believe in better things. "Return" is somewhat inaccurate because this seemingly schizophrenic procedure is not, in fact, a return to the confused poetry of the divided self, the agnostic agony (although the return is so nearly complete that, as titles like *Poems of the Past and of the Present* and *Late Lyrics and Earlier* would remind us, Hardy can afford to fill out volumes of new poems with lyrics left over from his youthful days). Nevertheless, in Hardy's later poetry, the will to believe is not a frustrated, insatiable drive, as it was in the 1865–67 poems. It is, rather, a delicate *pose*, a "romantic" fiction that makes life bearable, even lovely, but that always remains a pleasant fiction. When Hardy says that *"If* someone said on Christmas Eve, / 'Come; see the oxen kneel, . . . ' / I *should go* with him in the gloom, / *Hoping* it *might* be so," he makes it clear enough, without destroying the poem's lyrical charm, that no one is likely to issue the invitation, that the poet would not dream of instigating the barnyard quest, that hope is considerably less than faith and, therefore, that in this already conditional world no kneeling oxen would actually be found. It is only because the quest will forever remain trebly conditional, an hypothesis never to be tested, that the poet is willing to indulge this most reassuring "hope."

To explain the reason for this return or, more precisely, this transition, it is helpful to call upon certain biographical facts. During the later 1880's Hardy is said to have suffered from "excessive nervous sensibility" and "persistent melancholia."[6] He wrote in his autobiography of a recurring "horror of lying down in close proximity to a monster whose body had four million heads and eight million eyes."[7] On trips to London and Normandy he is reported to have seen "weird shapes,"[8] and in his diary he would write notes such as these: "in a fit of depression, as if enveloped in a leaden cloud"; "Sick headache"; "Everything looks so little—So ghastly little"; "Experience *unteaches*"; "The Hypocrisy of things. Nature is an arch-dissembler; a child is deceived completely"; *"nothing* is as it appears"; "Woke before it was light. Felt that I had not enough staying power to hold my own in the world."[9] It was during this period that, according to Evelyn Hardy, he "pondered" both the merits and the deceptions of "Positivism," "Christianity," and "general principles of life," especially "romanticism."[10] He wrote in his journal that "Romanticism will exist in human nature as long as human nature itself exists. The point is (in imaginative literature) to adopt that form of romanticism which is the mood of the age."[11] The growing sympathy for a sensibility, or at least a resurrected "form" of that sensibility, which Hardy had worked doggedly to unteach became an increasingly prominent aspect of his thinking. In 1887, after the success of *The Mayor of Caster-bridge*, he took Emma to Italy on what amounted to nothing less than an act of contrition, a pilgrimage to the homes, haunts, and tombs of Byron, Keats, and Shelley. It was during this same year that Hardy claimed, in the *Fortnightly Review*, that Byron's "Childe Harold" and Shelley's "*Lament*, 'O World, O life, O time' " are among "the most beautiful of English lyrics," and he hastened to add that his opinion "is a well-considered relapse on my part, for though in past years I have been very modern in this matter I begin to feel that mere intellectual subtlety will not hold its own in time to come against the straightforward expressions of good feeling."[12]

Sickness, financial troubles, hostile reviews, a disastrous marriage full of bitterness and conflict, the death of a beloved father (and of Carlyle, whose spiritual parentage was in some ways important to Hardy), all these things may have contributed both to the darkening view of things and to the romantic "relapse," the growing empathy with writers who, in Hardy's view, were poets of "straightforward . . . feeling," who had longed to escape the vicissitudes of the world through the powers of imagination.

All these biographical facts, however, may not have been fully responsible for Hardy's abandonment of a stoical philosophy and an ironic aesthetic in certain late works for a more schizophrenic vision of reality which the author described (in a letter to Swinburne) as an irreconcilable "contrast" between the "ideal life" a man lives in his mind "and the squalid real life" he is "fated to lead."[13] Without doubt, literary causes were also responsible for the poet's darkening vision of reality on the one hand and, on the other, his renewed interest in "romanticism" or, at least, that "form of romanticism which is the mood of the age." Carlyle's works, which Hardy had read carefully and often, had borne witness to a similar metamorphosis of sensibility. The commitment to earth and man in the "Everlasting Yea" had become, in "Shooting Niagra," a commitment to a double vision, a vision of mythologized heroes or messiahs and a counter-vision of frighteningly real human machines, or "niggers." Pater, having begun to weave physical, intellectual, and moral strands into one seamless garment of sensation, impression, reflection, gradually allowed his fabric to unravel into two pieces: visual impressionism and a kind of Ruskinian, neo-Christian ethic. And Dickens's near-perfect merger of passion and reason, ideal and reality, myth and chronicle in Mr. Pickwick and his *Pickwick Papers* had shattered into the worlds of grotesque caricatures and gothic dreamers found in *Bleak House, Great Expectations,* and *Little Dorritt.*

Swinburne, too, had gradually lost grip on that cohesive personal and social vision attained in the *Songs before Sunrise* and in *Erechtheus.* The stirring hymns to an integrated physical, imaginative, and political life sung by these poems of Swinburne's middle period had gradually been replaced by new romantic arias dedicated to a deathlike life of pure "song" or "art" ("Thalassius," "The Lake of Gaube"). Like Hardy and other Victorian contemporaries, Swinburne had emerged from a period of spiritual and aesthetic crisis, had nurtured a new sensibility by which the world could be perceived and even celebrated through art, only to discover, in his later years, that this world without God, without a moral force of nature, without divine and immortal human selves, without transcendent spiritual passions, without hope for perfect, social unions, was not a world he could continue to celebrate. To some extent, then, "decadence" (and I believe that Swinburne's and Hardy's moments of vision, far phantasies, are decadent in the truest sense of the word) was the inevitable result of aesthetic, spiritual, and moral prematurity. Swinburne and Hardy were raised on Christianity and romanticism—their youthful devotions are a matter of record—and their heroic, preeminently modern labors to raze the temples of all dead or doubtful gods seem almost fated to end in a second spiritual and aesthetic crisis, in a "return" to some "form of" an old faith to fit "the mood" of their "age," in decadence, for their joy is not in the faith but in the form, not in the mysteries of which their songs sing but, rather, in the mysteries of song, the power of poetry to fantasize worlds so sweet that they almost seem real.

In Swinburne's poetry, this return is first evident in the second series of *Poems and Ballads* (1878). Jerome McGann reveals his awareness of the change when he says, in a comparison of this volume with its namesake of 1866, "Brilliant as it is, the later volume remained innocent of the world as the earlier volume had not."[14] It is a perfectly accurate appraisal. Poets cannot grow in innocence; they can, however, write artificially innocent poems.

Just as Hardy's incipient return was accompanied by a period of physical and emotional crisis, Swinburne's was complicated by periods of acute depression. He told Edmund Gosse, in 1875, that "he found his intellectual energy succumbing under a morbid distress at his isolation, and that he had been obliged steadily to review before his conscience his imaginative life in order to prevent himself from sinking into despair."[15] He finished the volume in Glasgow during January 1877; recalling this period of the poet's life, Gosse remarks that "No one would have guessed at the distracted and even alarming physical condition of the author from the serene volume" that was published.[16]

What makes this volume so "innocent," so "serene," is a handful of poems that choose to exist apart from distractions, from alarming physical conditions, from isolation and despair. They protect their poet from reality and from the distressing agnostic knowledge that he has gained and disseminated, not by fully returning him to a lost faith but, rather, by hypothesizing in art an utterly imaginative realm, a lovely, quiet, and harmonious place, where such a faith *might* exist.

It is just such a hypothetical world that Swinburne would attain in "A Vision of Spring in Winter." It is true that the vision the poet claims to seek is both an anticipation of a real spring to come and a memory of some pleasant and painful seasons past. At one point the poet says "I stretch my spirit forth to the fair hours," and later in the same stanza he counters with the claim, "I send my love back to the lovely time" (3:94). But the spring the poet seems to seek most urgently, indeed the only spring depicted by the poem, is not a real season—past or future—it is a spring that exists only in winter, an utterly intangible place that exists utterly apart from winter's ruin. (I would go so far as to suggest that a proper reading of the poem's title would emphasize that this is to be a vision of spring-in-winter more than a vision of spring, in winter.) Thus, the spring envisioned is more a tone or mood, a sweet and intangible presence, than a past or future time. Keats's returning presence ("tender-coloured night," "Chill foster-father of the weanling spring") subliminally suggests that the spring to which Swinburne flies is something like the darkling nightingale's unheard melodies, the urn's cold pastoral (3:95).

Keats's poetry, however, can no longer be written, and Swinburne's poem cannot repress that fact either, for the speaker cries out, "I would not bid thee . . . give back" the time when "youth with burning lips and wreathless hair / Sang" of "hopes that triumphed and fell dead":

> These may'st thou not give back for ever; these,
>   As at the sea's heart all her wrecks lie waste . . .
> But flowers thou may'st, and winds, and hours of ease,
>   And all its April to the world thou may'st
>   Give back, and half my April back to me.
>
> [3:97]

Getting back half of April, that is, getting back not the romantic power for vision but, rather, the power to write hypothetically, wistfully, elegiacally about those moments of vision, "hopes that" once "triumphed and" then "fell dead," is a concept that could apply to almost any poem in this volume. In a lyric entitled "At a Month's End," Swinburne, posing once again as a lover losing his *inamorata*, admits the demise of an April dream of transcendent love when he speaks of "the old love's love-sake" now "dead and buried" (3:29). What is interesting about the poem is that, as its speaker confirms the fact that the beloved's physical longings for another supercede any spiritual affinities she might have with him, that the poet can never etherealize the mundane, can "Transmute . . . not form or feature," that is, cannot "Change feet for wings or wings for feet" (3:31), he neither cries out in bitterness (as he might have in his early volumes) nor celebrates the earthy realities of nature and man (as he might have in his middle period). Rather, he gets back *half* of an old, impossibly ethereal love by writing a dreamy poem that may allow the beloved (including, I should think, the post-romantic reader, the confirmed inhabitant of the here and now) the luxury of momentary escape. "This one broken foam-white feather," Swinburne writes, "I throw you off the hither wing," a "song for sleep to learn and sing"

> . . . in your ear when, daytime over,
>   You, couched at long length on hot sand
> With some sleek sun-discoloured lover,
>   Wince from his breath as from a brand. . . .
>
> [3:32–33]

Such poems cannot be taken, nor would Swinburne have us take them, as true romantic visions of possibility. They are, rather, in the words of two of Swinburne's 1878 titles, "Pastiche" or "Relics." The latter poem describes subtly the poetic attempt to recapture half of a romantic April. Its perfect, metapoetic image of book-pressed flowers (plucked in the paradisiacal gardens of poems like Shelley's "Hymn to Intellectual Beauty"?) both admits to its witheredness and, at the same time, makes a claim for its useless but special delicacy. It is "A white star made of memory long ago / Lit in the heaven of dear times dead to me":

> How sweet the day was with them, and the night!
> Such words of message have dead flowers to say.
>
> This that the winter and the wind made bright,
> And this that lived upon Italian light,
>   Before I throw them and these words away,
> Who knows but I what memories too take flight?
>
> [3:26, 28]

Similarly, in "A Forsaken Garden," the poet recaptures half an April by finding a *ghost* of a garden. He comes indirectly to a vision of garden and sea, roses and lovers, by wistfully confirming the reality only of weeds and of rocks, of thorns and of death. (Just as Hardy reveals and qualifies his moments of vision by bracketing them within parentheses, past tense, or conditional mood, so Swinburne both creates and brackets his dreams of love in Paradise by telling us that we can discover their remains.) Like the pressed flower, this is a "relic," an "inland island" of the belated poetic imagination which, in its witheredness, neither cries out against loss nor celebrates fibrous, organic life. Rather, it luxuriates in the timeless poetic place of elegy, the one place where "death may deal not again for ever; / Here change may come not till all change end" (3:24).

For no accidental reason, Swinburne's "return" to a "form" of "romanticism," exactly like Hardy's, is accompanied by an exploration of the elegiac mode. Nearly every poem in *Poems and Ballads*, Second Series and Third (1889), is elegiac in tone, and no fewer than sixteen poems in these two volumes are either formal elegies or tributes to dead writers or dead children. In his elegy on Baudelaire, "Ave atque Vale," Swinburne, in the wake of Arnold's modest poetic resurrection not of Clough but of a tree, attempts a lyric that will return to the Shelleyan hope of "Adonais" that, as Swinburne puts it, "the end and the beginning / Are one thing to thee, who art past the end" (3:52). But here, too, Swinburne can "give back" only "half" of poetry's "April" season, for "Ave atque Vale" brackets its hope, not in past tense, conditional mood, or parentheses, but in question marks:

> Hast thou found any likeness for thy vision?
> . . . .
> What of despair, of rapture, of derision,
> What of life is there, what of ill or good?
> . . . .
>   Are there flowers
> At all, or any fruit?
>
>   [3:52–53]

In "A Birth Song" (3:77–80), a poem written for Olivia Frances Madox Rossetti, Swinburne returns, as he does in "Olive," to a Wordsworthian conception of childhood in order to hope for news of the recent dead (specifically of Oliver Madox Brown). But even here romantic cosmography is compromised by the conditional mood ("If death and birth be one, / And set with rise of sun . . . / Some word might come with thee / From over the still sea"), by question marks ("What note of song have we?"), and by a combination of the two ("If love be strong as death, . . . / Could love send word to say / He lives and is not dead?"). "Neap Tide" can only ask, "Who knows if haply the shadow of death / May be not the light of life?", and a poem "In Memory of John William Inchbold," having posed a possibility—"change . . . shall . . . / Cease too, perchance, and perish. Who shall say?"—comes full circle and ends on the word with which it began: "Farewell" (3:240, 254). Thus the word with which Swinburne begins and ends his poem compromises the faith implicit in the circular, or rondel, structures the poet is finding more attractive year after year. To believe, in the words of "Ave atque Vale," that "the end and the beginning / Are one" is to abandon, necessarily, that additive structure of linear emergence which had formed Swinburne's stoical, middle poems. But to begin and end a poem with "Farewell" is to affix a somber question mark to the hope implied by structural circularity. Having begun his career with poems founded in uncertainty and ending with question marks, Swinburne, as he enters his decadence (which is, by definition, a second period of crisis and transition), recapitulates some of the moods and methods of his earliest efforts.

In his volume *Songs of the Springtides* (1880), Swinburne writes a poem that, like the "Prelude" to *Songs before Sunrise*, seems to offer a portrait of his own artistic development. "Thalassius" opens with a description of the poet's birth, a description that, by subtly fusing the cosmography of the "Intimations Ode" and the imagery of Shelley's *Prometheus*, would seem to indicate something of Swinburne's own aesthetic and spiritual parentage. The child ("it seemed / Nor man nor mortal child of man") drifts into life "on a reach of shingle and shallower sand . . . something nearer sea than land," a symbolic, transitional place where he emerges into the light of day ("Left for the sun's love") from that more glittering, imperial, palatial light of the sea ("Inlaid with starrier glimmering jewellery" [3:295]). He is the child of earthly nature (the sea) and that more dazzling parent, the sun, who, described synesthetically, descends to inspire (i.e., breathe life into) and influence (flow into) the "ebbs and flows" of Wordsworthian nature like nothing less than a Shelleyan spirit. He is felt, seen, and heard as

> A noise of songs and wind-enamoured wings
> And lutes and lyres of milder and mightier strings,
> And round the resonant radiance of his car
> Where depth is one with height,
> Light heard as music, music seen as light.
>
> [3:296]

But the child, not unlike the latecomer Swinburne, is abandoned both by the maternal ebb and flow and by the audacious, blazing, post-Miltonic father (for whom "depth is one with height"). He is nurtured, consequently, by an adopting spirit similar to the spirit of Swinburne's own Victorian age, a "warrior grey," perhaps akin to the Arnoldian or Tennysonian Ulysses, who teaches "wisdom" from "grave glad lips" in "songs" that carefully revise and reduce what the Victorians generally assumed to be romantic expectations (3:296). "Time" and "fate," this almost Carlylean or Arnoldian voice warns him, cannot be transcended, but through good works, works which may lead to "loss" and even "death," the man who "much less loves" life "than he hates / All wrongdoing" "Shall live a mightier life than time's or fate's." There can be no freedom in, no harmony found with, nature save in these actions through which man works for social brotherhood ("man's earth was not, nor the sweet sea-waves / His . . . / Except they bred not, bore not, hid not slaves" [3:297]). Thus, although "Love" is part of the warrior's instructive song, it is anything but the love which mystifies, eternalizes, or deifies souls. It is more like brotherhood, or loving-kindness, which bestows only the quiet immortality of historical influence (a man dies "not wholly as all men . . . / If aught of deed or word / Be seen for all time or of all time heard"), a love which might even be defined as hate ("hate of all / That brings or holds in thrall . . . / The holy body and sacred soul of man") (3:299–300).

At this point, the poem has arrived at that period of Swinburne's development represented by *Songs before Sunrise* and *Erechtheus*. But the poem does not end here. Rather, it describes a confrontation with "Death," the fact of life that, the child had been taught, is natural, inevitable, acceptable, even the hero's crowning glory. Does the "wisdom" of the "grey" "foster-father" carry the poet through his crisis? It does not. Swinburne, like Hardy, although born too late to embrace any faith, was born too early and too much a child of faith to accept what he thought he had accepted, that is, the unmediated vision of the here and now.

The result is the return, the decadence, the autumnal attempt to relocate at least half of April, to relearn at least some form of faith to fit the mood of the age. This decadence, exactly as in some of Hardy's late poems and novels, inevitably involves a panicky feeling of metaphysical union with a horrible, monstrous, grotesque nightmare world of supernatural forces. The poet of "Thalassius" tells us that suddenly the "earth / Shook underfoot as toward some timeless birth, / Intolerable and inevitable," that "all / Heaven" blared forth "a noise of tempest and a light / That was not of the lightning; and a sound . . . / That was not of the thunder." "[A]nd with songs and cries"

> That sang and shrieked their soul out at the skies
> A shapeless earthly storm of shapes began
> From all ways round to move in on the man,
> Clamorous against him silent. . . .
>
> [3:305]

And, just as in Hardy's late novels and poems, the return also involves longings for escape into a dream of harmony with an immortal and divine world of things. Thalassius leaves Erigone, his earthy pantheress, and travels "Back to the grey sea-banks." (The fact that they are now grey, not glorious, is important.) He falls asleep and awakens into song, a perilously late romantic song that, no "less than when his veins first leapt for joy" (shades of

Blake's *Songs of Innocence*, Wordsworth's "My Heart Leapt Up," and Shelley's "Hymn to Intellectual Beauty"), sings "from the love and largess of old time" (3:308–9).

But the return is only half a return, for in becoming a "song," the poet tells us that he ceases to be a "singer," implying that the end of the poem, though a form of romantic vision, is only half romantic. For the pervasive "I" of romanticism, the strong personal presence of the romantic poet which stood strongly committed to its expansive or apocalyptic vision, has disappeared, giving us the exquisite garden of unearthly delights, but admitting that it is a garden forsaken of commitment. "Thalassius" is a decadent poem that illustrates the implications of decadence. It is a poem that implies that the resurrection of an old song, a birth song, however necessary the resurrection may be, is, at the same time, death for the singer. That is why, having first written songs of sunsets and sunrises, then paeans to the glory of day, Swinburne, as he enters his last period, writes autumnal songs between "sundown" and "moondawn" (3:311). The return, the decadence, implies at once reflected light and the coming of the singer's night. These are poems which, like "On the Cliffs," address the nightingale shrouded in darkness, a dim, aviary symbol of the power of song to subsume nature in the death-loving "dream [man] weaves him for shadow." The poet admits that he cannot accept mere joy and sorrow, grief and delight, that he cannot be the poet of reality who, in "Itylus," knew, suffered, and understood. On the contrary, he admits to the nightingale (who is at once God and death, Sappho and a vision of reality, himself and pure song, a real bird and the Keatsian sister misunderstood by the post-romantic nightingale of "Itylus") that "We were not marked for sorrow, thou nor I," nor "were we made, / To take delight and grief," "Assuaged by pleasures or by pains affrayed" (3:314–15).

In some of the greater lyrics of the poet's *Studies in Song* (1880), the barely repressed association of return and renunciation almost breaks into admission. Swinburne's meditation on tombs "By the North Sea," perhaps his greatest lyric and certainly a poem deserving of closer analysis than this study can afford, half admits, often through pun, that the faith in immortality, in a God in and beyond "Time and the sea," is a faith that will have to be carefully built over a residing skepticism. At its most despairing, the poem breaks down into a claim for the pitiful absurdity of all faith, as when it resolves Shelley's hopeful celebration of an "unpastured sea hungering for calm" (*Prometheus*, 3.2.49) with a description of just how "Time brings pasture to the sea." The disheartened poet explains in the sixth of the long lyric's seven meditations that, "Displaced, devoured, and desecrated / Now by Time's hands darkly disinterred,"

These poor dead that sleeping here awaited
    Long the archangel's re-creating word,
Closed about with roofs and walls high-gated
    Till the blast of judgment should be heard,

Naked, shamed, cast out of consecration,
    Corpse and coffin, yea the very graves, . . .
Desolate beyond man's desolation,
    Shrink and sink into the waste of waves.
                         [5:107]

In the earlier, fourth meditation of the poem, Swinburne had sounded more hopeful while speaking of what seems to be a group of seafarers. (The stanzas of "By the North Sea" are left so powerfully indistinct that any critical interpretation is at worst a vulgarization and at best a development—in the photographic sense—of a narrative line that Swinburne has only barely exposed.) These shipboard "folk" (5:97) had sung a sort of lyrical prayer to "The lord of the sea":

And their hearts are as harps that approve him
    And praise him as chords of a lyre
That were fain with their music to move him
      To meet their desire. . . .
                        [5:100–101]

The poem goes on to suggest that the songs of the faithful *did* move "his song," that the notion of a meaningful correspondence between internal and external powers which lies at the heart of Christianity, romanticism, or that hybrid "church of Blake and Shelley" *was* validated. For "The godhead of wind" did "descend through the darkness to grace them," did "encompass . . . their weakness," did inspire them ("with the blast of his breath"), did "bless them" with "the mouths of his thunders." But here puns serve to remove the singer from the song, for "grace" may be no more than a *coup de grâce* or death-stroke; the inspiration that comes with his ardently sought "breath" may be a wind that slams voyagers into fatal rocks (hence the pun on "encompass"—the godhead's "encompass[ing] . . . caress" may well throw their compass into fateful spin); as for the word "blessing," surely it puns on the French *blesser*, to wound.

And yet this poem, which almost certainly lies somewhere behind Thomas Hardy's "Channel Firing," like Hardy's poem manages to transcend despair in the music of its triumphant final movement. In a moving song to the "Sun, whereof all is beholden," the poem almost manages to find a form-giving, romantically revised Miltonic God of light (his height is one with depth, not beyond all height) in a surrounding, almost Shelleyan heaven ("From the depth of his dome deep-vaulted / Our father is lord of the day" [5:108]). But even here, through pun, image, poetic structure, and allusion, we see that the lyric is only half a triumph. To begin with, to say we are "beholden" to the sun is to imply, at the literal level of the pun, only that the sun illuminates and that we can see. Secondly, since the poem itself is our source of light, since it illuminates the world it envisions, there is, here as in so many of the *Studies in Song*, an implicit equation made between a poem and a god. Consequently, when we realize that Swinburne's sun god recalls Apollo, god of poetry or art, we see that Swinburne is admitting the possibility that whatever order the poem claims to have found in chaos it has really only found, that is, made, in itself. Only in the self-sufficient world of the bright, impeccably ordered *objet d'art* can Swinburne make the claim that the world is "never" "void" of form and of light (5:109). That is why "By the North Sea" is at once a song to its own light and, at the same time, a poem whose metapoetic image must be, as it is in Hardy's late romantic lyric, "The Darkling Thrush" (1900), an image of a growing gloom that makes *any* song and *any* light, including its own, seem bright:

> When the ways of the sun wax dimmer,
>   Wings flash through the dusk like beams;
> As the clouds in the lit sky glimmer,
>   The bird in the graveyard gleams. . . .
>
>   [5:89]

As a catch phrase, "graveyard gleams" is not an inappropriate description of Hardy's or Swinburne's winter words, for these are poems that venture forth into the darkness determined to make

light. In "A Nympholept," the poet, like a Tennysonian knight on
the grail quest, looks for moments of vision knowing that "any . . .
that hath sight of" the "might of a vision" would "straiten," his "lips
. . . close[d]" in death, "His heart . . . sealed as the voice of a
frost-bound stream" (6:128–29). The poem, then, begins by equating true vision with death, and, as it develops, makes no solid claim
for true vision. "My spirit or thine is it, breath of thy life or of
mine," the poet asks of the scene, or of Pan, or of the sun, "Which
fills my sense with a rapture that casts out fear?" (6:140). In "The
Lake of Gaube" (1904) Swinburne will respond to just such a
question with the admission that, in spite of Shelley and Wordsworth, "Deep silence" not "deep truth" awaits all our questions
and, therefore, "the glory / We dream of may be but a dream" of
our own making (6:287).

However full of serious questions, poems like "The Lake of
Gaube" or "A Nympholept" might seem to end on a note of
triumph. "The Terror that whispers in darkness . . . / The doubt
that speaks in silence . . . / Where are they?" the poet asks in "A
Nympholept." But one might answer that they are here, right here
in the last stanza of the poem. For this terror that whispers in
darkness, this doubt that speaks in silence is surely that very,
Satanic question the poet has just posed when he asked, "My spirit
or thine is it . . . / Which fills my sense with rapture?" Am I the
creator of the world that keeps me sane, articulate, alive? Has my
response to an unbearable world, a world uninfused by light,
power, and love, been to create *ex nihilo* a world where, because
there is nothing real to usurp me, I am that light and power, order
and love? The last lines of both poems are ambiguous, but they
almost answer such questions in the affirmative. "The Lake of
Gaube" ends on the word "fear," and the last line of "A Nympholept" revises Carlyle's claim that the mundane *is* divine and Hardy's
earlier, post-romantic assertion that the temporary is the all by
making a new equation that defines the return, the decadence, the
new "form of romanticism which is the mood of the age":

> nought is all. . . .

It is a new equation that Hardy, too, would come to affirm when,
in "A Two-Years Idyll" (1912), he refers to a magical, unpractical,
doomed summer romance, now lost in a past that was impatient for
something "larger, life fraught":

> "Nought" it was called . . .
> Yet, all the while, it upbore us like wings
>   Even in hours overcast:
> Aye, though this best thing of things,
>   "Nought" it was called!
>
> What seems it now?
> Lost: such beginning was all; . . .
> —A preface without any book,
> A trumpet uplipped, but no call;
> That seems it now.

The poems that D. H. Lawrence composed between 1901 and 1914 (and collected in *Love Poems and Others, Amores, New Poems*, and *Look! We Have Come Through!*), lyrics which Ezra Pound called "Pre-Raphaelitish slush,"[17] are poems which, in diction and sensibility, tone and meaning, betray their debt to Swinburne and Hardy. The problems of how to live and what to live for, how to write poems and what to write poems about, problems which had beset the two mentors in their *fin du siècle* creations, are precisely the concerns which give form to Lawrence's early works.

"The Wild Common" is identified by Lawrence as one of his very "earliest poems" and placed first in that 1928 edition of *Collected Poems* which, Lawrence tells us, is "arrange[d] . . . as far as possible, in . . . the order in which [the poems] were written."[18] The lyric initially depicts a nature which seems to reflect ("imitate") and even celebrate ("proclaim") some higher, eternal idea or order which flows through and beyond all things:

> The quick sparks on the gorse-bushes are leaping
> Little jets of sunlight texture imitating flame;
> Above them, exultant, the peewits are sweeping:
> They have triumphed o'er the ages, their screamings proclaim.

The pathetic fallacy, that tendency to "see everywhere the image" of one's "own mood" which the agnostic Victorians found so bothersome in the poems of their romantic predecessors (and which, for reasons of irony or, later, of romantic reconciliation, colors the world of their own poetry) is present everywhere in these opening lines. With the exception of the "mournful turf" the "common flaunts bravely." "King-cups surge to challenge the blossoming bushes" and a "lazy streamlet . . . wakes," "leaps, laughs, and gushes / Into a deep pond, an old sheep dip, / Dark, overgrown with willows."

The overgrown sheep dip recalls the gradual loss of a visionary sensibility through literary history, from the symbolic pastoral world of Spenser or Milton through Wordsworth's naturalized, internalized vistas and, finally, to the earthy, commercial, but somehow still timeless and sustaining pastoral world of Hardy's *Far from the Madding Crowd*. How will Lawrence bear the burden of the loss, of his own diminished inheritance? By questioning the existence of *anything* other than the physical stuff of the fleeting moment, by suggesting that all notions of soul or oversoul, theisms or pantheisms, are but insubstantial umbrages of that temporal substantiality which we have always (literally and figuratively) overlooked. "What if the waters ceased" and "I were gone?" Lawrence asks. "What is this thing that I look down upon?"

How it looks back, like a white dog to its master!
I on the bank all substance, my shadow all shadow
    looking up to me, looking back!. . .
And the white dog dances and quivers, I am holding
    his cord quite slack.

That realm of soul or spirit, idea or ideal, which the opening lines of the poem had seen reflected by the natural world here is seen as an empty shadow cast by man in his substance. (For Swinburne, "God" was the "shade cast by the soul of man"; Lawrence goes Swinburne one better, making the soul into the shade cast by the physical substance of man.)

But how splendid it is to be substance, here!
My shadow is neither here nor there; but I, I am
    royally here!
. . . .
Oh but the water loves me and folds me,
Plays with me, sways me, lifts me and sinks me,
    murmurs: Oh marvellous stuff!

The physical world, to be sure, still speaks to the poet, but now it speaks of its hereness, not its "triumph over the ages."

Lawrence, a post-Arnoldian "touchstone of caresses," uses the unmusical language of common speech ("But how splendid it is," "but I, I am royally here"), together with the rough, spontaneous diction that such a language implies ("spurting," "stuff," "blobs") and the playful wit common to conversation ("I am holding his cord quite slack"). He would seem to do so in order to assert that the shadow world of metaphysical speculation is a post-Cartesian dog, utterly enchained to its purely physical master, which, because of its absolute insubstantiality, could never exist independent of the physical life of the world, no matter how "slack" the cord is "held." This seems a world where poetic "elevation" would be impossible; where to transcend in vision is to overlook reality; where, because we physically feel, therefore, we are; where poetry will communicate solely through its own, rough physicality; where "songs" cannot exist apart from the "singer."

"The Wild Common" would seem to make such a proclamation, but in fact it does not. The poem compromises itself, in its final stanza, by singing that

> All that is right, all that is good, all that
>   is God takes substance! a rabbit lobs
> In confirmation, I hear sevenfold lark-songs pealing.

Having arrived at the poetic statement that substance is merely substance, poetry merely the textured record of its temporal substantiality, Lawrence now injects into the poem a quiet allusion to Philippians 4:8, a mention of God (oversoul to man's shadow soul, very shadow of very shadows), and a pun which implies that a sanctified nature responds "In confirmation" to man's imagination. The poet's thoughts, however we may explain them, find an echo in the "sevenfold" skylarks "pealing" out in sabbatical celebration of the holy life of things. If poetry reflects reality's palpable chaos, then figures of speech such as "pealing" or "confirmation," because they imply physical/metaphysical relations, may admit afterthoughts about spiritual and poetic liberation. They may even reveal that, like a dog, sheep, or shadow, it is not easy for a poet to break free, no matter how overgrown the pasture, no matter how loose the "cord" may feel. The poem, having opted for skepticism, now hastily builds a faith over skepticism. Having defined the nothingness of the aphysical realm of shadows, it would seem, at the end, to suggest that nothing is all.

This poetic indecisiveness, this tendency towards decadence, is implicit in every one of these early poems, even if only by virtue of the fact that Lawrence writes muscular poems declaring the death of what he believed to be an old and idealistic sensibility but does so using highly traditional, even ecclesiastical images and, in most cases, a rhyme scheme. Both are carefully arranged poetic orders that, given the poet's obvious attempts to fit poetic language to the world-view it espouses, amount to Lawrence's own version of the conditional mood, for they either declare the poet's uncertainty about the world-view, or the necessity of imposing artificial orders on dappled chaos, or both. The speaker of "Renascence," for instance, attempts to declare that he possesses the "apple" of an earthy knowledge that was never "forbidden," that he is therefore Adam to a new world happy with the here and now. He claims to be content, as lover, to learn only the "warm, dumb wisdom" of the "quickened . . . pulse," content, as poet, to record, not mystify, the swirling impressions of the moment. And yet the symmetry of the rhyme scheme, the sanctified liturgical colors, and an allusion to Meredith's "Love in the Valley" forced into biblical and Miltonic contexts would seem to contest the notion that a "dappled" valley, not one which is "purple and white," is all the poet wants or expresses, that he really believes a world of sex and of death, of the "sow . . . grabbing her litter / With snarling red jaws," to be "wider than Paradise."

This poetic division is immanent in poems like "Weeknight Service" and "Red Moon-Rise." The former lyric concludes with a kind of philosophical and aesthetic contradiction in terms. It remarks that, to the tune of country church bells calling the faithful to worship, "The wise old trees / Drop their leaves with a faint, sharp hiss of contempt." The personification (and the serpent image and the rhyme) all quietly suggest an intelligent natural order or presence which undercuts the scorn of the agnostic declaration. Similarly, the perfectly Swinburnian sound of the line declares its poet to be an agnostic but an agonized one. When Lawrence says "the damned bells cease, and we are exempt," the reader feels a tension (why damned? why exempt? doesn't exempt imply exemption from something?); when he describes parishioners entering church as "last ghosts lurch[ing] / Towards" their "cenotaph," we are mindful of Lawrence's agnosticism, but also of the agonized, transitional poetry of Swinburne and Hardy (lurching ghosts being Hardyesque, "the soul's cenotaph" being a purely Swinburnian concept, even phrase).[19] Even the word "cenotaph" manages to remind us of transcendence and resurrection (*kenos*) as it declares the church to be a tomb (*taphos*).

"Red Moon-Rise" struggles even more arduously to be free from faith in mere shadows. It decries not only the folly of faith in God but, like Hardy's poem, "The Mother Mourns," it also ridicules the hope that nature can be read, can be interpreted as if it were the "confirmation" of all dreams and the Original of all poems. "The open book of landscape" shall be read and interpreted "no more,"

> for the covers of darkness have shut upon
> Its figured pages, and sky and earth and all between
> are closed in one.

"Crushed between the covers, we close our eyes," Lawrence says, for this is a "night-time" that "makes us hide our eyes." The sensual poet of "Red Moon-Rise" claims to "drown" his "fear," claims to be utterly glad to be visionless. He couches his claim, however, in archaic, self-consciously literate, allusive, even mystical language that betrays the lingering fear to give up "vision" (both in the natural and supernatural sense) and become a poet of touch, of feeling, of linguistic spasm. "I am glad," he says,

> Glad as the Magi were when they saw the brow
> Of the hot-born infant bless the folly which had
> Led them thither to peace;
> for now I know
> The world within worlds is a womb, whence issues all
> The shapeliness that decks us here-below. . . .

Here there is a significant tension created by following "within" ("world within worlds") with "below" ("us here below"), by ending a poem about the necessity of visionlessness with apparent allusions to Matthew, Plato, Shelley, and Hardy's "The Unborn," by balancing free, asymmetrical poetic form with self-consciously artificial poetic diction made up of "thither"s and "whence"s, and by allowing an agnostic manifesto to rival the hope and the reverence of Hardy's "The Oxen." Lawrence wants to admit that the world is a blank not in focus with his fancies, but, in short, he is afraid. "Like a man in a boat on very clear, deep water, space frightens and confounds me," he says in his "Song of a Man Who is Not Loved." It is more pleasant, even if it is absurd, for Lawrence to escape into an imaginary world of song where

> I could convulse the heavens with my horror.
> I think I could alter the frame of things in my agony.

I think I could break the System with my heart.
I think, in my convulsion, the skies would break.
["Mutilation"]

If Lawrence's poetry is torn, philosophically and formally, between subservience to and revolt from belief in such notions as timelessness, soul, ideal, God, vision, natural supernaturalism, or transcendence, it is equally uncertain about that state of being which Victorians had simply come to call romantic love. The speaker of "Lightning" reminds us that romantic circuitry establishes interfluence at the cost of a terrible shock or jolt to individuality. The poem's critique of romantic mergence, however, is somewhat offset by its mood, which suggests that the speaker is being denied his thrill by a prude:

I leaned in the darkness to find her lips
    And claim her utterly in a kiss,
When the lightning flew across her face
And I saw her for the flaring space
    Of a second, like snow that slips
From a roof, inert with death, weeping "Not this! Not this!"

"Tease," a critique of that love which would open up souls as well as bodies, is similarly compromised, in this case by a playful, even affectionate tone. "I will give you all my keys, / You shall be my châtelaine," the speaker "teases,"

When I hear you jingling through
    All the chambers of my soul,
How I sit and laugh at you
    In your close housekeeping rôle!

Jealous of the smallest cover,
    Angry at the simplest door. . . .

In his poem longing for a "New Heaven and Earth," Lawrence realizes, as Clough realized in his "ἐπί λάτμῳ," that epipsychic love, or union of self and soul, is really little more than love of one's own self. "I was a lover, I kissed the woman I loved, / And God of horror, I was kissing also myself," the poet exclaims:

I was the God and the creation at once;
creator, I looked at my creation;
created, I looked at myself. . . .

Unlike a more prurient Clough, however, Lawrence does not find the self-copulative passion of romantic love to be a comical mistake. Rather, as he tells us in "Manifesto," it is a kind of love which makes a sham of our so-called liberty, democracy, and way of life. The romantic revolutionary ideal, Lawrence thinks, is perfectly at odds with and undermined by the romantic ideal of love. Until all lovers be "two and distinct," until they "shall have each" their "separate being," there can be no "pure existence, real liberty."

> Till then, we are confused, a mixture, unresolved,
>   unextricated one from the other.
> It is in pure, unutterable resolvedness, distinction
>   of being, that one is free. . . .

Other poems, however, notably "Mystery" and "Excursion Train," are not just less critical of the popular faith in romantic "mixing" and "merging," but they even seem to lapse into that very faith, or at least some artificial, purely poetic form of that faith, in the mystical oneness of souls in romantic love. The former lyric describes love's mystery in terms not unlike those Swinburne uses in "Laus Veneris" and Arnold in "The Strayed Reveller" to describe the painful but precious wine of temporary bliss. "Now I am all / One bowl of kisses," the lover proclaims, and in a moving hymn he begs and "cr[ies]" on bended knee that his "Most High" should "stoop" and "drink me up"

> That I may be
> Within your cup
> Like a mystery,
> Like wine that is still
> In ecstasy.
> Glimmering still
> In ecstacy
> Commingled wines
> Of you and me
> In one fulfil
> The mystery.

"Still," that favorite ambiguity of poets, belies a latent uncertainty in what seems otherwise a decidedly decadent poem. When the poet finds love "Like . . . wine that is still / In ecstasy," does he tell us that he has found the quiet, perfect, world-within-world of epipsychic love (still as a Chinese jar is still) or does the word betray the poet's knowledge that such love is a dream of the past and therefore that its belated attainment offers a fragile, vulnerable life in borrowed time (still unravished bride of quietness)?

Ambivalence is instinct to Lawrence, especially in his earlier poems. Though romantic love makes him "half substanceless," the poet of "Release" "cannot but cleave" to his "Helen." Like Swinburne's love-tortured Anactoria, the speaker of "Excursion Train" is half tortured, half deified by the romantic longing for impossible unity. "You hurt my heart-beat's privacy; / I wish I could put you away from me," the love "bitten" speaker declares, adding that he "suffocate[s] in this intimacy / In which I half love you." Having "longed for this night," now "every fibre of me cries in pain / To God to remove you!" "Excursion Train," not unlike many of Swinburne's and Hardy's love poems, first a "dream" quest of the "soul" for impossible ecstacy, then a protest against the impossibility of such transcendence, finally longs for the quiet wholeness of oblivion:

> Though surely my soul's best dream is still
> That a new night pouring down shall swill
> Us away in an utter sleep, until
>   We are one, smooth-rounded!

Lawrence's "Hymn to Priapus," in its title and through its Christian and pagan allusions, invokes Swinburne's "Hymn to Proserpine" and in sound, tone, and story seems to complete Hardy's "After the Club-Dance," in order to make an even more despairing (and decadent) comment upon the fated passing of the "soul's best dream" of love. With his beloved, Althaean mother dead, "underground / With her face upturned to mine, / And her mouth unclosed in a last long kiss / That ended her life and mine," the poet now "dance[s] at the Christmas party / . . . with a ripe, slack country lass" who,

> Sweet as an armful of wheat
> At threshing-time broken, was broken
> For me, and ah, it was sweet!

Feeling "Fulfilled" but also "alone" after his brief and anonymous tryst, the poet finds his mind wandering to her who "fares in the stark immortal / Fields of death." The allusions first to the eucharist ("was broken / For me"), then to Proserpine in the barren underworld, together with the title and the subject of two kinds of love, invoke Swinburne's great "Hymn" subtly to suggest that mere Priapian sex with a soft country lass seems as pale and grey after the mystery of that more profound and perfect union as the love of Christ seemed to Swinburne's mourner, born and raised a devotee, even a lover, of the old gods. (Lawrence uses the image of the mother here in at least two ways. Like Swinburne in *Atalanta* he employs incest as a metaphor for that near perfect commingling of identities which is the goal of romantic love. He also uses the mother to suggest that the "faithful" love he feels for her was an old way of love taught him in his youth which now, like her, is dead, buried, unattainable, whereas the "faithless" love of the country girl is a love in nature, in the moment, in the realm of the possible.) The poem thus completes "After the Club Dance," published in 1913, the probable year of composition for Lawrence's "Hymn." The country lass who speaks in Hardy's lyric, like her Lawrentian counterpart, walks home from a dance which turned into more, but, as Hardy would have it, in a different direction:

> The roadside elms pass by me, —
>   Why do I sink with shame
> When the birds a-perch there eye me?
>   They, too, have done the same!

Lawrence seems to realize, in "Excursion Train," in his grudging "Hymn to Priapus," and in his fine lyric entitled "Dreams Old and Nascent," that which his predecessors had so often realized in their own moments of vision. "The old dreams are beautiful, beloved, soft-toned, and sure," and yet they're "worn out, they hide no more the walls they stand before." The problem lies in liberating oneself from the shadow world of dreams when you've been taught all your life to believe, as Conrad's Stein believed, that "A man that is born falls into a dream like a man who falls into the sea."[20] "The whole wide world is interior now," Lawrence, a late-coming romantic who would be otherwise, complains. "We're all shut up" in "air" so "close and poisonous" that we "sleep / A sleep that is writhing stupor." It is, then, Lawrence admits, an age of "Restlessness," a time that prods the poet to dream, to decadence, to desire of death:

I will trail my hands again through the drenched,
   cold leaves . . .
Till at length they induce me to sleep, and to forget.

In many of Lawrence's poems discussed thus far, the shaping power of Swinburne and of Hardy can surely be felt. However, there are other poems that, although no more profoundly influenced (indeed, there may be an inverse relationship between degree of influence and blatancy of allusions), bear more literal witness to their Victorian (and occasionally romantic) inheritance. "Elysium" restates, rather literally, some of the terms of Hardy's "The Temporary the All." Having emerged from a dream of "Paradise" thanks to the sensual presence of a new Eve, Lawrence says that "She found the source of my subjection / To the All, and severed the connection." And the metrics, not to mention the theme, of "The Bride" are perfectly imitative of a pattern all but patented by Hardy:

My love looks like a girl to-night,
   But she is old.
The plaits that lie along her pillow
   Are not gold.

R. P. Blackmur said, in 1935, that some of Lawrence's earlier poems "are so strongly under the influence of . . . Hardy" that "there was very little room for Lawrence himself in the poems." He continues his argument by mentioning only two Hardy poems— and quoting a third—that he believes to be most influential.[21] Unfortunately, several excellent critics since Blackmur have followed his lead. Sandra Gilbert several times mentions, but never really describes, the considerable influence of Hardy, and Tom Marshall, in *The Psychic Mariner*, is often seeing connections between poems that I am now, I hope, beginning to trace.[22] Perhaps the greatest disappointment to anyone interested in Hardy's Lawrentian legacy has been an essay entitled "A Doggy Demos" and included in an otherwise energetic book by Donald Davie on *Thomas Hardy and British Poetry*. It never becomes clear just what Davie sees as Hardy's relationship to Lawrence, except that both poets are "confessional" and that "Bibbles," Lawrence's poem to a dog and against democratic sentimentality, "could be directed indeed against the Thomas Hardy who wrote poems to and for the Royal Society for the Prevention of Cruelty to Animals."[23]

Lawrence's debt to Hardy—as well as to Swinburne, whose profound influence has never before been described—runs considerably deeper than Davie lets on. Lawrence's early interest in writing folk ballads or dialect poems, an interest not unusual given his provincial upbringing but no doubt piqued by Swinburne's and Hardy's experiments with the ballad form, led him to write a number of folk monologues bearing more than a casual relationship to published Hardy poems. "Violets," for instance, composed between 1905 and 1911, offers a graveside comparison of the quality of an anonymous lover's grief with the more official bereavement of a dead man's family. In 1898, Hardy had published "She at His Funeral," a monologue spoken by a lover unknown to the family of the deceased:

> Unchanged my gown of garish dye,
> Though sable-sad is their attire;
> But they stand round with griefless eye,
> Whilst my regret consumes like fire!

"Monologue of a Mother" is still another poem that directly annexes Thomas Hardy (the narrative method is derivative of monologues like "The Trampwoman's Tragedy"; the presiding imagery is straight out of "Neutral Tones") and makes some indirect use of Swinburne's revision of Shelley's *Prometheus* in *Atalanta in Calydon* (Lawrence attempts to validate Swinburne's correction of the tense of Shelley's claim that "the hungry hours were hounds").

"Neutral Tones" had suggested the inevitability of time's triumph and the impermanence of all forms (imaginative, romantic, and natural) through a scene from the past where life seemed only "alive enough to have strength to die," where "grey . . . leaves" "fallen from an ash" are the only lingering reminders of burnt-out springtime hopes. Lawrence's maternal lover declares that, her last son departed, she "must fold [her] hands and turn" her "face to the fire":

> And watch my dead days fusing together in dross,
> Shape after shape, and scene after scene of my past
> Clotting to one dead mass in the sinking fire

Where ash on the dying coals grows swiftly, like
   heavy moss.

Later, when this same mother suggests that she is like a "hound pursuing" her son "Till he chafes at my crouching persistence," she seems to realize, as Althaea and Mrs. Yeobright did not, that to attempt to elude the hounds of time, her own fated loss, is to become her son's own fate, a kind of familial embodiment of the "hungry hours" of nature, first Shelley's, later Swinburne's, "mother of months."

In the poems Lawrence wrote during his affairs with Helen Corke, Louise Burrows, and Frieda Weekly (1909–12), he is even more obviously revealing his debts. Swinburne, in his "Ballad of Death," had buried his tears in "the place," the "tender interspace," where his Lady's "breast-flowers" are "cloven apart." In Lawrence's playfully irreverent "Song of a Man Who is Loved," we learn that it is a place that he, in his twentieth-century ballads of life, intends to annex for his own. In the off-balanced first line Lawrence literally makes his "home" between "two breasts":

Between her breasts is my home, between her breasts.
Three sides set on me chaos and bounce, but the
   fourth side rests
Sure on a haven of peace.

The "Ballad of Another Ophelia" appropriately invokes "The Triumph of Time" to speak of the loss of hope and of love to time:

Nothing now will ripen the bright green apples
Full of disappointment and of rain;
Brackish they will taste, of tears, when the
   yellow dapples
Of autumn tell the withered tale again.

The obsessed speaker of "Kisses on the Train," his heartbeat "bound, / Like a magnet's keeper" to the pulse of his beloved, sounds like the love-shackled speaker of "Laus Veneris." "And still as ever / The world went round," the speaker excitedly declares in Swinburnian tones, "My mouth on her pulsing / Throat was found, / And my breast to her beating / Breast was bound." And "Snap Dragon" relies equally heavily upon "Laus Veneris" and "Anactoria"; seeing the feet of a woman "press / The grass deep down with the royal burden of her," the lover first admits that "gladly" he would offer his "breast to the tread of her," then uses the flower to declare the agony of his lover's ache:

> I pressed the wretched, throttled flower between
> My fingers, till its head lay back, its fangs
> Poised at her. Like a weapon my hand was white
>   and keen,
> And I held the choked flower-serpent in its pangs
> Of mordant anguish, till she ceased to laugh,
> Until her pride's flag, smitten, cleaved down to
>   the staff.

In a fierce poem entitled "These Clever Women," Lawrence, like Swinburne in "Anactoria," sees the romantic desire for an impossible, perfect cleavage or mixture of soul and body to be the source of agony and pain, even a Godlike hatred and cruelty. As the beloved rejects the only "solution" possible of individual men and women, the sexual moment where identities are "Dissolved in the blood," and demands an epipsychic solution that the merely physical poet cannot bring about, he screams out,

> I would kiss you over the eyes till I kissed you blind . . .
> Then perhaps in the dark you'd get what you want to find:
> The solution that ever is much too deep for the mind. . . .

In "Lilies in the Fire" Lawrence speaks to this same lover, calling her first a "star called down to me to-night," a Shelleyan splendor turned to fragrance, then a more Hardyesque, "glistening toadstool shining here,"

> Among the crumpled beech-leaves, phosphorescent,
> My stack of lilies once white incandescent,
> My fallen star among the leaves. . . .

But the fall that the poet records (or perhaps precipitates), a fall from the high old ideal of stellar love to the naturalized purity of lily-love and, finally, to the unpetaled sliminess of the glistening woodland toadstool, is, again, a fall into love too Satanic, unholy, revisionary, to be accepted by a lover (or a world) grown grey with the breath of idealism:

You hold yourself all hard, as if my kisses
Hurt as I gave them; you put me away—

Nay, never, I put you away: yet each kiss hisses
Like soft hot ashes on my helpless clay.

This lovers' contest is one which goes on, as the somewhat vague dialogue form of "Lilies in the Fire" suggests, not only between lover and beloved but also within the superficially aggressive speaker. Beyond that, it is a division that obsesses the mind, flesh, and spirit of Lawrence, a poet raised on "high . . . old dreams . . . beautiful, beloved," now utterly "worn out." It is a division that gave power to Thomas Hardy's last novels for precisely the same reason: the conflict between Jude's earthiness and Sue's Shelleyan ethereality was a conflict within Jude and, beyond that, within Hardy himself. It is a conflict that, early and late, hurt Hardy into poetry, one so central to Lawrence's consciousness that, when he writes a poem about Jude and Sue, he might just as well be writing a dialogue of self and soul, a poem about the subject of all his poems: the struggles of the physical self to raze the temples and rape the divinities of the past and the soul's decadent resistance. I quote "And Jude the Obscure and His Beloved," taking a few small, illustrative liberties with the text:

SELF: Oh my God what a bitter shame,
                After all this time of patience and pain
                Still to answer me just the same,
                Still to say: "I want no flame
                To lick me up, but only the warm
                The steady glow."

SOUL: Oh heart
                Of love and beauty loose no more
                Your reptile flames of passion: store
                Your beauty in the casket of your soul. . . .
                For in the firing all my porcelain
                Would crack and shiver with keen pain,
                My ivory and idols split in twain,
                My temples broken, then I should remain
                A priestess execrated, full of stain.[24]

Lawrence did not write a great deal in prose about the aesthetic and spiritual proximity of Hardy and Swinburne to himself. If he had, we might suspect that their influence had not been profound, for it is with profound literary debts as it is with pecuniary, it seems neither pleasant nor wise to talk about them. Sometimes Lawrence reveals his indebtedness through his own tastes. His public adoration of Whitman, for example, is a tacit, private adoration .of Swinburne and of his influential poem "To Walt Whitman in America," both of which championed Whitman for revolutionary political, social, and sexual principles very nearly akin to Swinburne's own. The more direct remarks that Lawrence makes about Swinburne and Hardy in essays and in letters tend to be both more copious about and complimentary to the grandfatherly Swinburne, a fact which would seem to be in accord with Lawrence's tendency to scream out allusions to Swinburne in his poetry and to make lesser, quieter, and, especially in the case of his fiction and later poetry, more substantial use of Thomas Hardy, his spiritual and aesthetic parent.

When Lawrence discusses Hardy at all, he usually attacks him for what Lawrence sees as his pathetic compromises with Laws, metaphysical and aesthetic. Lawrence, who finds in all nineteenth-century writers a tension between what he calls "Love" (which might loosely be defined as spiritual or imaginative will or aspiration) and "Law" (something like self-repression, -restriction, -limitation, or -restraint), says that the agonizing failure of Hardy's work is that it declares "There is no reconciliation between Love and the Law. . . . The spirit of Love must always succumb before the blind, stupid, but overwhelming power of the Law."[25] In a 1912 review of *Georgian Poetry*, an anthology in which his own poetry appears, he half-praises Hardy for being an agent of the "age of demolition," for realizing that "faith and belief and the temple must be broken." But Hardy, who ended up "demolishing our faith in our own endeavor," became one of our *fin du siècle* "nihilists," Lawrence says, one of "the intellectual hopeless people" who "represent the dream we are waking from. It was a dream of demolition," Lawrence goes on to say. "Everything was taken from us. And now our lungs are full of new air, and our eyes see that it is morning, but we have not forgotten the terror of the night . . . and the anguish of it leaves us rather eager."[26]

Swinburne, to be sure, is occasionally attacked in these very terms. At first complimenting his precursor—and, indirectly, himself—for making great "concession to the body, so that the poetry becomes almost a sensation," he goes on to twist what is, for the most part, inaccurate praise into criticism, thus offering an erroneous critique of Swinburne and an accurate, if subconscious, assessment of his own triumphs and limitations. I use italics to suggest that moment at which the critique of Swinburne swerves into profound self-analysis:

> So that in Swinburne . . . we find continual adherence to the body, to the Rose, to the Flesh, the physical in everything, in the sea, in the marshes; there is an overbalance in the favour of Supreme Law; Love is not Love, but passion, part of the Law; there is no Love, there is only Supreme Law. And *the poet sings the Supreme Law to gain rebalance in himself, for he hovers always on the edge of death, of Not-Being, he is always out of reach of the Law, bodiless, in the faintness of Love that has triumphed and denied the Law, in the dread of an over-developed, over-sensitive soul which exists always on the point of dissolution from the body.*
> But he is not divided against himself.[27]

Lawrence's associations with Swinburne, of course, pre-date the above-quoted critique (which appears, of all places, in the 1914 *Study of Thomas Hardy*) by at least twelve years. Jessie Chambers, Lawrence's Muriel, identifies Swinburne, along with Hardy and all the romantics (plus Whitman, Meredith, Tennyson, Browning, Thompson, and Baudelaire), as the authors Lawrence read most frequently and passionately during their tempestuous six-year friendship, 1902–8.[28] And Helen Corke, with whom the poet had an affair between 1909 and 1912, recalls Lawrence reading Swinburne out loud to her, a habit he evidently imposed upon others as well, for Mrs. Ivor Vinogradoff, remembering his visit to Gariston in 1915, says that Lawrence insisted that "he read poetry aloud to us, mostly Swinburne," and a year later, Lawrence writes in a letter to Barbara Low admitting that, wherever he goes, he reads "Swinburne . . . in a loud and declamatory voice—it gives me great satisfaction."[29]

In letters written in 1911 to Louise Burrows, third light in Lawrence's distant romantic heaven, he had quoted "The Garden of Proserpine" and spoken of "Tristram of Lyonesse" ("Some parts of it are very fine," other "parts . . . are barren to excess"), and by 1916, several years after his marriage to Frieda, his affection for

Swinburne had increased in inverse proportion to his affection for Louise. I quote from two letters to Barbara Low:

> And if you see Mrs. Eder, do ask her if she could send the Swinburne Frieda left at her house at Christmas. I love to read him. . . .
>
> You sent atlases and Swinburne—then the cake and sweets Frieda ordered. This is [a] most surprising array. . . . I will have Swinburne and Shelley and Herodotus and Flaubert: just the four, round the round table in the tower. . . . Thank you very much indeed for the Swinburne. I lie in bed and read him, and he moves me very deeply. The pure realisation in him is something to reverence: he is very like Shelley, full of philosophical spiritual realisation and revelation. He is a great revealer, very great. I put him with Shelley as our greatest poet. He is the last fiery spirit among us. . . . There was more powerful rushing flame of life in him than in all the heroes rolled together. One day I shall buy all his books. I am very glad to have these poems always by me.[30]

Hardy, unlike Swinburne, is never called "our greatest poet" by Lawrence, nor is he ever described as any sort of hero. And yet Hardy was the father of Lawrence's aesthetic and philosophy, the one force that, repressive only by its anteriority, nearly liberated Lawrence from the prison of his own tortured selfhood.

Debtor's Prison

Swinburne, Hardy, Lawrence, and the Burden of Belief

7

In 1914, while in a deep depression, D. H. Lawrence was struggling to write a *Study of Thomas Hardy*. In that book, which was finished the same year, well over a decade before its subject's death, but which was first published in its entirety in 1936, Lawrence complains that the "tragedy of Hardy" is "always the same":

> the tragedy of those who, more or less pioneers, have died in the wilderness. . . . This is the theme of novel after novel: remain quite within the convention, and you are good, safe, and happy in the long run . . . : or, on the other hand, be passionate, individual, wilful, you will find the security of the convention a walled prison, you will escape, and you will die, either of your own lack of strength to bear the isolation and the exposure, or by direct revenge from the community. . . .[1]

The *Study of Thomas Hardy*, of course, may be of dubious value to an inquiry into Lawrence's deep-seated or subconscious assessment of Hardy's limitations or value. Nevertheless, an examination of his own first novel, *The White Peacock* (1911), does suggest that Lawrence, through the forms of his own fiction, consciously or perhaps subconsciously, attempts to correct his mentor on this issue, that is, endeavors to demonstrate that in passionate, willful individuality lies the only hope for survival and that the dutiful, responsible, careful, and conventional life is a sure road to spiritual, often even physical, death.

One of the weaknesses (and there are many) of the novel is that it never really transcends its most basic purpose, that is, to be a Hardy novel that shows Hardy was wrong. The character who perhaps stands closest to the novel's center of interest, George Saxton—shepherd, dairy hand, farmer, thresher, and orchardist— is little more than a reductive composite of Gabriel Oak, Diggory Venn (who was originally a dairyman), Donald Farfrae, and Giles Winterborne, a caricature or trivialization of that "conventional" Hardy hero. His "passion," Lawrence says, was "bound down by his caution and self-instinct."[2] George Saxton is "a young farmer, stoutly built, brown eyed, with naturally fair skin burned dark and freckled in patches" (p. 1). He is a fellow of "lazy curiosity" (p. 1) who says things like "I shan't mow these fields any more. . . . But merely to have mown them is worth having lived for" (p. 246), of whom the narrator, Cyril Beardsall, says "Your life is nothing else but a doss. I shall laugh when somebody jerks you awake" (p. 2).

In a certain sense of the word which the more effete (and more Lawrentian) Cyril might not understand, George Saxton is more than awake, for this farmer who drawls in country dialect is as practical and resourceful as he is humble, unassuming, and provincial. When a dog attacks a flock of sheep, George (which happened to be the name of Gabriel Oak's older, cleverer, and more trustworthy shepherd dog) is first to "burst into sight pursuing. Directly, there was the bang, bang of a gun" (p. 75). Like Oak, Diggory Venn, and Giles Winterborne, Farmer Saxton seems to have great trouble romancing (let alone marrying) the coquettish woman he loves (p. 214) who, in turn, like Bathsheba, Thomasin, and Grace Melbury, is in the meantime unfortunately but suc-cessfully pursued by and engaged to a more dashing, if less deserving, suitor. Like Oak and Farfrae, George Saxton thinks of putting his past behind him by journeying to the Americas to set up a farm of his own, but, like Hardy's duo, George is prevented from having to make any such major change in environment by circumstance, together with no small amount of characteristic inertia.

Lawrence not only touches on the characterizing details of George's originals—Oak, Venn, Farfrae, and Winterborne—but he even manages to use the scenes of his novel to make him the perfect anti-type to his Hardyan opposites, namely, those more yearning intellectual idealists, Angel and Jude, and that always unsatisfied Faustian, Michael Henchard. Lawrence fashions George into

Michael Henchard's opposite by having him get drunk in a tavern and, suddenly and unexpectedly, propose marriage to a "quaint" and "quite uneducated" woman (p. 274), thereby, in a moment of inebriation and with a "voice . . . husky and strangulated with excitement," happily committing himself to a life which promises to be humdrum at best. "You know," he says to Cyril afterwards, "She—She's a clinker" (p. 156). When he finally marries this "crude . . . barmaid," Meg, George resigns himself to a life similar to the one Angel Clare may well have avoided, namely a life working for his provincial in-laws and tending to a family "milk business" (pp. 274, 276). And, unlike Jude, who, because he cannot bear to hear the sharp cries of a mangled rabbit caught in a trap, puts the animal out of its misery, Lawrence's Farmer Saxton is expert at chasing rabbits in the corn stubble, falling on them, cuffing them to death (p. 56).

Lettie Beardsall, sister of the character who supplies the novel's narrative and the quintessence of the nearly always unsatisfied (and often cruel) romantic heroine of Hardy's fiction, objects, perhaps too much, to George's earthy hunting instincts. "I think a man is horrible," she says in the presence of George and of Leslie, her more wealthy, educated, and pale fiancé, "who can tear the head off a little mite of a thing like a rabbit, after running it in torture over a field." It is a remark that her intended, no harborer of animal instincts himself, is nevertheless unwilling to allow her. " 'Why, women are cruel enough,' said Leslie, with a glance at Lettie. 'Yes,' he continued, 'they're cruel enough in their own way' " (p. 59).

Lettie, who happens to be the woman George spends his life admiring from a distance, is Eustacia, Bathsheba, Elfride, Grace Melbury and, at times, even Sue Bridehead, rolled into one. Here is a woman who would, like Hardy's romantic heroines, shape the world according to the dictates of her own fancy and then, because she had what she longed for, become dissatisfied. "I would shape things—oh, wouldn't I have my own way!" Lettie exclaims, admitting later that, as for the world she would shape, she wouldn't "want it particularly—when" she'd "got it" (p. 232). She is the epitome of emotional and spiritual vacillation, for she is one who wants all the world to conform to her own romantic hopes and dreams and then, when it doesn't, she finds her own disappointment written in every detail she sees. "We had lived between the woods and the water all our lives," Cyril says, and she had sought the bright notes in everything. She seemed to hear the water laughing, and the leaves tittering and giggling like young girls; the aspen fluttered like the draperies of a flirt, and the sound of the wood-pigeons was almost foolish in its senti-mentality.

Lately, however, she had noticed again the cruel pitiful crying of a hedgehog caught in a gin, and she had noticed the traps for the fierce little murderers, traps walled in with a small fence of fir, and baited with the guts of a killed rabbit.

[p. 50]

Like so many of Hardy's more pouting, petulant heroines, Lettie defines love as "want[ing]" something you "can't have" (p. 21). When Leslie Tempest is all affection, she couldn't be less interested in him, and, therefore, looks in the direction of George (who is, for the most part, bashfully pawing the ground and looking the other way). But when Leslie, understandably, turns his attentions to the likes of Margaret Raymond, Lettie is all eagerness and desire, at least until Leslie proposes, at which point she demurs:

"Oh, wait till Christmas—till I am twenty-one."
"Nearly three months! Why on earth—!"
"It will make no difference. I shall be able to choose thee of my own free choice then". . . .
"What are you making so many words about? You don't know now, do you?"
"No—that I don't."

[p. 96]

Lawrence's characterization of Lettie is, superficially as well as basically, reminiscent of Hardy's characterization of his own bored and unsatisfied women. Like Hardy, Lawrence manages to make his heroine all lips and hair (these were practically the only visible aspects of Eustacia Vye's anatomy) and, like Hardy, Lawrence makes them into sensuous symbols of their owner's paradoxical mixture of wildness and ethereality. "Twisting a curl round his finger," Leslie says to Lettie, "Look how fond your hair is of me," only to have Lettie respond that her hair "is like me—it won't be kept in bounds" (p. 94). To Leslie's retort that he desires to "feel" his "arms full of" her, to "touch that red mouth," Lettie piques her ardent lover with a reminder that the boundlessness to which she has referred is no mere sexual liberation: "I'm afraid," she says with a sigh, "you'll never sing hymns with me in heaven" (p. 95).

Leslie, no dynamo of worldly passion and power himself, is nonetheless piqued by the inexhaustible discontent of his romantic *inamorata*, tiring especially of her etherealized brand of love-making. She likes to "Suppose" them "two angels," or to think of herself as the "Blessed Damosel," her lover the poor mortal listening below to her "fragrant prayers—that your thin soul might mount up." To which Leslie, who when frustrated calls her his "Atalanta," responds: "Hang thin souls, Lettie! I'm not one of your souly sort. I can't stand Pre-Raphaelites" (pp. 94–95).

However Atalantan and Pre-Raphaelite, however "proud, scornful, difficult to please" Lettie may be, her disappointed suitor is certainly not a character with whom Lawrence sympathizes in the novel (indeed, he manages to mangle Leslie through an automobile accident coincidental enough to earn Thomas Hardy's grudging approval.) Neither is Lettie Beardsall conceived by Lawrence as an ineffectual angel, a restless fool, or a Satanic overreacher who, in Hardy's words, was that kind of "elevated . . . soul" so "dangerous to the commonwealth" (*The Return of the Native*, 1:158). The fact of the matter is, the *Study of Thomas Hardy* tells us that Lawrence preferred the always restless and never satisfied heroes and heroines of Hardy's fiction to the Oaks and the Farfraes, the Venns and the Winterbornes. They—Elfride, Troy, Boldwood, Wildeve, Eustacia, Henchard, Fitzpiers, Felice Charmond, and Jude—are among the characters Lawrence finds full of raw, untamed life. These are the men and women who, in Lawrence's words, "are always twisting suddenly out of bud and taking a wild flight into flower, always shooting suddenly out of a tight convention . . . into something quite madly personal. . . . They are people each with a real, vital, potential self . . . and this self suddenly bursts the shell of manner and convention and commonplace opinion and acts independently, absurdly, without mental knowledge or acquiescence" (p. 410).

What *The White Peacock* suggests, then, is the failure of Hardy's novels to marry what Lawrence calls "Love" with "Law." Hardy, Lawrence complains, always leaves his lively imaginative men and women to die in the wilderness even as he permits his practical, resourceful types to strangle in the clutches of "tight convention," never allowing one to inform the other, never realizing that passionate willfulness is as necessary to survival as survival is for passionate willfulness. This is the purpose of the failed marriage in

The White Peacock, the always expected but never consummated union of passionate, willful Lettie and tight, conventional George, the union which would have reorganized Hardy's fiction, consummating the union of Angel and Tess, marrying Giles to Grace, Henchard to Lucetta, Eustacia to Diggory, and Bathsheba to Oak *before* she had to learn all those numbing lessons about not aiming too high, not feeling too much, and not rejecting all the humdrum that life throws in your path.

So why doesn't Lawrence fully revise Hardy, marrying the unmarried, turning the consummation of tragedy (for Lawrence would call even *Far from the Madding Crowd* a tragedy of human spirit) into the consummation of marriage, the marriage of "Love and Law"? Because Lawrence, as a young man, like Hardy before him, is anxious and, consequently, didactic: before he can write his own fiction he must first write a novel showing why Hardy's novels went wrong, thus convincing himself of the need of that which he fears may be utterly redundant and thus unnecessary—more novels by D. H. Lawrence.

That is why *The White Peacock* attempts to turn inside out novels like *A Pair of Blue Eyes*, *Far from the Madding Crowd*, *The Return of the Native*, *The Mayor of Casterbridge*, and *The Woodlanders* by making the humble, controlled, practical, and adaptive character the one who is, through his unassuming drudgery, dangerous to the commonwealth and, ultimately, the spiritual destroyer of his counterpart. Through contrived, almost painful scenes, Lawrence dramatizes the destructive ineffectuality not of the angelic romantic but of the humble, muted, post-romantic hero. Just after Lettie has finally acquiesced in Leslie's marriage proposal, her fiancé, less than potent, is symbolically emasculated in the automobile accident. That evening, when Cyril goes to see George, "he too" is "very despondent":

> "It's no good now," said I. "You should have insisted and
> made your own destiny."
> "Yes—perhaps so," he drawled. . . .
> "I would have had her—she'd have been glad if you'd done as
> you wanted with her. She won't leave him till he's strong, and
> he'll marry her before then. You should have had the courage to
> risk yourself. . . ."
> "But—" he began, not looking up; and I laughed at him.
> [p. 214]

Derision is, indeed, called for. George says things like "I don't see . . . why we can't" be "free" (p. 229), but even in the wake of Cyril's hint (and two even stronger ones from Lettie herself) he cannot transcend his own provincial reticence enough to propose marriage. Before marrying Leslie, Lettie gives George one last chance by playing his role and trying to jolt him into dissatisfaction and, consequently, into life. Picking wild flowers and watching larks wheeling over a meadow, she says, "I wish we" could be "free like that":

> "Why can't you?" he asked.
> "You know we can't . . . ," she replied, and her whole soul challenged him. "We have to consider things" she added. He dropped his head. He was afraid to make the struggle, to rouse himself to decide the question. . . . She turned away and went kicking through . . . the blossoms. . . .
>
> [p. 229]

In Hardy's *Far from the Madding Crowd,* Oak had won his beloved Bathsheba in a scene just such as this one. " 'Bathsheba,' " Oak had said, " 'If only I knew one thing—whether you would allow me to love you and win you and marry you after all—If only I knew that!' "

> "But you never will know," she murmured. . . ." Because you never ask."
> "Oh—Oh!" said Gabriel with a low laugh of joyousness. "My own dear—"
>
> [2:330–31]

George's reticence pays no such dividends. Shortly before her wedding, when Lettie takes George "into the wood" and says things like "If you were a faun, I would put guelder roses round your hair" and "we're netted down here; if we were free in the winds—Ah!" George's plea, "don't go—don't go away," comes too late to establish union. " 'No, my dear, no,' " Lettie rejoins,

> "The threads of my life were untwined; they drifted about like floating threads of gossamer; and you didn't put out your hand to take them and twist them up into the chord with yours."
>
> [pp. 235–36]

Whereas Oak, Venn, and Elizabeth-Jane Henchard won their lovers by watching, waiting, and even promoting a rival out of respect for the wishes of their beloved, George Saxton condemns Lettie to the stultifying life of a society matron and himself to the life of an alcoholic who eventually loses his business and whose drunken melancholy—later, irascibility—horribly victimizes his wife and family.

Thus, through George, Lawrence affords himself one last argument with *The Mayor of Casterbridge*, for Saxton's Henchardian end is the direct result of being too little of a Henchard, of lacking that dissatisfaction, imagination, impulsiveness, willfulness, and irascible assertiveness that ruined Henchard but which might have saved George from disaster. (Even Saxton's short-lived immersion in politics revises Henchard's political career, for in Lawrence's novel, politics serves as a symptom of George's loss of self-respect, his irresponsibility, and his relative uselessness to the community in which he lives!) Hardy's tragedies, as Lawrence sees them, are caused by "passionate, individual, wilful" characters who "dare" to "escape" from "convention." *The White Peacock*, Lawrence's denial of Hardy's fiction, suggests that tragedy results when a man or woman is "afraid . . . to dare to play with life" (p. 269).

There are ways, of course, in which Lawrence attempts to make his novel more than an illustration of Hardy's mistakes. For one thing, he posits Cyril Beardsall as an almost transparent narrator and, by allowing him to overhear conversations to which he was not party, to know facts and situations of which he could not possibly be aware, and to introduce us, *via* indirect discourse, to all the thoughts and feelings of all the other characters, makes him into hardly less than an omniscient author who, as he reveals the lessons implicit in the plot he sees unfolding (or unfolds), becomes that sadder but wiser author who survives, physically and spiritually, who unites those principles of Love and Law which Hardy merely contained and who will go on to be D. H. Lawrence, author of *Women in Love, The Rainbow, Lady Chatterly's Lover*.

But it is not quite so simple as this. For one thing, Cyril is attracted to George Saxton's sister, Emily, who is as much the spiritual sister of his own sister, Lettie, as he is the spiritual brother of Emily's brother, George. Cyril, who tells us that Emily values the "exhilarating, almost intoxicating" feeling of "freedom" and doesn't want to "have to be anything to anybody, but just to please [her]self," seems occasionally uncomfortable with what he calls "the little woman's wildness" (pp. 284–85, 293). And, though he tells us that her engagement to Tom Renshaw comes as a completely unexpected and disappointing surprise, it seems fair to say that Cyril, to the extent that he is authorial, brings Emily and Tom together, as by coincidence, because he cannot marry her, that is to say, he has not yet found, in himself, anything as good as, let alone superior to, Hardy's conventional, practical, and provincial hero. For Tom is a farmer, "exceedingly manly: that is to say he did not dream of questioning or analysing anything. . . . He did not imagine that anything could be other than just what it appeared to be:—and with this appearance, he was quite content. He looked up to Emily as one wiser, nobler, nearer to God than himself" (p. 337). Emily, like Bathsheba before her, is somehow liberated, through marriage to this simple and satisfied man, from what she thought was liberty into that truer freedom that Cyril, or Lawrence, comes to find in the shackles of domesticity. "Emily," Cyril says, "in her full-blooded beauty was at home." She "had at last found her place, and had escaped from the torture of . . . modern life. She was making a pie, and the flour was white on her brown arms. . . . I was quiet, subdued before her" (p. 349).

It is strange, this ending. After writing a novel that attacks the inadequacy, the ineffectuality, of one quintessentially Hardyan hero, the author suddenly and *ex nihilo* creates another one and quickly gives to him the woman who, from the beginning, had seemed the hand-picked mate for his own *persona* in the fiction, Cyril Beardsall.[3] Having written a novel that screams out in defiance against Hardy's fiction, especially *Far from the Madding Crowd*, Lawrence maneuvers his ending in such a way that *The White Peacock* very nearly *becomes Far from the Madding Crowd*. (He would later recapitulate in life what he had done in this fiction; in his dying months he proclaimed, evidently for the first time, *Far from the Madding Crowd* to be one of his very favorite novels.)[4] The final scene of *The White Peacock* pictures Tom Renshaw, standing outlined against the sky, deftly stacking corn in "an exquisite, subtle rhythm" (p. 354). By so ending his first work, Lawrence subconsciously makes himself no more (and hopes that we will think him no less) than Thomas Hardy.

This super-sublimation of Hardyan aspiration, even imitation, in a book which attempts to deny the validity of Hardy's fiction is apparent not only in the novel's conclusion but also in the blatant unfairness of its anti-Hardyan discourse. For one thing, Lawrence must make himself utterly oblivious to those clear transitions in Hardy's aesthetic, philosophy, and sensibility (some of which have been outlined in this study) to be able to suggest that Hardy is always the "poet of the Law," that he always degrades passionate, willful men and women even as he teaches us that if we "remain quite within the convention" and always strive to be "good, safe, and happy," we will survive in security. As early as *The Return of the Native*, Hardy seems to be elevating his romantic protagonist at the expense of the persevering commoner (Venn) and the other character who learns the value of humble contentment (Clym). By the time of *The Mayor of Casterbridge*, he seems so unsure about the relative values of "Love" and "Law" that we wonder if we know who his hero is, who is *the* Mayor of Casterbridge elevated to titular prominence. *The Woodlanders* annihilates the Oakian Giles Winterborne and allows Faustian Fitzpiers to survive (thus Lawrence's statement that Hardy "always" makes his eccentrics die in the wilderness and "always" allows his more practical, conventional commoners to survive is utterly untrue), and *Tess* and *Jude* defy all Lawrence's categories, for their four protagonists (Tess, Angel, Jude, and Sue) are equally and perfectly divided against themselves with regard to Love and Law, willfulness and conventionality, and the two common, earthy characters who are their monolithically sensual foils (Alec and Arabella) are more convincingly hideous than human.

But such a profoundly unfair, even myopic, interpretation of a parent as Lawrence dares to purvey through *The White Peacock* is part and parcel of adolescent life. Lawrence, after all, does no worse by Hardy than Hardy had done by Wordsworth when he had objected, in *Tess*, to that babe in the woods who told us of "Nature's holy plan," by Shelley or Keats when he called Boldwood's love a "too unhappy happiness" and Angel Clare's unpractical idealisms "angelic" and therefore "Shelleyan," than he did by his romantic predecessors as a group when he labeled Wildeve "the Rousseau of Egdon," Fitzpiers a "Transcendentalist," and Troy the epitome of "Romanticism." What one writer does to his predecessors, of course, often reveals more about himself than it does about his subject or subjects. In two letters written in 1914, Lawrence says as much himself. "My book about Thomas Hardy," he writes to J. B. Pinker on 5 September, "will be about anything but Thomas Hardy, I am afraid—queer stuff—but not bad."[5] And in a letter to Amy Lowell dated 14 December he goes one step further. "My book on Thomas Hardy," he says, "has turned out as a sort of Story of My Heart."[6]

Many critics have pointed out the failures of Lawrence's first novelistic effort, and most have attempted to account for the novel's shortcomings. Julian Moynihan has insisted that the novel is a young author's almost autobiographical record of his own spiritual and psychological confusion. "The measure of the unsuccess of *The White Peacock*," Moynihan remarks, "is precisely the measure of the writer's emotional insecurity at the beginning of his career."[7] F. R. Leavis doesn't disagree with Moynihan's claim that the work is unsuccessful; Leavis, in his own study of *D. H. Lawrence: Novelist*, says that *The White Peacock* is "painfully callow." And he agrees that the book suffers because its author does not make something orderly of his own internal turmoil. Lawrence, Leavis claims, had "no certain grasp of his emotional purpose" while writing *The White Peacock*. But whereas Moynihan believes that Lawrence's weak grasp of "emotional purpose" is due to adolescent chemistry, Leavis sees it as the result of an attempt, on Lawrence's part, to shy *away* from autobiography and to write a "serious," even abstract, novel. The young author of *The White Peacock*, according to Leavis, "is too much preoccupied with writing a novel: he feels obliged to transpose his experience into 'literature' . . . and doesn't deal directly with what is at the centre of his own emotional life."[8] Graham Hough, in *The Dark Sun*, would have it both ways. On one hand he sees the novel as "autobiography," Cyril as Lawrence's "mouthpiece," and the plot as an all too accurate history of "the period which *Sons and Lovers* describes" more imaginatively and with greater control. On the other hand, however, he would convince us that *The White Peacock* is very nearly *pastiche*. "The presiding genius at the birth of *The White Peacock*," Hough insists, was "George Eliot."[9]

My own reading of the novel leads me to offer a synthesis of these various views. I cannot agree fully with Moynihan when he states that the "country settings" and homespun "figures" of *The White Peacock* are "taken directly from the pastoral northern slope of Lawrence's . . . home valley";[10] I believe them to be taken just as directly from Hardy's Wessex country. Yet my disagreements with Moynihan are not absolute. With Leavis, I would have to see

Lawrence's failures arising from a preoccupation with "literature," and yet I cannot agree that Lawrence does not write out of "his emotional life" in *The White Peacock*. Moynihan is correct in seeing "emotional insecurity" at the core of the novel; I would add, however, that the barely repressed emotional distress arises out of Lawrence's insecurity as a writer, not as a young man. So while I would reject Graham Hough's claim that the novel fails because it is a scenes-of-my-childhood autobiography, I concur with his strong sense of the book as a new generation of novel with a "genius" of the past "presiding" over its birth. I cannot reject the notion that George Eliot strongly influenced Lawrence, since I have already seen her as a formative power over several of Hardy's influential novels. If by "presiding genius at the birth of *The White Peacock*" Hough means that Eliot was Lawrence's midwife, then I am perfectly content. But Thomas Hardy, quite clearly, was the unnamed father.

The same spectrum of opinions which surrounds *The White Peacock* confuses our view of *The Rainbow*. At one end are critics like George H. Ford, who would have it that *The Rainbow* is a "myth" about modern "emancipation"—from ignorance, from religious forms, and from provincial social patterns.[11] At the other end of the spectrum is the view of Middleton Murray (and even H. M. Daleski) that the novel recounts some kind of "history of Lawrence's . . . sexual failure."[12] Hough, by contrast, contends that *The Rainbow* is "the least autobiographical of Lawrence's major novels," and yet his own analysis would argue that the novel is a deeply personal creation. Lawrence's "need," in *The Rainbow*, is "no longer to come to terms with a pressing personal imbroglio: it is rather to clarify and develop a philosophy of life which is present only in embryo."[13]

The Rainbow, from this study's point of view, is a highly personal novel, especially in its later chapters. It is personal, however, not so much because some of Ursula Brangwen's experiences or philosophies parallel Lawrence's own but, rather, because her position as a young artist whose independence is threatened by a figure who would marry her to his ancient lineage, is a position shared by Lawrence. *The Rainbow* is, indeed, an embryo, but one which grows out of a literary imbroglio. It is an autobiography and myth—a myth about an emancipation which, because all embryos are born of a past, can never quite occur, an autobiography in a new sense of the word. *The Rainbow* relates its own history. Through its saga of families and generations, the novel traces its own line of descent from its romantic grandparents (Tom and Lydia) through an incestuous, agonized relationship between its parents (Swinburne and Hardy, sublimated in Will and Anna), accounting for its own beliefs, doubts, and divisions through self-analysis (grandchild Ursula). *The Rainbow* is, in every possible sense of Freud's term, a family romance.

The novel declares from the outset that its setting is in the romantic nature revised by Thomas Hardy, that world in which nature's communions and conversations with man have been literally translated into intercourse. Making subliminal use of the weighty "udders ponderous" as "sandbags" in *Tess* (1:211), the almost sensual scene of the sheep shearing in *Far from the Madding Crowd* (and specifically alluding to the "throbs" of nature's "body," her "common pulse" [*Madding Crowd*, 1:13]), the "teeming . . . life" of "loving, hating, coupling, parting" depicted in *Jude* (p. 144), and the lyrical depiction of the rising of "saps in noiseless streams" in *Tess* (1:257), Lawrence says, of the ancient Brangwen family, that

> . . . heaven and earth was teeming around them, and how
> should this cease? They felt the rush of the sap in spring. . . .
> They knew the intercourse between heaven and earth. . . . Their
> life and interrelations were such; feeling the pulse and body of
> the soil, that opened to their furrow for the grain . . . and clung
> to their feet with a weight that pulled like desire, lying hard and
> unresponsive when the crops were to be shorn away. . . . They
> took the udder of the cows, the cows yielded milk and pulse
> against the hands of the men. . . . [14]

The greatest landowner in the region is Mrs. Hardy. The huge estate which she has inherited is none other than Shelley Hall. Placing Mrs. Hardy at the center of Beldover life, Lawrence adds that "The male part of the poem was filled in by such men as the vicar and Lord William, lean, eager men . . . who had command of the further fields" (p. 5).

Perhaps this makes too much of a Shelleyan estate, a Hardyan tenant, and a landscape depicted as a poem. Nevertheless, the life of the first Brangwen described by the novel is a life of romantic yearnings. Tom Brangwen is one who sits "betrayed with emotion"

when he hears poems like "Shelley's 'Ode to the West Wind'" (p.
10). A "sensitive and emotional" man, he "dreamed of foreign
parts" even as he "held himself stubbornly resistant to . . . the
commonplace" (p. 20). "Dormant always on the brink of ecstacy,
like a creature evolving to a new birth," Tom "seemed to live . . .
in contact with the unknown, the unaccountable and incalculable"
(pp. 32, 52). His "ravening soul . . . was not satisfied" with the
everyday events of a man's existence (p. 118). "There was" an
"infinite world, eternal, unchanging," he fervently believed, "as
well as the world of life" (p. 73).

When he first meets Lydia Lensky, his *inamorata*, Tom loves her
for her strangeness, her mystery, her ethereality, in short, her
distance from him and his world. (This tendency to idealize the
unknown, of course, is characteristic of Hardy's "romantics" from
Eustacia to Angel; the romantic grandfather, here called Tom
Brangwen, is therefore an image of the romantic inherited by
Lawrence from his Victorian parents.) "He felt . . . a curious
certainty about her," the narrator says of Tom's feelings for Lydia,
"as if she were destined to him. It was to him a profound
satisfaction that she was a foreigner. . . . [H]e dared not know her,
even acquaint himself with her by thinking of her. . . . The world
was submitting to its transformation. He made no move: it would
come" (p. 25).

Tom Brangwen is a lover of the All who has not yet learned that,
in the words of Hardy's poem, the "temporary" *is* the "All" of life.
Like the naïve Henry Knight of *A Pair of Blue Eyes*, he believed
that "There was an inner reality, a logic of the soul, which
connected" his beloved "with him" (p. 34). His post-Miltonic
definition of an "Angel" is "the soul of man and woman in one"; his
union with Lydia seemed to give him "a completeness and an
inviolable power" (pp. 128, 39). Like the Shelley of "Epipsychidion" (ll. 573–86) and unlike both the belated Swinburne (whose
"Anactoria" makes the lover "crueller than God" [l. 152]) and
Hardy (who says of love-hungry Eustacia, "Had it been possible
for . . . mankind to be entirely within her grasp . . . there would
have been . . . the same perpetual dilemmas . . . we endure now"
[1:148]), Tom sensed that the "strange, inviolable completeness" he
found in romantic love "made him . . . as sure and as stable as
God" (p. 39). Once again, we see that his faith is that romantic
faith as conceived by later writers; Swinburne's disappointed

romantic in "The Triumph of Time" believed that, had the beloved returned his somewhat ethereal desire, "We had stood as the sure stars stand," "We had grown as gods" (ll. 37–41).

Anna Brangwen, Lawrence's representative of the next, more skeptical generation, may be the biological daughter of her mother and Paul Lensky, but she is the naturally rebellious spiritual daughter of Tom and Lydia. Whereas Tom lived in contact with an "infinite world, eternal, unchanging," whereas his wife, Lydia, "had some fundamental religion" by which she "worshipped God as a mystery, never seeking in the least to define what He was" (she only knew that He was "gleaming, imminent . . . immediate beyond all telling"), Anna lives tormented by her sense of a painful gap between the visions of the faithful and the blankness of reality (p. 94). She is, on one level of discourse, the tormented, agonized agnostic who is born too late for any kind of faith, the fictional embodiment of Lawrence's own spiritual and aesthetic parent, Algernon Charles Swinburne.

Although the mysteries of the church always fascinated Anna, they did not quite mean anything to her. Her rosary—like the Christ of Swinburne's "Hymn to Proserpine"—was "pale." What it *"meant"* was "not right, somehow." "Her mind reverted often to the torture cell of a certain Bishop of France, in which the victim could neither stand nor lie stretched out. . . . [S]he could feel the horror of the crampedness" (pp. 95, 97). Her love for her cousin, Will, is no less painful a pleasure, a fact Lawrence implicitly reveals through Swinburnian narrative and dialogue which recall the rapt, devotional lover of "Laus Veneris," who "must cleave" to Venus with "Lips that cling hard"; the passion that "rends" in "Anactoria"; and the licentious lover Swinburne called "Faustina Imperatrix." Soon after meeting Will in church, Anna "had her arms round him, was clinging close to him, cleaving her body against his, and crying in a whispering, whimpering sound. 'Will, I love you, I love you, Will, I love you.' It sounded as if it were tearing her" (p. 108). In her desire to mix with him perfectly, "She wanted to rend him" (p. 149). She "kissed his breast with a slow, rapt, half-devotional movement," but her very devotion was torture to herself and to her beloved. The narrator entitles the chapter describing the romance "Anna Victrix" (p. 179).

Her lover Will, like Thomas Hardy, is something of a lapsed Protestant. He is also, of course, his lover's cousin (Hardy had recognized Swinburne as "that brother poet"); thus, the romantic theme of incest is here extended to encompass the realm of literary intercourse. Like Hardy, Will Brangwen is a draughtsman, a fan of Gothic revival especially interested in church and cathedral restoration. A man half in love with and half sick of shadows, he knows that all the mysteries celebrated by the faithful are dreams, are fictions, but he finds it even more difficult to accept the banality of mere fact. "He knew it was so: wine was wine, water was water, for ever: the water had not become wine. The miracle was not a real fact." But

> Which was stronger, the pain of the denial, or the desire for affirmation? He was stubborn in spirit, and abode by his desire. But he would not any more affirm the miracle was true.
> Very well, it was not true, the water had not turned into wine. . . . But for all that he would live in his soul as if the water *had* turned into wine. For truth of fact, it had not. But for his soul, it had.
>
> [p. 161]

The church, with all the metaphysical speculations it stands for in Will's mind, offers an escape "Away from time, always outside of time! Between east and west, between dawn and sunset, the church lay like a seed in silence." In "the church, 'before' and 'after' were folded together, all was contained in oneness." It is a pure artifice which, nevertheless, has truth for "his soul"; its great dome suggests that which he wants to believe in but cannot, namely, a white radiance of eternity barely stained by life's colorful illusions. "His soul would have liked it to be so: here, here is all, complete, eternal . . . no illusion of time, of night and day passing by, but only perfectly proportioned space" (pp. 189–90). Will Brangwen is, in a new sense, the decadent Mr. Hardy who has inherited Shelley Hall.

But his more cynical lover, his young Sue Bridehead (who serves, even as she did in Hardy's *Jude*, both as her lover's image of "Absolute Beauty" (p. 222) and as an irreverent, Swinburnian agnostic scornful even of her authorial cousin's *will* to believe) claims she would not even "like it to be so." "His passion in the cathedral . . . made her angry. After all, there was the sky outside," and "the open sky was no blue vault, no dark dome hung with twinkling lamps, but a space where stars were whirling in freedom" (p. 190). Like Swinburne, whose "defiant, exultant verse undermined [Hardy] emotionally,"[15] Anna "soon came to combat [Will's] deepest feelings. . . . She hated his blind attachments"; she "forced him to let . . . go." Like any artist influenced by an aesthetic or spiritual forerunner, "he almost loved her for this, though at first it maddened him like an insult. . . . But at length he came to accept her judgments, discovering them as if they were his own" (160).

Not unlike Swinburne, however, Anna is herself a child of romanticism. Her father, after all, had been somewhat reductively portrayed as a quintessential romantic social revolutionary somewhat in the mold of Hardy's Clym Yeobright. A social visionary who dreamed of "inciting his countrymen," he lived in a realm of "words" and "great ideas," working "very hard, till nothing lived in him but his eyes." When Anna was born "he seemed nothing but skin and bone and fixed idea," for he had grown "thinner and thinner, till his cheeks were hollow and . . . [he] wasn't handsome anymore" (pp. 43–44, 243). (Eyes, thinness, hollowness, and the loss of handsomeness are the four almost caricatured aspects of Clym which Hardy persistently explores in *The Return of the Native*.)

The article of romantic faith toward which Anna is drawn, of which she does not "force" Will to "let go," is faith in the bliss of romantic love in a world beyond time and trouble. In love, Anna and Will think themselves "as remote from the world as if the two of them were buried like a seed in darkness. . . . Here was a poised, unflawed stillness that was beyond time, because it remained the same, inexhaustible, unchanging, unexhausted" (p. 135). With the loss of self implicit in epipsychic passion, the lovers believe, comes the annihilation of time, a new paradise in nature, and a perfect society unto itself. "And now, lo, the whole world could be divested of its garment," the Carlylean-sounding narrator says, reflecting the youthful, Teufelsdröckhian optimism of his pre-lapsarian lovers, "the garment could lie there shed away . . . and one could stand in a new world, a new earth, naked in a new, naked universe. It was too astounding and miraculous!" (p. 140).

But it is, of course, a miracle guaranteed to precipitate a fall, a fall into lovers' hell, for post-romantic man was not meant to live in romantic paradise, was born too late for an age of miracles. Soon their love is invaded by the world it thought it had transcended.

"The world *was* there, after all. And he had felt so secure, as though this house were the Ark in the flood, and all the rest was drowned. The world was there: and it was afternoon" (p. 137). Occasionally the miraculous sense of achieving an eternal world apart recurs, but then, just as quickly as it came, it vanishes, both with the triumph of time and with "The Triumph of Time," the poem in which a love that hoped to stand "as the sure stars stand" was "spoilt," "Smitten," "ruined at root":

> So it went on continually, the recurrence of love and conflict between them. One day it seemed as if everything was shattered, all life spoiled, ruined, desolate and laid waste. . . . The next day she loved and rejoiced in the way he crossed the floor, he was sun, moon, and stars in one.
>
> [p. 156]

As conflict gradually comes to outweight cosmic satisfaction, however, the lovers, disappointed by a dream that cannot be attained and a reality that is "unsatisfy[ing], unfulfill[ing]," become, as Dolores and Bathsheba, Anactoria and Eustacia had become, crueller than hell, cruel in their fierce desire for self-satisfaction, cruel because unfulfilled desire is necessarily unfulfilling. "He was cruel to her. . . . It was horrible that he should cleave to her, so close, so close, like a leopard that had leapt on her, and fastened" (pp. 170, 174). Like Swinburne's recurrent "pantheress" ("At a Month's End," "Fragoletta"), like the lover of Venus who "fastens sharply" ("Laus Veneris") or Michael Henchard, who tends toward "tigerish affection," Will and Anna Brangwen prove what Swinburne and Hardy, together, learned: romantic love does not establish a perfect circuitry, a galaxy apart, rather, it amounts to the destructive discharge of negatives into positives. For this reason, in *The Rainbow*, the romantic metaphor of electricity is purposely degraded into the battery, a baser metaphor that tells of the self-corroding union of opposites in love. "From his body through her hands came the bitter-corrosive shock of his passion. . . . She rose from her knees and went away from him to preserve herself. . . . To him also it was agony" (p. 170). The love position, of course, has also here been appropriately revised into a suggestive comment upon the never equal mixture of individuals in love, perhaps even of artists in history. There is little interfluence and much influence, the fellation *tableau* suggests, as does Ursula, the child of Anna and Will's union. She, like Lawrence, says she "love[s]" her "volume of Swinburne's poetry" (p. 400). But she, like Lawrence, is a child more nearly like her Hardyan than her Swinburnian parent.

She is more Hardyan than Swinburnian because, whereas the problem Swinburne has wrestled with had been concerned primarily with artistic expression (early and late Swinburne's volumes had wondered how to sing and what to sing about), Ursula's besetting trauma, like Hardy's, is over a question about how to be. In fact, in some sense she is Lawrence's revision of a specific Hardy character, the third and youngest Avice of Hardy's last published novel, *The Well-Beloved*. The challenge of her life is to do approximately what Avice did when she defied the wishes of her parent, rejected that grandfatherly suitor who would have possessed her and surrounded her with his own art, and thus broke free from those ideal, neo-Platonic constraints to her liberty and her very being embodied in Jocelyn Pierston. These same constraints had left Avice's romantic grandmother first disappointed, then dead in the prime of her youth and had, in the last years of her more Victorian (i.e., practical and conventional) mother's life, fired her mother's fancy for the second time, and, also for the second time, left her alone, disappointed, disenchanted.

Ursula's problem of how to be, then, is that of escaping a grandfatherly idealism, transcendentalism, or romanticism like the one that Lawrence believed her original, Avice, to have escaped when she jilted sixty-year-old Pierston in *The Well-Beloved*. Consequently, Ursula's tale, *The Rainbow*, and its teller, Lawrence, are caught in a larger question of how to be which involves escaping from the one man whom Lawrence would no doubt see as Pierston's Great Original, namely, Thomas Hardy. Thus, the personal image of an idea or an ideal that, for Hardy's Pierston, is manifested through three generations, is, in *The Rainbow*, a collective, even historical idea or ideal that, by rejecting its perpetrator and his authorial original, Thomas Hardy, Lawrence and his novel can escape, or at least avoid.

That is why, in its final chapters, the novel does all it can to suggest that Ursula (and, in and through Ursula, itself) is utterly free from the hopes, faiths, disappointments, failures, and divisions which plagued both her troubled parents and grandparents. In her rejection of her suitor's, the Baron's, proposal (and of marriage in general), she would seem, both as a person and as an agent of literary history, to reject the idea of carrying on the family line and all those traditions, rules, beliefs (even landscapes) which families pass on through time. For her suitor, after all, is a symbol not only of family continuity, he is also an agent of religious belief (his father was the rector Ursula's grandmother had "nursed") and, beyond that, a symbol of lingering faith in romantic love and social idealism. A chapter entitled "First Love," for instance, is ambiguous in its referent. It first describes Ursula's youthful, Swinburnian, painful passion for Jesus:[16] "She leapt with sensuous yearning to respond to Christ." She "wanted Jesus to love her deliciously." She "was in such a daze, such a tangle. How could she get free? She hated herself, she wanted to trample on herself, destroy herself" (p. 270). Then, immediately following, it describes her love for Anton, a romantic attachment that recapitulates the loves of Dr. Fitzpiers and Eustacia Vye. Like the romantic of *The Woodlanders*, who falls in love with an "idea or an ideal" when he sees Grace Melbury in a mirror (1:296), Ursula "was in love with a vision of herself: she saw as it were a fine little reflection of herself in his eyes" (p. 276). "She laughed upon him, blind to him, never doubting but that he was the same as she was." Like Hardy's Eustacia, who, for one brief shining moment, "lived . . . in a luminous mist" with Clym (2:234), Ursula, in the first days of her "first love," "lived . . . radiant as an illumined cloud" (p. 286). Her lover's proposal, however, is, along with his family name, eventually rejected, accepted, then, finally, rejected again. For the Baron, Ursula realizes, however much he may seem the mirror image of herself, the very image of her "Well-Beloved," also implies an end to her individuality. (Even his social vision is romantic-democratic; "he did not consider the soul of the individual sufficiently important. He believed a man was important in so far as he represented all humanity" [p. 309].)

Lawrence sees to it, in the novel's final pages, that his last heroine in *The Rainbow* utterly rejects the Baron and all he stands for. And he generates all the new heaven and new earth imagery and rhetoric he can in order to assert that she will "never" be "married" (p. 440). But the liberating last chapter seems just that, a short flight of imagery and rhetoric. For one thing, the sequel to *The Rainbow*, *Women in Love*, will suggest that Ursula's commitment not to marry (and thus not to be influenced in all senses of that word) will be short-lived. More important, the powerful, penultimate chapter of *The Rainbow* (four times as long as its sequel between sequels) makes us aware, through landscape, of just how uncertain, unliberated, and spiritually paralyzed Ursula is.

> Suddenly, cresting the heavy, sandy pass, Ursula lifted her head, and shrank back, momentarily frightened . . . uttering a cry. . . .
> The sands were as ground silver, the sea moved in solid brightness, . . . and she went to meet the advance of the flashing, buoyant water. He stood behind, encompassed, a shadow ever dissolving.
> She stood on the edge of the water, at the edge of the solid, flashing body of the sea, and the wave rushed over her feet.
> "I want to go," she cried. . . .
>
> [p. 451]

For Ursula, the choice is between a world of shadows and a world of death. So it was for Swinburne and Hardy, and so it is for Lawrence too. The difference is, for Lawrence, that Hardy and Swinburne are among those shadows.

If *The White Peacock* did not, *The Rainbow* makes one fact absolutely clear: however much indebtedness Lawrence incurs or repudiates with respect to his post-romantic predecessors, the deep source of that debt is, necessarily, to a remoter vision of things, a romantic view of nature and of love, of the self, time, and society, which has come down to him both directly and in a somewhat garbled, secondhand form, shaping his own understanding of things, influencing his own aesthetic expressions. This deeper debt, always subliminally recognized by Lawrence's early poems and by most of his greater novels, underlies and almost even controls both Lawrence's prose criticism and those last, great volumes of verse which almost seem to have been conceived as illustrations of their author's critical principles.

In his relatively few critical essays on poetry, Lawrence manages to do to his romantic inheritance much as his Victorian elders had done, that is, he trivializes it into a vision of things which utterly ignored reality as it searched obsessively for a world of perfection which is nowhere to be found. In an essay entitled "The Nightingale," first published in 1919, Lawrence declares his predecessors to be those who must always make reality into what they want it to be, something smooth and perfect and mystical which can exist only in the solipsistic fancies of the romantic poet. As for the real nightingale, Lawrence says,

> He is the noisiest, most inconsiderate, most obstreperous and jaunty bird in the whole kingdom of birds. How John Keats managed to begin his "Ode to a Nightingale" with: "My heart aches, and a drowsy numbness pains my senses," is a mystery to anybody acquainted with the actual song. You hear the nightingale silverily shouting: "What? What? What, John? Heart aches and a drowsy numbness pains? Tra-la-la! Tri-li-lilylilylilyily!"[17]

Here is a passage that manages to revive Carlyle's complaint that Coleridge never bothered becoming "acquainted" with "the actual world," Ruskin's *outré*, horticultural analysis of "The Sensitive Plant" ("Dew with a breeze is impossible," "Sensitive plants don't grow in gardens," "the blockhead!") and, more generally, that fierce, philistine tone common to so many Victorian attacks on those ineffectual angels who, ever singing their "Tra-la-la" songs of innocence, spent their lives beating the void with luminous wings in vain.

In his essay on the "Poetry of the Present," published a year earlier (in 1918), Lawrence at once makes the blunt and familiar claim that romantics were pathetic perfectionists and, in a symbolic landscape and timescape, declares the poetry of romantics to be the art of the dim past and the inconceivable future, at the same time implying that his own rough songs are the only true songs of the day. "Poetry is, as a rule," according to Lawrence, "either the voice of the far future, exquisite and ethereal, or it is the voice of the past, rich, magnificent." All our poets, it seems to him, "sing on the horizons. They sing out of the blue, beyond us, or out of the quenched night." They "sit by the gateways, some by the east, some by the west," but their songs are ever the same, for both "The poetry of the beginning and the poetry of the end must have that exquisite finality, perfection which belongs to all that is far off." Both are songs sung "in the realm of all that is perfect" and about "all that is complete and consummate. This completeness, this consummateness," Lawrence adds, is "conveyed in exquisite form: the perfect symmetry, the rhythm which returns upon itself like a dance. . . . Perfected bygone moments, perfected moments in the glimmering futurity, these are the treasured gem-like lyrics of Shelley and Keats":

> But there is another kind of poetry: the poetry of that which is at hand: the immediate present. In the immediate present there is no perfection, no consummation, nothing finished. The strands are all flying, quivering, intermingling into the web, the waters are shaking the moon. There is no round, consummate moon on the face of running water. . . . [18]

Specifically as well as generally, Lawrence makes his romantic predecessors into poets of a perfection so unearthly that his own more muscular shouts seem, by comparison, to be as alive as they are imperfect. As for Shelley, he "is pure escape," Lawrence says, for in his poems "the body is sublimated into sublime gas." In Keats "the body can still be *felt* dissolving in waves of successive death—but the death business is very satisfactory."[19] Not about to forget Wordsworth, Lawrence next adds that the "Wordsworthian child" is nothing more than a "simpleton" whom he, unlike the more respectful Yeats, is not prone to "admire,"[20] and, as for Wordsworth's "faith" in the oneness of himself with nature, he believes that to be the same pathetic mistake Swinburne thought Blake to have made, that is, the mistake of "seeing everywhere the image of [one's] own mood." When Wordsworth finds his feelings confirmed by a "primrose," we "must assert" this is "an impertinence on William's part. He ousts the primrose from its own individuality. . . . It must be identical with *his* soul. Because, of course, . . . there is but One Soul in the universe. This is bunk."[21]

Bunk or no bunk, the business of trivializing one's predecessors into maudlin, weak-eyed sensibilities is, as Lawrence himself admits in *Apocalypse*, "an old story." (Lawrence is speaking here of the text of *Ezekiel*, "deliberately corrupted by fanatical scribes, who wanted to smear over the pagan vision.") "Every rising civilisation must fiercely repudiate the passing civilisation," Lawrence reminds us, but these repudiations are not to be taken too seriously. They result, after all, not from a true argument with the past but, rather, from "a fight within the self" and, therefore, if we read them carefully, they implicitly admit that "Every profound new movement makes a great swing also backwards to some older, half-forgotten way of consciousness."[22]

Once Lawrence's patently Victorian critical equation of romanticism with "perfection-seeking" and "oversouling"[23] is understood, the fundamental concerns of many of his own later poems become clear. *Birds, Beasts, and Flowers,* surely Lawrence's finest single volume of poetry, was written between 1920 and 1923 and published only seven years before the poet's death. In that late work, however, Lawrence reveals that, no less than Swinburne or Hardy, he is still enough drawn to romantic poetry, or to that idealized vision of things which he seems to (want to) think most romantic poetry contains, that he feels the need constantly to counter "romanticism" with criticism, thus implicitly making his own "great swing backwards" by admitting, quietly, that his own work is undeniably a form of romanticism to fit the mood of his own age.

In "Pomegranate," the poem which he places first in the volume, his speaker addresses an audience (which I believe to be made up of the spirits of the romantic poets) and, in tones of insecure security, nags that

> You tell me I am wrong.
> Who are you, who is anybody to tell me I am wrong?
> I am not wrong.

That which the Lawrentian speaker is "not wrong" about is the earthy imperfection of his own poetic vision, that is, his own, none-too-secure belief that poetry must not attempt to transcend the painful pleasures of the mundane, must not seek a perfection that is nowhere to be found. Pointing to a symbolic, if rotting and ruptured, pomegranate, a veritable microcosm of the Lawrentian self and cosmos, the speaker bullies, "Do you mean to tell me you will see no fissure? / Do you prefer to look on the plain side?"

> Do you mean to tell me there should be no fissure? . . .
> Do you mean it is wrong, the gold-filmed skin,
>   integument, shown ruptured?
> For my part, I prefer my heart to be broken.

The poem is nothing less or more than an attack, however unfair, on "romantic" modes of seeing (Lawrence claims he will not "prefer to look" on only those aspects of nature which reinforce his ideas or ideals, he implicitly claims not to want to "add the gleam, / The light that never was, on sea or land"), on romantic modes of being (he says he doesn't even desire to "quite forget / The weariness, the fever, and the fret" of the world, rather, he "prefer[s]" his "heart to be broken"), and even on his romantic precursors' modes of expression or of "showing" ("Do you mean it is wrong, the gold-filmed skin, integument, shown ruptured?"). "Pomegranate," like its somewhat inferior successor, entitled "Peach," is designed to bait the romantic audience that Lawrence sees as too refined in its squeamishness about reality. In "Peach," the speaker, having teased his more orthodox critics about the slick, bloody redness of the inside of a peach ("Blood-red, deep; / Heaven knows how it came to pass"), will not let them avoid seeing "the groove" of the fruit, and then, with all the humor a Philistine can muster, ends his address with a reminder that a peach, that all of nature, is not "round and finished like a billiard ball":

And because I say so, you would like to
  throw something at me.
Here, you can have my peach stone.

Where the Victorians had trivialized their influential predecessors into cherubs and children, Lawrence similarly trivializes those supposedly "perfectibilian" predecessors into gutless society matrons, old ladies who, unable to cope with the here and now, construe the world into something more amenable to their denatured tastes. That, at least, is what the poet seems to be doing in "Figs," where the mannered opening up of that fruit seems to stand as a metaphor for the romantic way of opening up the world through poetry. "The proper way to eat a fig," Lawrence says,

Is to split it in four, holding it by the stump,
And open it, so that it is a glittering, rosy,
  moist, honied, heavy-petalled four-petalled flower.

But the vulgar way
Is just to put your mouth to the crack, and take
  out the flesh with one bite.

Those who, unlike the spontaneous, crack-sucking Lawrence, poetically open the fig carefully, properly, imaginatively, manage to make the ripe fruit, which on its own is a glaring, red reminder of the inevitability of sex and of death, into a heavenly flower for our vision, something it is not and never has been. As for the fig, Lawrence almost angrily declaims,

> There never was any standing aloft and unfolded
> on a bough
> Like other flowers, in a revelation of petals . . .
> Shallow wine-cups on short, bulging stems
> Openly pledging heaven.

The unheavenly flower of this fruit, Lawrence reminds us, is always "Folded upon itself," an unseen and indescribable phenomenon, a reminder to all visionaries and poets that all cannot be seen and known. "Folded upon itself," it is a "secret unutterable," "Its nakedness all within-walls, its flowering forever unseen." The attempt at making the ripe fruit into an open flower, therefore, is a vain and pathetic attempt to reveal that which cannot be revealed.

Anyway, as for ripeness, Lawrence almost screams out at his romantic critics in "Pomegranate," "Peach," "Figs," and in a companion piece entitled "Medlars and Sorb Apples," it is not the perfect flower of being, the state of wholeness, perfection, and heavenly tranquility which poets like to think it is. It is, rather, quite the opposite, the time when the groove of the peach, the cleft of the pomegranate, and the "purple slit" of the fig split open "Like a wound," like the ill-concealed "secret" of "a prostitute," to remind us that all those things like beauty and fullness and fruition and perfection for which romantic poets quested are inextricably bound up with the momentary, almost painful ecstacy of sex and the inevitable, stinking rottenness of death. That is why "Medlars and Sorb Apples" tries to fly in the face of Keats's poem, "To Autumn," by turning what Lawrence somehow must have seen as that ode to culmination, fulfillment, and perfection (in fact, it is only Keats's autumnal bees who "think warm days will never cease") into a revisionary hymn to the "Intoxication of final loneliness" "among decaying, frost-cold leaves," a paean to rottenness, a celebration of "Autumnal excrementa," the "grape turning raisin," the skins of medlars and apples turning to "Wineskins of brown morbidity."

To make his swerve from the onward and upward pursuit of ripeness, stasis, and tranquility apparent, Lawrence turns the direction of his poetic quest downwards and backwards: to counter the transcendentalists, he refuses to seek the apex, or flowers, of experience, and to respond to the meliorists, he seeks not some far-off divine event toward which all creation moves, but, rather, the primitive life of the deep past, what Lawrence refers to in

"Medlars and Sorb Apples" as the "dark," the "hellish experiences" out of which, unfortunately, all creation has arisen. (Lawrence thus defies Milton as well as the romantics, for he equates all ascents, spiritual or imaginative, with lapses, and suggests that in the fall into blindness and hell lies our only hope for regaining Paradise.)

In "Grapes," Lawrence struggles to precipitate that fall by celebrating the dark, green, sticky, and sappy pre-floral world that Hardy, too, had chosen (in *Far from the Madding Crowd*, *The Woodlanders*, and *Tess*) as a symbolic scenario for his own didactic arguments with a so-called romantic vision of nature. "Long ago, oh, long ago," Lawrence wistfully reminisces, "Before the rose began to simper supreme, / Before the rose of all roses, rose of all the world, was even in bud,"

> There was another world, a dusky, flowerless,
>   tendrilled world
> And creatures webbed and marshy. . . .
>
> Of which world, the vine was the invisible rose,
> Before petals spread, before colour made its
>   disturbance, before eyes saw too much.
> In a green, muddy, web-foot, unutterably songless world
> The vine was rose of all roses.

The primitivism of "Grapes" is a fierce complaint against "romantic" poets from Milton to Yeats, for this "still, and sensitive, and active" world that existed "before eyes saw too much," before "song" had disturbed the lively quiet of "invisibility," is a world not just of the Paleolithic past but, rather, is a world that existed, in some sense, until the laser-like blindness of Milton and all subsequent visionaries illuminated and, in illuminating, destroyed the Paradise of sensual darkness. They, so the evolutionary historical metaphor suggests, managed to make visionary "roses" appear on what were previously just "Audile, tactile" vines, but in so doing they shrouded the dark life of things, the flowerless roots and stems that support and feed all that the eyes (physical and imaginative) can see, in a darkness more terrible than hell.

This necessary quest for the primitive world lost underlies all of the poems in *Birds, Beasts, and Flowers*. The poet's attraction to the great pikes described in "Fish," after all, is that "Loveless, and so lively," they were "Born before God was love, / Or life knew loving"; they were "Beautifully beforehand with it all."

What Lawrence means by "Love," here, it seems to me, is what we might call "correspondence," that is, the hope of the romantic self that nature, or that another self, or that the temporal process, or that social forms, will in some way correspond with and will, in any case, offer little resistance to one's hopes and fancies and projections, that is, the self's intentions to love and, by loving, appropriate the world. (Arnold meant exactly this when he complained of that "promiscuous" intercourse with reality whereby the romantic poet too-personally "adopt[s]" all the "matter offered to [him] by life.") The beauty of the "Fish," for Lawrence, is their uncompromised, unself-conscious society of selfhood; they manage to be "Many suspended together, forever apart." They have "No tender muzzles, / No wistful bellies / No loins of desire, / None." They are creatures the poet, delving into his conditioned romantic vocabulary of sympathy and negative capability, cannot comprehend, creatures that force the poet who would flow into and through all things into ellipses:

> I said to my heart, *who are these*?
> And my heart couldn't own them. . . .
>   [italics and ellipses are Lawrence's]

The "Fish" is that in nature which gives the lie to the "Love" or correspondence that, in their *cor cordium*, the poets of perfection wanted to believe in, for once the poet has felt "his gorping, water-horny mouth, / And seen his horror-tilted . . . mirror-flat bright eye; / And felt him beat in my hand, with his mucous, leaping life-throb," his "heart accused itself"

> Thinking: *I am not the measure of creation.*
> *This is beyond me, this fish.*

The nature of nature, Lawrence suggests through his most famous poem, "Snake," is forever beyond man's anthropocentric understanding; in fact, because Milton has invaded the sleeping body of the serpent with Western man's conception of evil, contact —primordial, physical, passionate, and primitive—is all but impossible, for after the violence of words and ideas can only come the bone-breaking violence of sticks and stones ("I picked up a clumsy log / And threw it at the water-trough with a clatter"). Even the regret that may follow such an anthropocentric "pettiness" is falsified, is ruined, by that consequent and equally anthropocentric

"sympathy" or "love" of nature (Arnold would see it as promiscuous intercourse, Lawrence more nearly as rape) which followed
Milton's violence to the serpent in the form of Coleridge's mariner's
sympathetic declaration of brotherhood with the coiling, twining,
sea-snakes:

> And immediately I regretted it.
> I thought how paltry, how vulgar, what a mean act!
> I despised myself and the voices of my accursed
>   human education.
>
> And I thought of the albatross. . . .

The at once pathetic and fallacious "Love" of that which, because
it cannot truly be seen or known, could never be loved, is a "Love"
or a sense of correspondence which Lawrence believes (even as his
Victorian predecessors believed) leads naturally (or, Lawrence
would say, unnaturally) to a perfectly consistent (and therefore, in
the agnostic's eyes, equally inaccurate) definition of romantic love,
a theory of affection based on absolute correspondence and
therefore perfect unity of lovers' flesh and spirit which Lawrence, in
his topically, thematically, and aesthetically primitive "Tortoise
Shout," intends to defile. For love, translated into sex in this poem,
becomes that which "breaks up" all "unity," all "integrity," all
"inviolability," leaving "That which is whole, torn asunder."
Beyond this act of defiance and denial, Lawrence even plays with
the "Ode to a Nightingale" and a scene from *Jude the Obscure* to
insinuate, almost inaudibly, that Keats's desire to fade away into
the forest dim and, through Jude, Hardy's kindly sympathies with a
nature that knows no love or sympathy are anthropocentric rapes
of reality, utterly defensive sublimations of the divisive urges of sex
into the false and fantastical vision of unifying correspondence,
sympathy, or loving-kindness. "I remember," Lawrence says,

> The first time, out of a bush in the darkness, a
>   nightingale's piercing cries and gurgles
>   startled the depths of my soul;
> I remember the scream of a rabbit as I went through
>   a wood at midnight.

Lawrence also follows in the footsteps of his Victorian parents
(perhaps, though how Lawrence would hate it, *brothers* would be
a more accurate term) by seeing the false, forced, foul ideal of

romantic love as inseparable from an equally cloying and, ultimately, equally divisive romantic definition of society, one which
says that, although on the surface all men are divine individuals, at
base they are all divinely the same, born of the same holy family.
That is why, in "The Evening Land," Lawrence cries out against
America, for him a symbol of the pitiful romantic lover transformed into an equally unfortunate romantic revolutionary ideal.
"I confess I am afraid," the poet says, of "The catastrophe of your
exaggerate love," "You who . . . only lose yourself," always
"decomposing":

> You who in loving break down
> And break further and further down
> Your bounds of isolation,
> But who never rise, resurrected, from this grave of mingling,
> In a new proud singleness. . . .

Lawrence calls America "the false dawn that precedes the real"
and, in a companion poem to "The Evening Land," refers to himself
as "The Revolutionary." (He thus identifies himself as at once a
kind of an Athenian herald and Chthonian martyr of the new,
post-romantic dawn.) In "The Evening Land" the poet denounces
those idealists who have, under the aegis of democracy, given us a
"bright motor-productive" social "mechanism" fostering only an
"iron click of . . . human contact." In "The Revolutionary" he
manages to trivialize the so-called romantic idealists of the past into
"Pale-face . . . / Caryatids," stone-faced upholders of a "temple"
that "The Revolutionary" would destroy. "What a job they've got
to keep it up," Lawrence muses, "Their poor, idealist foreheads
naked capitals / To the entablature of clouded heaven." "Oh and I
wish the high and super-gothic heavens would come down now, /
The heavens above, that we yearn to and aspire to," he cries out;
and then he proceeds to give us a perfect metapoetic scenario, a
depiction of himself, a blind Samson about to raze the brittle
temple of what Swinburne had called "the dead and doubtful
gods":

> I do not yearn, nor aspire, for I am a blind Samson.
> And what is daylight to me that I should look skyward?
> I only grope among you, pale-faces, caryatids, as
>   among a forest of pillars that hold up the dome
>   of high ideal heaven

Which is my prison,
And all these human pillars of loftiness, going
   stiff . . .
I stumble against them.
Stumbling-blocks, painful ones.

To keep on holding up this ideal civilisation
Must be excruciating . . .

I shall be so glad when it comes down.
I am so tired of the limitations of their Infinite.
I am so sick of the pretensions of the Spirit.

The curious thing about this poem is that, like Swinburne's "Itylus," it is a poem about disagreement or separation in which no one really moves, no one really breaches or even escapes the sanctity of the other. Like "Itylus," "The Revolutionary" is a poem of stasis which ends exactly where it begins. Its speaker, having begun on a note of definite exclamation, ends his piece by saying conditional things like *"When* your world is in ruins" (italics mine), "See *if* I *am not Lord* of the dark and moving hosts" (here the so-called "revolutionary" declaration is qualified by a conditional, a negative construction, and the inappropriateness of the word "Lord"). But this ambivalence, after all, is nothing new. It is something which caused Swinburne's and Hardy's seeming emergence from romanticism (as they conceived it) to boomerang back into forms of romanticism made to fit the mood of their age. It is something that keeps Lawrence's poetry and fiction ever divided against itself, form versus content, idea versus structure, vocabulary versus sentiment, music versus metaphysic. Even in "The Evening Land," that bitter diatribe against democratic social idealism, the poet admits halfway through that his "soul is half-cajoled." And, in its final lines, this sermon-like rhetorical attack on that nation which in "loving break[s] down" its "bounds of isolation" degenerates into something utterly different. "Modern, unissued, uncanny America," Lawrence says, you "Allure me till I am beside myself, / A nympholepht."

Often, Lawrence is less straightforward about his pledges of allegiance. Sometimes, in fact, the extent of his respect for romantic poetry in general and its supposed ideals can only be ascertained from the absurd, the embarrassingly overstated, even the grotesque nature of his attacks. In "Bibbles," for instance, he trivializes a "romantic" lust to merge with and be at one with everyone and everything into a "Whitmanesque" dog. "I'd never have let you appropriate me," Lawrence says, "had I known . . . you love *everybody*," had I known "You . . . / Believe in the One identity." For, he continues, becoming more and more audacious as his address progresses, because of your feelings that all nature can be internalized,

> . . . I have to clean up after you, filth which even
> blind Nature rejects,
> From the pit of your stomach;
> But you, you snout-face, you reject nothing, you
> merge so much in love
> You must eat even that.

Lawrence thus goes Browning, who made Shelley into over-ruminated cud and himself into the new, fresh food, one better, or one worse, making the romantic sensibility an old, shit-eating bitch gone in the teeth who never saw that "Nature" was "blind," and himself into the "new poet" (Browning's phrase) who must "clean up after" her before he can begin his daily business of writing his own nourishing poems.

As a poem about a dog, "Bibbles" is cute, if a bit unseemly. As a poem about idealists, about those who would be more than what they are, who would make nature more than what it is, who would transcend limitations and boundaries, the poem is too fiercely, too grotesquely overstated to declaim anything more than the burden of belief.

Indeed, in two of Lawrence's last volumes of poetry, *Pansies* (1929) and the posthumous *Last Poems* (1932), the poet totally succumbs to that burden and, somewhat like Yeats, rather seems to enjoy it. If we were to believe all that the poet would have us believe in "Bibbles," we would surely refuse to believe he went on to write "Spiral Flame," a poem collected in *Pansies* in which the now maturer lyricist says "Yet,

> . . . O my young men, there is a vivifier.
> There is a swan-like flame that curls round the
> centre of space
> and flutters at the core of the atom,
> there is a spiral flame-tip that can lick
> our little atoms into fusion

So we roar up like bonfires of vitality
and fuse in a broad hard flame of many men in a oneness.

In *Last Poems*, this "swan," a notion of a creative force or collective imagination in debt to Blake, Wordsworth, and Shelley *via* William Butler Yeats, returns even closer to its source, namely, that Judeo-Christian idea of God the Creator which (and here, it seems to me, Victorians from Carlyle to Lawrence are absolutely correct about the romantic "faith") underlies all romantic revisions, all spilt religions. In "Silence," a very different (and yet in many ways, a very much the same) Lawrence from the youth who decried "faith" in "shadows" in poems such as "The Wild Common," prays, "Come, holy Silence! reach, reach / from the presence of God, and envelop us."

Lift up your heads, O ye Gates!
for the silence of the last great thundrous laugh
screens us purely, and we can slip through.

Lawrence is, perhaps even more than Swinburne and Hardy, a poet condemned to life in a debtor's prison. And yet, as Wordsworth reminded us in his sonnet on the sonnet, often "the prison, unto which we doom / Ourselves, no prison is." Certainly, for Lawrence, as for Swinburne, Hardy, and a no less imprisoned contemporary named Dylan Thomas, the prison of literary history is never one that silences, rather, it always manages to hurt its poets into song. It is a prison that, in the words of Thomas's "Fern Hill," always

held me green and dying
Though I sang in my chains like the sea.

It is a prison that can occasionally liberate the poet of the here and now into inspiration, turn, or rather return, poems of chance and circumstance into moments of vision. It is the poetic prison that is also somehow a muse, a place Hardy seems to be describing in a lovely, eerie, and totally ignored late lyric, "On a Midsummer Eve," when he says,

I went, and knelt, and scooped my hand
As if to drink, into the brook,
And a faint figure seemed to stand
Above me, with the bygone look.

I lipped rough rhymes of chance, not choice,
I thought not what my words might be;
There came into my ear a voice
That turned a tenderer verse for me.

Notes

Chapter One

1. Thomas Carlyle, "On History," in *Selected Works, Reminiscences, and Letters*, ed. Julian Symons (London, 1955), p. 49.

2. H. G. Wells, *The Outline of History*, ch. 40.

3. Walter Pater, "Pico della Mirandola," in *Works* (London, 1901), 1:35. Terence's phrase comes from *Heauton Timorumenos*, 1:i.

4. Thomas Carlyle, *The Life of John Sterling* (London, 1851). The passage I have quoted is just one of a number of spleenful remarks collected in the very short chapter, "Coleridge."

5. Quoted by Walter Pater. See Pater's essay on "Coleridge," in *Works*, 5:73.

6. Ibid., p. 104.

7. Quoted by Amy Cruse in *The Victorians and Their Reading* (Cambridge, Mass., 1962), p. 177.

8. Pater, "Wordsworth," in *Works*, 5:55.

9. Matthew Arnold, "Byron," in *The Complete Prose Works of Matthew Arnold*, ed. R. H. Super (Ann Arbor, Mich., 1960), 9:218.

10. Thomas Carlyle, "Characteristics," in *Carlyle's Works*, Sterling Edition (Boston, 1869), 14:373.

11. John Ruskin, *Fiction, Fair and Foul*, in *The Works of John Ruskin*, ed. E. T. Cook and Alexander Wedderburn (London, 1905), 34:397.

12. Algernon Charles Swinburne, "Notes on the Text of Shelley," in *The Complete Works of Swinburne*, Bonchurch Edition (London, 1926), 15:380.

13. Robert Browning, "An Essay on Shelley," in *The Poetical Works of Robert Browning* (Boston, 1974), pp. 1009–10.

14. Carlyle, "Goethe" and "Burns," in *Works*, 13:213, 311.

15. Swinburne, "Wordsworth and Byron," in *Complete Works*, 14:169.

16. Arnold, "Byron," in *Complete Prose Works*, 9:221.

17. Arnold, "John Keats," in *Complete Prose Works*, 9:205–06.

18. Carlyle, "Burns," in *Works*, 13:274.

19. Charles Eliot Norton, ed., *The Correspondence of Thomas Carlyle and Ralph Waldo Emerson* (Boston, 1888), 1:92–93, 190; 2:11–12.

20. Cecil Y. Lang, ed., *The Swinburne Letters* (New Haven, Conn., 1959), 1:159–60.

21. Arnold, "Heinrich Heine," in *Complete Prose Works*, 3:108.

22. Carlyle, "Life and Writings of Werner" and "Burns," in *Works*, 13:113, 308.

23. Swinburne, "Matthew Arnold's New Poems," in *Complete Works*, 15:72.

24. Swinburne, *William Blake*, in *Complete Works*, 16:87, 93.

25. Arnold, "Byron," in *Complete Prose Works*, 9:221–22, 227.

26. Arnold, "Obermann," in *Complete Prose Works*, 5:296, 303.

27. Arnold, "George Sand," in *Complete Prose Works*, 8:226.

28. Carlyle, "The Diamond Necklace," in *Works*, 15:283.

29. Carlyle, "Characteristics," in *Works*, 14:346–47.

30. Swinburne, *William Blake* and "Matthew Arnold's New Poems," in *Complete Works*, 16:231, 15:74–75.

31. Ibid., 15:83.

32. Arnold, "Wordsworth," in *Complete Prose Works*, 9:50.

33. Arnold, "On Translating Homer," in *Complete Prose Works*, 1:102.

34. Swinburne, "Matthew Arnold's New Poems," in *Complete Works*, 15:115, 87.

35. Quoted by F. E. Halliday in *Thomas Hardy* (Bath, Eng., 1972), p. 16.

36. Thomas H. Huxley, *Evolution and Ethics* (London, 1947), p. 60.

37. Quoted by Jerome Buckley in *The Triumph of Time* (Cambridge, Mass., 1966), p. 67.

38. Sir William Thomson, Lord Kelvin's *Mathematical and Physical Papers* (Cambridge, 1882–1911), 1:514.

39. H. G. Wells, *The Time Machine* (London, 1895).

40. Alfred, Lord Tennyson, *In Memoriam*, 123.5–9.

41. The remarks on Tennyson and Arnold are Jerome Buckley's, (*The Triumph of Time*, p. 3).

42. Carlyle, *Sartor Resartus*, in *Works*, 1:42.

43. Carlyle, *On Heroes, Hero-Worship, and the Heroic in History*, in *Works*, 1:242.

44. Swinburne, *William Blake*, in *Complete Works*, 16:92.

45. G. Robert Stange, *Matthew Arnold: The Poet as Humanist* (Princeton, N. J., 1967), p. 202.

46. Carlyle, *Sartor Resartus*, in *Works*, 1:103, 109, 111.
47. Arthur Hugh Clough, *The Poems of Arthur Hugh Clough*, ed. A. L. P. Norrington (London, 1968), p. 42.
48. Emily Brontë, *Wuthering Heights*, chaps. 9, 32.
49. Carlyle, *Sartor Resartus*, in *Works*, 1:143.
50. Swinburne, *William Blake*, in *Complete Works*, 16:55, 92.
51. Percy Bysshe Shelley, *A Defense of Poetry*, ed. A. S. Cook (New York, 1890), p. 14.
52. A. Dwight Culler, *Imaginative Reason* (New Haven, Conn., 1966), p. 110.
53. Northrop Frye, *A Study of English Romanticism* (New York, 1968), p. 38.
54. Frederick Pottle, "The Eye and the Object in the Poetry of Wordsworth," *Yale Review* 40 (1950):28.
55. Owen Barfield, *Saving the Appearances: A Study in Idolatry* (London, 1957), p. 132.
56. Paul de Man, "Intentional Structure of the Romantic Image," in *Romanticism and Consciousness*, ed. Harold Bloom (New York, 1970), p. 76.
57. Misao Miyoshi *The Divided Self* (New York, 1969), p. 47.
58. Harold Bloom, "The Internalization of Quest Romance," in *Romanticism and Consciousness*, p. 9.
59. Georges Poulet, *Studies in Human Time*, trans. Elliott Coleman (Baltimore, 1956), p. xxxii.
60. Frye, *Study of English Romanticism*, p. 38.
61. Northrop Frye, "The Road of Excess," in *Romanticism and Consciousness*, p. 127.
62. M. H. Abrams, "English Romanticism: The Spirit of the Age," in *Romanticism Reconsidered*, ed. Northrop Frye (New York, 1963), p. 43.
63. Frye, *Study of English Romanticism*, p. 20.
64. See *Romanticism and Consciousness*, pp. 1, 133–37, 217.
65. Geoffrey Hartman, "Romanticism and 'Anti-Self-Consciousness,'" *Centennial Review* 6 (1962):553.
66. This is the subject of Abrams, "English Romanticism."
67. Bloom, "Internalization of Quest Romance," p. 6.
68. Samuel Taylor Coleridge, *Biographia Literaria*, ed. J. Shawcross (Oxford, 1907), 2:207.
69. Arnold, "Wordsworth," in *Complete Prose Works*, 9:51.
70. Swinburne, "Wordsworth and Byron" in *Complete Works*, 14:219.
71. Ibid., p. 198.
72. Arnold, "John Keats," in *Complete Prose Works*, 9:212.
73. The approach, of course, was introduced in *The Anxiety of Influence* (New York, 1973) and applied in *A Map of Misreading* (New York, 1975).

74. Arnold, "The Function of Criticism . . . " in *Complete Prose Works*, 3:281–82.

75. John Stuart Mill, *Autobiography* (Indianapolis, Ind., 1957), p. 153.

76. Arnold, "On the Modern Element in Literature," in *Complete Prose Works*, 1:21–22.

77. Carlyle, "Diderot," in *Works*, 15:85–86.

78. Swinburne, "Notes on Poems and Reviews," in *Complete Works*, 16:356.

79. Carlyle, *Sartor Resartus*, in *Works*, 1:175, 179.

80. Ibid., p. 191.

Chapter Two

1. Cecil Y. Lang, ed., *The Swinburne Letters* (New Haven, Conn. 1959), 1:115.

2. Ibid., 2:82–83.

3. Sara Bailey, ed., *John Bailey, 1864-1931, Letters and Diaries* (London, 1935), p. 174.

4. *The Swinburne Letters*, 3:14.

5. Algernon Charles Swinburne, *The Poems of Algernon Charles Swinburne* (London, 1904), 4:249–50. All future references to Swinburne's poetry in this study will be cited parenthetically in the text and will refer to volume and page numbers of this edition.

6. Jerome H. Buckley, *The Triumph of Time* (Cambridge, 1966), p. 3.

7. Charles Eliot Norton, ed., *The Correspondence of Thomas Carlyle and Ralph Waldo Emerson*, (Boston, 1888), 1:91.

8. Morse Peckham, *Victorian Revolutionaries* (New York, 1970), p. 280.

9. Algernon Charles Swinburne, *Swinburne: Selected Poetry and Prose*, ed. John Rosenberg (New York, 1968), p. xxiv.

10. Algernon Charles Swinburne, *The Complete Works*, Bonchurch Edition (London, 1926), 16:92.

11. Ibid., pp. 54–56, 133, 142–43, 179.

Chapter Three

1. Jerome J. McGann, *Swinburne: An Experiment in Criticism* (Chicago, 1972), pp. 248–49.

2. Cecil Y. Lang, ed., *The Swinburne Letters* (New Haven, Conn., 1959), 3:14, 1:115.

3. Thomas Carlyle, *Carlyle's Works*, Sterling Edition (Boston, 1869), 15:283.

4. Matthew Arnold, *The Complete Prose Works of Matthew Arnold*, ed. R. H. Super (Ann Arbor, Mich., 1960), 1:21–22.

5. Arnold, *Complete Prose Works*, 3:281–82.

6. Algernon Charles Swinburne, *The Complete Works of Swinburne*, Bonchurch Edition (London, 1926), 15:62–119 *passim*.

7. *The Swinburne Letters*, 2:251.

8. Swinburne, *Works*, 16:53–57.

9. J. Hillis Miller, *The Disappearance of God* (Cambridge, 1963), p. 140.

10. Carlyle, *Carlyle's Works*, 15:85–86.

11. Charles Eliot Norton, ed., *The Correspondence of Thomas Carlyle and Ralph Waldo Emerson* (Boston, 1888), 1:340.

12. *Empedocles on Etna*, 1.2.304–6.

13. William R. Rutland, *Swinburne: A Nineteenth-Century Hellene* (Oxford, 1931), p. 242.

14. I quote from Shelley's translation of the elegy, l. 107.

15. *Sartor Resartus*, 2.9, 3.5.

16. G. B. Tennyson, *Sartor Called Resartus* (Princeton, N. J., 1965), p. 328.

17. *Sartor Resartus*, 3.7.

18. D. H. Lawrence, "Phoenix," ll. 1–4.

19. McGann, *Swinburne: An Experiment in Criticism* p. 121.

20. Ibid., p. 129.

Chapter Four

1. Thomas Hardy, *The Complete Poems of Thomas Hardy*, ed. James Gibson (London, 1976), p. 4.

2. Florence Emily Hardy, *The Early Life of Thomas Hardy* (London, 1928), p. 22.

3. Florence Emily Hardy, *The Later Years of Thomas Hardy* (London, 1930), p. 83.

4. Florence Hardy, *The Early Life*, pp. 171–72.

5. Evelyn Hardy, *Thomas Hardy: A Critical Biography* (London, 1954), p. 60.

6. William R. Rutland, *Thomas Hardy: A Study of the Writings and their Backgrounds* (Oxford, 1938), p. 71.

7. All but four quotations of Hardy's poetry refer to the first edition of the volume in which the poem appears. (First editions are as useful as manuscripts here, for none of the poems that I quote vary between existing manuscripts and first editions.) Of course, neither existing manuscripts nor first editions are entirely suitable for my purposes, since most of the original working manuscripts of poems written thirty, even forty years

before their publication were destroyed by Hardy as he copied them into clean manuscripts that were sent to the printers. We cannot know whether he made significant changes between manuscripts; my own experience studying Hardy's other revisions, however, leads me to suspect that any changes would have been minor and cosmetic in nature. Nevertheless, some poems that I quote may not be exactly identical to the initial compositions. Hence, some of my findings in this chapter must remain slightly more speculative than my observations upon Hardy's fiction.

In the case of four poems written after the 1865–67 group, "The Temporary The All," "He Abjures Love," Nature's Questioning," and "Aquae Sulis," I have taken the liberty of quoting second printings. In all cases but the last, the revision is no more than a stylistic improvement: the first editions, awkward and embarrassing, convey the same ideas and feelings through the same poetic structure.

8. Jerome J. McGann, *Swinburne: An Experiment in Criticism* (Chicago, 1972), p. 85.

9. Ibid., p. 7.

10. Florence Hardy, *The Early Life*, p. 65.

11. Ibid., p. 84.

12. Florence Hardy, *The Later Years*, pp. 39–40.

13. Ibid., p. 41.

14. Ibid., p. 61.

15. Ibid., p. 82.

16. Florence Hardy, *The Early Life*, p. 313.

17. Florence Hardy, *The Later Years*, p. 111–12.

18. Ibid., p. 138.

19. Ibid., p. 137.

20. Ibid., p. 141.

21. Harold Orel, *Thomas Hardy's Personal Writings* (Lawrence, Kansas, 1966), pp. 38–39, 48–49.

22. A. Dwight Culler reminds us that Swinburne defended "Dolores" by calling it the first part of a "lyrical monodrama of passion of which 'The Garden of Proserpine' and 'Hesperia' are the remainder. Each is to be regarded not as a valid statement in itself but as a 'transitional state leading up to or succeeding upon another.'" See Culler's article entitled "Monodrama and the Dramatic Monologue," in *PMLA* 90 (1975):379.

23. The chronological distinctions made in this chapter (distinctions that, in all cases, merely separate poems of the 1865–67 group from all later poems) are based upon Hardy's dating, in manuscripts, in first editions, and in a list of poems compiled in *The Early Life* (p. 71) of his earliest poetic attempts. In the case of a few poems cited, however, I have relied upon dates of composition supplied by J. O. Bailey's study of *The Poetry of Thomas Hardy* (Chapel Hill, N. C., 1970) and by Richard L. Purdy's meticulous *Bibliographical Study* (Oxford, 1954).

24. *The Poems of Swinburne*, 1:1.

25. Thomas Carlyle, *Carlyle's Works*, Sterling Edition (Boston, 1869), 1:144.

26. Ibid., p. 143.

27. John Stuart Mill, "Nature," in *The Philosophy of John Stuart Mill*, ed. Marshall Cohen (New York, 1961), p. 456.

28. Algernon Charles Swinburne, *The Complete Works of Swinburne*, Bonchurch Edition (London, 1926), 16:93.

29. Walter F. Cannon, "Darwin's Vision in *On the Origin of the Species*," in *The Art of Victorian Prose*, ed. George Levine and William Madden (New York, 1968), p. 166.

30. Carlyle, *Works*, 1:132.

31. Thomas H. Huxley, "On the Physical Basis of Life," in *Method and Results* (New York, 1897), pp. 141, 147–48.

32. William Faulkner, *Go Down, Moses* (New York, 1942), pp. 328–29. Issac McCaslin revisits the grave of Lion and Sam, only to find that they are "not held fast in earth but free in earth and not in earth but of earth, myriad yet undiffused of every myriad part, leaf and twig and particle, . . . acorn oak and leaf and acorn again . . . in their immutable progression."

33. Philip Henderson, *Swinburne: The Portrait of a Poet* (London, 1974), p. 11.

34. *The Poems of Swinburne*, 2:117.

Chapter Five

1. "The Harvest Supper" lyrically described by George Eliot's novel is creatively reheated in *Far from the Madding Crowd* (at the dinner honoring Bathsheba's engagement) and at Henchard's harvest feast for the gentler folk of Casterbridge. Hetty Sorrel, having resisted the "unmistakeable avowals in luscious strawberries" made by the gardener of "The Chase," is seduced by the heir to that great property. The undoing of Hardy's Tess begins in a "fruit-garden" where "specially fine" strawberries are put in the heroine's mouth by one similarly above her station. It comes to its fateful consummation in the "primeval" forests of "The Chase." Hetty's excruciating walk from Stoniton to Stony Stratford is made all the more painful by the none-too-frequent milestones and relieved only by the sight of a large-eyed spaniel. In *Far from the Madding Crowd*, Fanny Robin, pregnant and betrayed like Hetty by an irresponsible lover, counts the milestones separating her from the work house and literally leans on a "great" and "mysterious" dog.

2. Thomas Hardy, *A Pair of Blue Eyes* (London, 1873), 1:3–5. (Because this study is a description of transitions, and because Hardy, unlike

Swinburne, revised and re-revised his works throughout his lifetime, nearly all quotations from Hardy's fiction refer to the first hardbound edition of the novel in question. I use the first edition as opposed to the first serialization because, in some cases, passages that appear in the manuscript and in the first hardbound edition do not appear in the first serialization, i.e., Hardy occasionally adulterated manuscripts to make them acceptable to magazine editors and magazine audiences.)

3. Thomas Carlyle, *Carlyle's Works*, Sterling Edition (Boston, 1869), 15:283.

4. Thomas Hardy, *Far from the Madding Crowd* (London, 1874), 1:11–12.

5. Cecil Y. Lang, ed., *The Swinburne Letters* (New Haven, Conn., 1959), 1:159–60.

6. Algernon Charles Swinburne, *The Complete Works of Swinburne*, Bonchurch Edition (London, 1926), 15:72.

7. Matthew Arnold, *The Complete Prose Works of Matthew Arnold*, ed. R. H. Super (Ann Arbor, Mich., 1960), 9:205.

8. Thomas Hardy, *The Return of the Native* (London, 1878), 1:8.

9. Arnold, *Complete Prose Works*, 9:227.

10. Walter Pater, *Works* (London, 1901), 5:104.

11. Arnold, *Complete Prose Works*, 9:206.

12. "Laus Veneris," l. 48.

13. F. E. Halliday, *Thomas Hardy: His Life and Work* (Bath, Eng., 1972), pp. 81, 174.

14. Carlyle, *Works*, 13:308; Swinburne, *Complete Works*, 16:93.

15. Thomas Hardy, *The Mayor of Casterbridge* (London, 1886), 1:59, 202, 206.

16. *Times* (London), 9 October 1908, p. 11.

17. Michael Millgate, *Thomas Hardy, His Career as a Novelist* (New York, 1971), p. 226.

18. Albert J. Guerard first delineated the grotesque, absurd, surrealistic aspects of Hardy's art in *Thomas Hardy* (New York, 1964).

19. J. I. M. Stewart, *Thomas Hardy: A Critical Biography* (London, 1971), pp. 113–14.

20. Thomas Hardy, *The Woodlanders* (London, 1887), 1:202.

21. This particular quotation is found in Chapter 23 of the manuscript of the novel (Hardy does not use the word "romantical" in the first edition). The manuscript resides in the Dorset County Museum.

22. Arnold, *Complete Prose Works*, 9:222, 227.

23. Pater, *Works*, 5:73; Thomas Carlyle, *The Life of John Sterling* (London, 1851).

24. John Ruskin, *The Works of John Ruskin*, ed. E. T. Cook and Alexander Wedderburn (London, 1905), 35:220.

25. Roger Ingpen and W. E. Peck, eds., *The Complete Works of Percy*

Bysshe Shelley, Julian Edition (London, 1926–30), 8:98.

26. Halliday, *Thomas Hardy*, p. 71.

27. Ibid., p. 110.

28. This quotation can be found in Chapter 20 of the manuscript of the novel, as well as in all subsequent editions with the exception of the first edition, where Hardy does not use the word "hurt."

29. Thomas Hardy, *Tess of the D'Urbervilles* (London, 1891), 1:38.

30. This passage appears in editions subsequent to the first edition of 1891.

31. Thomas Hardy, *Jude the Obscure* (London, 1896), pp. 10–11.

32. Florence Emily Hardy, *The Later Years of Thomas Hardy* (London, 1930), p. 41.

33. Misao Miyoshi, *The Divided Self* (New York, 1969), p. xv.

Chapter Six

1. Virginia Woolf, "Thomas Hardy," in *The Common Reader*, 2nd. ser. (London, 1932), p. 248.

2. Evelyn Hardy counts six poems written during the 1880's; Florence Emily Hardy, in *The Later Years of Thomas Hardy* (London, 1930), mentions that the lyrics produced during this decade were "few or none" (p. 66).

3. Florence Hardy, *The Early Life of Thomas Hardy* (London, 1928), pp. 77–78.

4. Ibid., p. 284.

5. Algernon Charles Swinburne, *The Complete Works of Swinburne*, Bonchurch Edition (London, 1926), 16:364–65.

6. Evelyn Hardy, *Thomas Hardy: A Critical Biography* (London, 1954), p. 176.

7. Florence Hardy, *The Early Life*, p. 179.

8. Evelyn Hardy, *Thomas Hardy: A Critical Biography*, p. 176.

9. Florence Hardy, *The Early Life*, pp. 230–31, 162.

10. Evelyn Hardy, *Thomas Hardy: A Critical Biography*, p. 176.

11. Florence Hardy, *The Early Life*, p. 189.

12. From the *Fortnightly Review*, August 1887, pp. 304–6.

13. Florence Hardy, *The Later Years*, p. 41.

14. Jerome J. McGann, *Swinburne: An Experiment in Criticism* (Chicago, 1972), p. 206.

15. Edmund Gosse, *Portraits and Sketches* (London, 1912), pp. 15–16.

16. Edmund Gosse, *The Life of Algernon Charles Swinburne* (New York, 1917), p. 239.

17. Tom Marshall, *The Psychic Mariner* (New York, 1970), p. 105.

18. "Preface" to the *Collected Poems of D. H. Lawrence* (London, 1928).

With one exception, all quotations of Lawrence's poetry in this study refer to this volume. Since my argument is that Lawrence's poetry, early and late, is fundamentally influenced by Swinburne and Hardy, and since I am not attempting to describe transitions in the Lawrence canon (save the most elementary changes, e.g., in choice of subject matter, basic imagery, or rhymed versus unrhymed diction), there is no reason to quote manuscript or first edition versions of the poems, versions which are, in my opinion, often decidedly inferior in quality. Also, since no poem to which I shall refer is more than two pages in length, I shall not give references to line numbers in the text.

19. See, for instance, the "Prelude" to *Songs Before Sunrise*, l. 62.

20. *Lord Jim*, ch. 20.

21. R. P. Blackmur, *The Double Agent* (New York, 1938), p. 108.

22. It was Marshall who made me realize that Lawrence's "Hymn to Priapus" might be influenced by Swinburne's "Hymn to Proserpine."

23. Donald Davie, *Thomas Hardy and British Poetry* (New York, 1972), p. 144.

24. "And Jude the Obscure and His Beloved" can be found in *The Complete Poems of D. H. Lawrence*, ed. Vivian de Sola Pinto and Warren Roberts (New York, 1964), pp. 878–79.

25. D. H. Lawrence, *Phoenix: The Posthumous Papers of D. H. Lawrence*, ed. Edward D. McDonald (New York, 1936), p. 480.

26. Ibid., p. 304.

27. Ibid., pp. 478–79.

28. E. T. [Jessie Chambers], *D. H. Lawrence, A Personal Record* (London, 1935), pp. 108–10. Also see her article on "The Literary Formation of D. H. Lawrence," in *European Quarterly* 1 (1934):36–45.

29. Helen Corke, *D. H. Lawrence: The Croydon Years* (Austin, Texas, 1965), p. 9; Edward Nehls, ed., *D. H. Lawrence: A Composite Biography* (Madison, Wisc., 1957), 1:310, 406.

30. James T. Boulton, ed., *Lawrence in Love: Letters to Louise Burrows* (Nottingham, Eng., 1968), pp. 80, 85. Harry T. Moore, ed., *The Collected Letters of D. H. Lawrence* (New York, 1962), pp. 454, 474.

Chapter Seven

1. D. H. Lawrence, *Phoenix: The Posthumous Papers of D. H. Lawrence*, ed. Edward D. McDonald (New York, 1936), p. 411. Future references to the *Study of Thomas Hardy* will, throughout the discussion of *The White Peacock*, be made in parentheses within the text.

2. D. H. Lawrence, *The White Peacock* (Carbondale, Ill., 1966), pp. 154–55. This edition restores original passages canceled from the first English and American editions. All future references to the novel will be

found within parentheses, in the text of my argument, and will refer to this edition.

3. Jessie Chambers has revealed that, while working on the early and middle sections of the novel's very first manuscript draft, Lawrence decided to have George and Lettie marry after Leslie's accident, but soon decided otherwise. This fact, combined with his later decision to marry Emily to Tom Renshaw, would suggest that, having balked at his initial plan to give Lettie to George, he failed to be able to keep them apart, and that failure is recognized by the marriage of Lettiean Emily to Georgian Tom.

4. Edward Nehls, ed., *D. H. Lawrence: A Composite Biography* (Madison, Wisc., 1959), 3:426.

5. Harry Moore, ed., *The Collected Letters of D. H. Lawrence* (New York, 1962), p. 290.

6. Ibid., p. 298.

7. Julian Moynihan, *The Deed of Life* (Princeton, N. J., 1963), p. 5.

8. F. R. Leavis, *D. H. Lawrence: Novelist* (New York, 1968), p. 6.

9. Graham Hough, *The Dark Sun* (New York, 1957), pp. 6, 23–24.

10. Julian Moynihan, *The Deed of Life*, p. 5.

11. George H. Ford, *Double Measure* (New York, 1965).

12. See H. M. Daleski, *The Forked Flame* (Evanston, Ill., 1965), p. 291.

13. Hough, *The Dark Sun*, pp. 54–55.

14. D. H. Lawrence, *The Rainbow* (London, 1926), p. 2. All future references to this readily available and only slightly revised version of the 1915 first edition will appear in parentheses within the text.

15. Evelyn Hardy, *Thomas Hardy: A Critical Biography* (London, 1954), p. 73.

16. Swinburne, in a letter to E. C. Stedman, says "as a child I went in for [Catholicism] as passionately as for other things (e.g., well-nigh to unaffected and unashamed ecstasies of adoration when receiving the sacrament)." (Cecil Y. Lang, ed., *The Swinburne Letters* [New Haven, Conn., 1959], 3:13).

17. Lawrence, *Phoenix*, p. 40.

18. Ibid., pp. 218–19.

19. Ibid., pp. 561–62.

20. D. H. Lawrence, *Phoenix II: Uncollected, Unpublished, and Other Prose Works by D. H. Lawrence*, ed. Warren Roberts and Harry T. Moore (London, 1968), p. 624.

21. Ibid., p. 447.

22. D. H. Lawrence, *Apocalypse* (London, 1932), pp. 63, 84, 56.

23. Lawrence, *Phoenix II*, p. 448.

Index